WELLNESS
THROUGH STRESS MANAGEMENT

WALT SCHAFER

D1557117

INTERNATIONAL DIALOGUE PRESS · DAVIS · CALIFORNIA

Cover Design: Deborah Dickson

Library of Congress Card Number 82-80484
ISBN 0-89881-012-4

WELLNESS THROUGH STRESS MANAGEMENT

WALT SCHAFER, Ph.D.

PROFESSOR OF SOCIOLOGY
CALIFORNIA STATE UNIVERSITY AT CHICO
FOUNDER AND DIRECTOR
STRESS AND HEALTH CENTER
N.T. ENLOE MEMORIAL HOSPITAL, CHICO, CALIFORNIA

FOREWORD

Wellness is a conscious, deliberate, and informed quest for a full life. It represents an entirely new way of viewing "health" — from an abstract notion akin to "not sick, disabled, or diseased" to an expanded expectation of and commitment to life satisfaction. The wellness movement is the most significant force in the contemporary health care system. Hundreds of hospitals have recently established wellness centers to promote self-responsibility, nutritional awareness, physical fitness, and environmental sensitivity. The movement is strengthened by the growing recognition in all medical quarters that the best way to stop and reverse the economically disabling rise in medical expenditures is to help people gain the motivation and skills necessary to stay well in the first place. One of the recognized leaders of this movement is Walt Schafer — and no one is better qualified to write of the relationships between stress management dynamics and techniques and a successful wellness lifestyle than this master teacher, theoretician, implementer, and athlete.

WELLNESS THROUGH STRESS MANAGEMENT is encyclopedic in scope. It will be a standard reference work in this field for many years to come. In stress management, it should soon become *the* text — and its author will finally receive the national acclaim that has been his due for many years. Too many writers versed in the minutia of one specialty have overlooked the relationships of their specialties to other, equally crucial fields. So many publications on single wellness dimensions, such as nutritional awareness and elements of it such as weight control, have ignored or poorly addressed issues or fields inextricably linked to that topic, such as physical fitness in general and adequacy requirements for endurance routines in particular. This has often been the case with books on stress, including those authored by the biggest names in the field, such as Cannon, Benson, Brown, Pelletier, and even the Godfather of Stress, Hans Selye. Walt Schafer would never overlook these connections; quite the contrary, WELLNESS THROUGH STRESS MANAGEMENT more than any other source specializes in their construction. The reader will find in these pages on-target analyses of stress management issues and their relationships to other wellness dimensions and a catalogue of reasons why an appreciation of these interconnections is crucial to a balanced and satisfying wellness lifestyle. As if all this were not enough, Walt Schafer has also shown how the enduring commitment to whole person excellence also encompasses an awareness of and involvement in the mega-issues, such as nuclear policies, pollution, crime, the economy, and so on.

You will find mines of rich wellness deposits in these pages. Extract what you need in the first phase of your exploration — and know that you can return time and again for added return on your investments in WELLNESS THROUGH STRESS MANAGEMENT.

This book is a winner and Walt Schafer is my candidate for this year's Nobel Prize for Wellness.

DONALD B. ARDELL

PREFACE

This volume contains few I's or me's, yet it is a very personal book. It is first and foremost an expression of my own learning, my own quest for wellness through wise stress management. I have learned from many sources. Most of all, I have learned by integrating information from others with my own internal search for a lifestyle of true wellness, a lifestyle with the proper balance between work and play, giving and receiving, mind and body, intensity and recovery. My profound hope is that, through this book, you also will be aided in your quest for wellness through effective stress management.

A key assumption here is that wise stress management is a kind of preventive medicine. If you succeed in harnessing stress — not avoiding it, but controlling and directing it — you will reduce risk of illness. As Rene Dubos wrote in *Man Adapting,* "To ward off disease or to recover health, man as a rule finds it easier to depend on healers than to attempt the more difficult task of living wisely." This book, then, is designed to assist you in living wisely, thereby enhancing your own wellness.

As you read, especially Part II, you will find many specific guidelines and techniques for managing stress. There is more here than any one person can hope to use, certainly in the short run. Do not be overwhelmed. Sort and select those few steps you can realistically apply during coming weeks and months. Then remember the principle of gradualism: lasting change comes in modest increments.

I am grateful to many persons for their contributions to this effort. Some who have influenced and inspired me the most have done so at a distance through their own research and writing. Most important among these are Hans Selye, Kenneth Pelletier, Kenneth Cooper, Herbert Benson, Meyer Friedman, Ray Rosenman, Robert Eliot, Donald Ardell, Joe Henderson, George Sheehan, Richard Lazarus, Albert Ellis, and Richard Rahe. I am fully accountable, of course, for my own writing, whatever the source.

Ideas in this book have taken shape through my interactions with two groups of learners to whom I am indebted. First, I am most grateful to past and present students in my classes, Harnessing Stress, Social Stress, Occupational Stress, and Sociology of Health at California State University, Chico. University colleagues also have been helpful in providing a supportive academic environment in which I could develop and teach courses central to my interests. Especially important have been Dean James O. Haehn and Sociology Department Chairpersons Jerry Maneker and William Martin.

The second group includes those community participants with whom I have experienced reciprocal learning at the N.T. Enloe Memorial Hospital Stress and Health Center, of which I am founder and Director. The Stress and Health Center is designed to assist three groups toward wellness through improving stress management and lifestyle habits: patients, healthcare professionals, and the public. During the past four years our workshops, clinics, and classes have included Reducing Body Tension, Running Clinic, Overcoming the Hazards of Being Male, Cancer Support Group, Coping with the Stresses of Single Parenting, Coping with Loss, and Walk-Run for Health. A comprehensive Twelve-Week Stress Control Program incorporates a stress and health assessment (carried out in cooperation with a cardiologist), goal setting, understanding stress and lifestyle concepts, altering stressors where needed, altering interpretations of stressful events, learning deep relaxation and brief relaxation techniques, starting a personal fitness regimen, nutritional planning, and discovering other new coping techniques. We also offer individualized biofeedback training, one-to-one stress consultations, and a five-session program called Fitness-Relaxation-Nutrition. Among our most popular recent programs has been a year-long group series called Reducing Perfectionism and Hurry Sickness, aimed at modifying coronary-prone behavior.

Participants join these programs upon self-referral, referral by physicians, or as members of the Enloe Hospital Cardiac and Pulmonary Rehabilitation Programs. At the other end of our age spectrum is our Infant Massage Program through which parents learn how to use carefully directed touch to improve bonding and reduce emotional and physical tension in small children. We are now the national headquarters for training and information on infant massage, a technique developed by Vimala Schneider of Denver. (See her book, *Infant Massage,* Bantam, 1982.)

Among our most powerful programs is an ongoing Career and Health Enhancement Program for law enforcement and other employees. The program incorporates many of the ingredients described in *Wellness Through Stress Management* in a concentrated effort to assess and improve health, morals, and productivity of employees, thereby reducing medical costs, disability leaves, and lost work time. Particular emphasis is placed on nutrition, relaxation, and fitness.

Through all these programs, my staff and I have sought artfully to apply scientifically-grounded guidelines and techniques of stress management and health promotion. In turn, our participants have taught us which practical applications do and do not work and which methods of instruction are most effective. To these many, many people I express my thanks.

Individuals too numerous to name have been invaluable in developing and operating the Stress and Health Center and indirectly therefore in development of this book. Particularly significant have been our Medical Directors, the late Fred L. Evans, M.D., F.A.C.C., and Charles Whitcomb, M.D.; two physicians and close friends, Bruce Aikin, M.D., and John Higgins, M.D., with whom I have worked very closely and who have provided patient referrals, feedback, and encouragement; Enloe Hospital Executive Director James P. Sweeney and Director of Nursing Services Nancy Muravez, R.N.; and past and present Center staff, including Nita Catterton, M.A., Richard Cohen, M.A., Audrey Downes, R.N., Randall Langeland, Melissa Nicholaw, M.S., R.D., Connie O'Connor, Ph.D., and Shirley Sait. My Center secretary, Dorine Sanders, has been patient, supportive and helpful in a thousand ways. To her I express a special thanks.

The manuscript was ably typed by Joanne Cannon and Edna Westlake. Nora Harlow provided invaluable editorial assistance. Ernst Wenk, President of International Dialogue Press, has been an inspiration and patient supporter both in completion of this book and in production and distribution of my previous book, *Stress, Distress, and Growth*.

My daughters, Kimberly and Kristin, have witnessed first-hand the evolution of these ideas in my own life and work. They have participated in my personal quest for a lifestyle that balances home and work, rest and activity, work and play, health and career. I am grateful for their friendship and for their living examples of many of the principles I have set forth in this book.

Finally, Teresa Kludt has been a source of ideas, caring, and energy. It is to her with loving gratitude that this book is dedicated.

December 1982, Chico, California,   Walt Schafer

CONTENTS

FIGURES

EXERCISES

ACKNOWLEDGEMENTS

We wish to thank the following for permission to reprint materials used in this book.

Richard H. Rahe and Thomas H. Holmes, "The Social Readjustment Rating Scale," *Journal of Psychosomatic Research, 11 (1967), pp. 213-18.* ©Pergamon Press, Ltd. Reprinted with permission of Pergamon Press, Ltd, Quotes appear here on pp. 200-201.

Herbert M. Greenberg, *Coping With Job Stress.* Englewood Cliffs, N.J.: Prentice-Hall, Inc., ©1980. Quotations used are from pages 142-143, 144. Reprinted by permission of Prentice-Hall, Inc. Quotes appear here on pp. 261-262.

Medical Self-Care, Number 16 (Spring, 1982), "How Organized Are You?" Quotation is from page 26. Reprinted by permission of publisher. Quote appears here on p. 205.

Cary L. Cooper. *The Stress Check.* Englewood Cliffs, N.J.: Prentice-Hall, Inc., ©1981. Quotations used are from pages 153-4. Reprinted by permission of Prentice-Hall, Inc. Quotes appear here on pp. 354-355.

Jane Madders, *Stress and Relaxation.* New York, N.Y.: Arco Publishing, Inc., ©1979. Quotations used are from page 48 to page 60. Reprinted by permission of Arco Publishing, Inc. Quotes appear here on pp. 289-294, 353.

Karl Albrecht, *Stress and the Manager.* Englewood Cliffs, N.J.: Prentice-Hall, Inc., ©1979. Quotations used are from pages 204-5, 228-230. Reprinted by permission of Prentice-Hall, Inc. Quotes appear here on pp. 228-230, 296, 331-333.

Herbert Benson, M.D. with Miriam Z. Klipper, *The Relaxation Response.* New York, N.Y.: William Morrow and Company, ©1975. Quotation used is from Figure 11, "Change in Oxygen Consumption." By permission of the publisher. Quotes appear here on pp. 55,56, 247, 248-249.

Daniel A. Girdano and George S. Everly, *Controlling Stress and Tension: A Holistic Approach.* Englewood Cliffs, N.J.: Prentice-Hall, Inc., ©1979. Quotations used are from pages 115, 116, 133. Reprinted by permission of Prentice-Hall, Inc. Quotes appear here on pp. 47, 185, 186, 187, 189, 190, 212, 213, 328.

John J. Parrino, *From Panic To Power.* New York, N.Y.: John Wiley and Sons, Inc., ©1979. Quotations used are from pages 120-1, 124, 136. Reprinted by permission of John Wiley and Sons., Inc. Quotes appear here on pp. 96, 297.

John Travis, M.D. and Regina Ryan, *The Wellness Workbook.* Copyright, 1980. Used with permission. Available from Ten Speed Press, Box 7123, Berkeley, CA 94707. Material used is from pages 14, 32, 33, 53, 132, 143, 166-7, 181. Quotes appear here on pp. 181, 182, 192-195, 249-250, 255-257, 295, 310-311, 323-324.

Kenneth Cooper, *Aerobics.* New York, N.Y.: Bantam Books, ©1968 . Quotation is from page 11. Reprinted by permission of publisher. Quote appears here on p. 236.

Alvin Toffler, *Future Shock.* New York, N.Y.: Bantam Books, ©1971. (Originally published by Random House, 1970.) This and all subsequent quotes from *Future Shock* are copyrighted by Alvin Toffler. Quotations used are from pages 11, 249, 250, 264, 266, 268-9, 299, 331, 344-5, 348, 365, 377. Reprinted by permission of publisher. Quotes appear here on pp. 22, 23, 41, 118, 119, 120, 128, 129, 263.

Walter McQuade and Ann Aikman, *Stress.* New York, N.Y.: Bantam Books, ©1974. Quotations are from pages 41, 76. Reprinted by permission of publisher. Quotes appear here on pp 84, 85, 86, 87.

Ronald W. Vander Zanden. *Sociology: A Systematic Approach.* (3rd edition). New York, N.Y.: The Ronald Press, Inc. ©1976. Quotations are from pages 65-6, 146-7. Reprinted by permission of publisher. Quotes appear here on pp. 134, 135, 136, 137.

John W. Farquhar, M.D., *The American Way of Life Need Not Be Hazardous to Your Health.* By permission of W.W. Norton and Company, Inc. ©1978 by John W. Farquhar. Quotation used is from pages 64-5. Quote appears here on pp. 208-210.

Hans Selye, *The Stress of Life.* (Rev. Ed.) Philadelphia: J.B. Lippincott Company, ©1974. Quotations used are from page 141. Reprinted by permission of publisher. Quotes appear here on pp. 43, 52, 53, 90.

William Glasser, *Positive Addiction.* New York, N.Y.: Harper and Row Publisher, Inc. ©1976 by William Glasser, Inc., Joseph P. Glasser, Alice J. Glasser and Martin H. Glasser. Quotations used are from pages 92-3, 108, 109, 113. Reprinted by permission of publisher. Quotes appear here on pp. 233-234, 248.

Judith G. Rabkin and Elmer L. Struening, "Life Events, Stress, and Illness, *Science,* Vol. 194 (December 2, 1976), pages 1013-1020. Quotation is from page 1017. Quote appears here on p. 129.

M.B. Marx, T.F. Garrity, and F.R. Bowers, "The Influence of Recent Life Experience on the Health of College Freshmen," *Journal of Psychosomatic Research,* Vol. 19 (1975) pages 87-98. Quotation is from page 91. Quote appears here on pp. 202-203.

Lawrence E. Hinkel, Jr., "The Effect of Exposure to Culture Change, Social Change, and Changes in Interpersonal Relationships on Health." in B. Dohrenwend and B. Dohrenwend, Editors, *Stressful Life Events: Their Nature and Effects.* New York: John Wiley and Sons, Inc. ©1974. Quotation used is from page 21. Reprinted by permission of publisher. Quote appears here on pp. 227-228.

John L. Roglieri, *Odds On Your Life.* New York: Seaview Books. ©1980 by John L. Roglieri. Reprinted by permission of publisher. Quotations used are from pages 204. Quotes appear here on pp. 281-282, 342.

PART I

UNDERSTANDING STRESS

STRESS: HELPFUL OR HARMFUL?

John's mounting tension level was increasingly apparent to him, his family, and his co-workers. His hands trembled as each day wore on, his stomach churned, his shoulders were tight, his lower back hurt. He felt edgy and anxious, too often depressed for several days. Communication became increasingly difficult, thinking more fuzzy, speech sometimes staccato. He snapped at secretaries, silently boiled inside as business sales slowed, then blew up at colleagues. Working lunches usually included two or three stiff drinks to dull the tension. His wife and children became targets of irritability and short-temperedness.

John knew that tension was inevitable in his work. He even had found in the past that some anxiety was useful before a difficult meeting or speech. Yet chronic tension was getting out of hand. Something had to change, and soon. Already his body showed signs of breakdown, his work was inefficient, his business partnership was threatened, his family was becoming depressively alienated. Finally, his drinking was nearly out of control.

Following a series of stress management consultations, John was determined to take positive steps.

After carefully weighing the options, he decided to leave his business partnership and enter a different field of work. He began a daily running and deep relaxation program and improved his diet. He learned new techniques of mental and physical relaxation (on-the-spot tension reducers), which reduced the frequency of destructive stress build-ups. He learned to perceive stressful situations more positively. He developed new communication skills for coping with colleagues and for supervising subordinates. He decided completely to eliminate alcohol consumption for at least the next year. Finally, he learned to accept moderate tension as a fact of life and sometimes even as a positive force.

As a result of these steps, John's health, productivity, life satisfaction, and relationships improved within a few months. These improvements were as apparent to him and others as his distress symptoms had been earlier.

John's experiences taught him a great deal. They also illustrate a number of basic features of stress, providing a useful starting point for this book.

SOCIAL AND PERSONAL CIRCUMSTANCES AND STRESS

The old adage still holds: "No man or woman is an island, no one stands alone." John's personal distress did not develop in a vacuum. It resulted from John's efforts to adapt to changing circumstances surrounding him — both in the immediate, day-to-day environment and in the larger national and international climate. For example, John's business had taken a downturn in recent months in response to high interest rates, rising unemployment, and inflation. Periodically, his business faced a cash-flow crisis, a problem that seemed to correlate directly with his physical ailments and flare-ups with employees.

John's experience was consistent with recent research showing that the personal impact of economic ups-and-downs is not limited to the pocketbook. Economist Ray Catalano, of the University of California at Irvine, recently stated, "The economy is pervasive in our lives, it affects our psychological and physical well-being, and it is felt throughout our society." The research of Catalano and others shows that a deteriorating economy markedly increases rates of stress-related illness, depression, suicide, child abuse, and alcoholism. "It seems to be clearly true in males. They get more depression and more clinical kinds of symptoms when the economy goes bad." During economic hard times, individuals and families face twin crises: tension from too little income and job insecurity mounts at the very time when options for day-to-day coping disappear because of limited funds — for example, taking a weekend trip, eating out, or beginning a new project around the house.

In addition to economic strains of inflation, unemployment, and high interest rates, we all face other chronic pressures from our environment: the threat of nuclear war, air pollution, rising crime rates, social tension, daily international tensions, the energy shortage, and urban noise. Like John, each of these pressures intrudes into our daily lives in a multitude of small ways. For many, the effect is a build-up of physical, psychological, and interpersonal tensions.

Alvin Toffler may well have been correct when he wrote more than ten years ago in *Future Shock:*

The assertion that the world has "gone crazy," the graffiti slogan

that "reality is a crutch," the interest in hallucinogenic drugs, the en-
thusiasm for astrology and the occult....the attacks on science, the
snowballing belief that reason has failed man, reflect the everyday
experience of masses of ordinary people who find they can no longer
cope rationally with change. [1]

Faced with these challenges, some people adapt with strength and dignity, pressing onward toward their goals while maintaining good health and a positive attitude toward life. Others collapse, get sick, abuse others, or become seriously demoralized.

Managing stress effectively has been vital throughout history, of course. But now more than ever, personal well-being depends on knowing how to harness stress.

WHAT DO GOOD "COPERS" DO?

You need not be helpless. Your fate is not sealed at birth or by the circumstances of your life. You can take affirmative steps to build personal protection against the mounting forces creating distress for millions. You can learn from those who handle life's pressures without illness or unnecessary strain. What distinguishes "good copers?"

Social Support

Good copers know the importance of social support. Family, friends, church, and neighborhood can lend stability, guidance, and caring. And strength flows from giving as well as receiving.

Anchors

Good copers know that other personal anchorages are vital. Included are religious and personal beliefs, daily routines, enduring and meaningful objects, favorite spots in nature.

Physical Care

Good copers take good care of their bodies, no matter what. When times get tense, some don't bother. Too little time. Too many pressures. By contrast, successful copers practice sound health and fitness habits during both bad and good times. They eat well, exercise daily, and take twenty minutes a day for deep relaxation.

Involvement

Good copers get involved. Helpless alienation breeds depression and

23

disease. Active participation in community and political affairs adds to a sense of control and belonging. Not only do individuals benefit, but so does the community. Economic and political strains always produce personal stress. But harmful, destructive distress can be avoided by applying these lessons in your own daily life, even in rough waters.

Perception

Good copers see the world in a generally positive way. They don't see events through rose-colored glasses, but they do try to see the good even in adversity and even in "bad" people. Most of all, they perceive themselves as competent and in control. They see difficult times as challenges to be mastered rather than as threats.

Reactions to Distress

Good copers respond to distress in ways that are adaptive and constructive, thereby reducing the tension. They avoid maladaptive reactions, which escalate stress and tension.

This book is intended to assist you in practical, concrete ways to manage your own stress effectively. Along the way, you will learn what stress is, how it affects you, and what scientific research tells us about stress management techniques.

WHAT IS STRESS?

John's emotional and physical symptoms clearly suggest too much stress. In order to understand why his body began to break down, his emotions became less stable, his thinking grew more confused, and his relationship turned sour, he had to learn more about stress. This required a clear definition, first of "stressor," then of "stress."

A STRESSOR IS ANY DEMAND ON MIND AND BODY.

STRESS IS AROUSAL OF MIND AND BODY IN RESPONSE
TO DEMANDS MADE UPON IT.

Definitions are neither right nor wrong. They are useful in varying degrees according to scope and clarity. Definitions can be inclusive or narrow, fuzzy or clear. My definition of stress has several distinct advantages.

First, the definition makes clear that stress is ever-present, a universal feature of life. Arousal is an inevitable part of living. We constantly think, feel, and act with some degree of arousal. Stress cannot and should not be avoided. Rather it must be contained and managed.

Second, this definition points to the multi-faceted nature of stress. As you will read in more detail in Chapter 2, the stress response (arousal) involves virtually every set of organs and tissues in your body. Thoughts and feelings are clearly intertwined with these physiological processes. John's anxiety and depression, for example, were not feelings alone. Rather, they were inseparable emotional-physiological states. Body influences mind, and mind influences body. Behavior, while not included in the definition, often is an outward expression of stress — for example, short-temperedness, fast talking, accidents, and harried movement.

Third, this definition is neutral. Arousal of heart rate, blood pressure, muscle tension, emotional tension, and perception are intrinsically neither helpful nor harmful. Most often arousal is simply a fact of life, neither particularly helpful nor harmful. It simply is. As we shall see in the next section, however, stress can become positive or negative. This feature of our definition is significant because it calls attention to a wide range of experiences with stress, from the positive tension of a Wimbledon tennis tournament finalist to the recurrent colds or flu of the unstable college student who plans time poorly.

Chapter 2 will deal with the precise nature of physical and psychological arousal. Meanwhile, let us look at the two kinds of stress.

POSITIVE STRESS

John's experience illustrates the curious duality of stress. On the one hand, moderate, occasional elevations of anxiety helped prepare him for meetings, difficult conferences, or complex business negotiations. On the other hand, excessive chronic arousal seriously threatened his health, productivity, satisfaction, and relationships. Let us examine more closely the two sides of stress.

POSITIVE STRESS IS AROUSAL THAT CONTRIBUTES TO HEALTH, SATISFACTION, AND PRODUCTIVITY.

Positive stress is useful in a wide range of circumstances. Below are several illustrations:

Positive stress helps us to respond quickly and strongly in physical emergencies, such as averting an auto collision, avoiding a dropped brick, lifting a heavy object off a child, fighting a fire, or administering cardio-pulmonary resuscitation to a heart attack victim.

25

Positive stress is useful in performing well under stress, such as in tennis at Wimbledon, on the Law School Admissions Test, in a job interview, or during a speech to the Rotary Club.

Positive stress helps us to prepare for deadlines — a term paper due date, five o'clock check-out time, or filing date for tax returns.

Positive stress helps us realize potential over a period of years in athletics, academics, and occupations.

Positive stress adds zest and variety to daily life.

Positive stress calls attention to the need to resolve a situation of disharmony with others.

Clearly, then you do not want to avoid stress altogether. Without it, life would be stagnating and unsatisfying.

DISTRESS

When arousal occurs at too high or too low a level, either temporarily or chronically, then positive stress gives way to harmful distress. The challenge is to identify your own zone of positive stress and to maintain a lifestyle that will enable you to stay in that zone most of the time.

DISTRESS IS TOO GREAT OR TOO LITTLE AROUSAL WHICH IS HARMFUL TO BODY OR MIND

As John became more aware of himself, he saw that he displayed:

Trembling of hands	Depression
Stomach churning	Poor concentration
Tight shoulders	Fuzzy thinking
Sore lower back	Accelerated speech
Edginess	Irritability
Anxiety	Short-temperedness

These distress symptoms served as early-warning signs — messages that something was wrong and needed to be changed, either in John's attitude or in his external situation. Physical, emotional or intellectual change may signal distress if the health, satisfaction, productivity, or emotional well-being of others is threatened. Harmful distress must be avoided whenever possible.

26

Minor distress signals such as trembling of hands and tension headaches serve as useful early warning signs when we listen to them and respond by doing something about them. Too often, however, such symptoms remain undetected, become chronic, and turn into full-blown illnesses requiring medical attention. As we shall see in Chapter 3, a number of diseases are influenced by stress. Below is a partial list of stress-related illnesses among individuals recently referred by physicians to our Stress and Health Center for consultation:

Migraine headaches	Non-cardiac chest pain
Tension headaches	Heart attack
Psoriasis	Cancer
Gastritis	Rheumatoid arthritis
Ulcers	Dizzy spells
Colitis	High blood pressure
Chronic lower-back pain	

Experts estimate that between 60 and 90 percent of illness episodes are stress-related. Stress contributes to illness in three ways: by imposing long-term wear and tear on the body and mind and reducing resistance to disease, by directly precipitating an illness as in a heart attack or tension headache, and by aggravating an existing illness as in increased arthritic swelling and pain or flare-up of psoriasis.

Psychological distress may include severe depression, debilitating anxiety, disorientated thinking, paranoia, lack of motivation to perform daily routines. Here too the line between distress symptoms and full-blown distress illnesses is not distinct. Symptoms tend to shade gradually into more serious disturbed states. Most often such psychological distress symptoms accompany physical illness because of the intricate interplay of mind and body.

DISTRESS AND DISHARMONY

By definition, distress is something to avoid whenever possible. Yet a period of distress can be transformed into positive stress. For distress almost always is a sign of some kind of disharmony among different wants or needs within the person or between the person's inner wants and needs and outside circumstances. John learned from his growing distress. Among other things, he listened to his own inner voice telling him it was time to change career directions. He also determined to take better care of his body. When distressed, then, ask:

1. What is the disharmony within me or between myself and my outside reality?

2. What can I do to resolve this disharmony?

Stress is a neutral term. Most arousal in daily life is neutral. As it mounts or falls, however, stress can turn into positive stress or distress. Positive stress is useful for expansion of talents, variety of life, and maximum performance. Distress is to be avoided whenever possible. Even when unavoidable, it can yield benefits by providing the basis for new learning, a change of direction, resolution of disharmony.

COSTS OF DISTRESS

Costs to the individual of prolonged and recurrent distress in mind and body include:

Physical illness
Lowered energy
Lowered productivity
Wasted potential
Lack of career advancement
Dissatisfaction with life, work, and relationships
Low self-esteem
Non-involvement in public issues
Joylessness and meaninglessness
Absence of fun and play

Unfortunately, the costs of distress do not stop with the individual. They ripple outward, creating negative effects in the social world as well. For the family, high personal distress of one member, especially a parent, can contribute to:

Tension "in the air"
A damper on freedom of expression
Open conflict
Psychological put-downs
Physical abuse
Low self-esteem of others in family
Loss of potential earnings by an ailing family member
Inattentiveness to emotional and physical needs of others
Family break-ups
High health-care costs

Similarly, in the workplace the costs are great. For example, they include:

Low productivity	Absenteeism
Worker dissatisfaction	Worker turnover
Conflict with co-workers	Higher health insurance costs

A recent study put dollar values on these costs. The probable costs of stress to an industrial firm employing 2,000 people with gross sales of about $60 million per year were estimated at $3,560,000, slightly more than the five percent profit of $3,000,000 for a given year. Albrecht, in *Stress and the Manager,* points out that if we multiply the $1,780 stress-related cost per employee in the above study by 80 million workers, we end up with a mind-boggling cost of stress to industry alone of $142,400,000,000 — a high cost indeed for stress-induced loss of effectiveness and efficiency.[2]

This figure says nothing of a multitude of other estimated costs to society as a whole. Included by way of illustration must be the following for a given year:

$30 billion in alcohol and drug abuse
$2.5 billion in prescribed medications (50 percent of all such prescriptions)
$2 billion in legal non-prescription drugs
$242 billion in disease care costs (75 percent of 1983 estimated total costs)
$18 billion in tobacco sales.[3]

These figures do not include costs for counseling and therapy, law enforcement and corrections, added educational costs, costs of vandalism and violence, or many other hidden expenditures. In short, a substantial part of the gross national product is devoted to distress and its harmful consequences.

Finally, note the ten leading causes of death in 1981 in the United States, as shown in Figure 1-1. Every one of these clearly is related to lifestyle. Even deaths from diseases of early childhood are related to such factors as nutrition, smoking, and poor prenatal care. (The United States ranks only sixteenth in the world in infant mortality, so many other countries are proving that there is nothing inevitable about a high childhood death rate.) But focusing only on non-infant deaths, stress contributes a notable share through the mediating pathways shown in Figure 1-2.

29

FIGURE 1-1

CAUSES OF DEATH, 1981[4]

	Annual Deaths per 100,000 Population
Heart Disease	408.2
Cancer	175.6
Accidents	42.1
Chronic obstructive pulmonary diseases	23.3
Pneumonia and influenza	20.3
Diabetes mellitis	13.7
Cirrhosis of the liver	12.2
Diseases of early infancy	11.9
Suicide	11.4
Homicide	11.2

Roglieri, in *Odds on Your Life*, estimates that mismanagement of stress alone probably will contribute to more than one-quarter of all deaths during the next five years in a typical group of white males, ages 40-45.[6] Excessive distress is extremely costly to individuals, families, employers, schools, and the entire nation. Many experts predict that these costs will rise.

SIX WAYS OF RELATING TO STRESS

People vary in the ways they relate to stress and distress. Recognizing that no one is ever clearly one or the other, we can distinguish among the following types of people and their approaches to stress:

FIGURE 1-2

MEDIATING PATHWAYS TO STRESS-RELATED DEATHS[1]

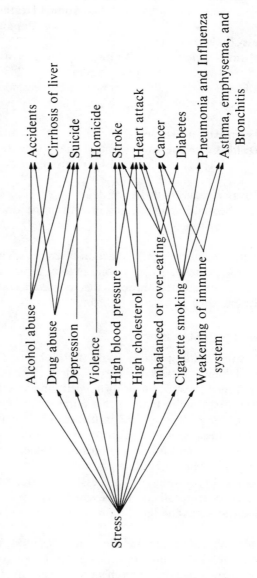

Stress-seeking/provoking

Stress seekers thrive on challenge, risk and sensation

Stress avoiders thrive on security and familiarity, avoiding challenge, sensation, and risk. May be based on realistic appraisal, needs, chemistry, and preference, or on irrational fears of risk-taking, failure, or success.

Distress-seeking/avoiding

Distress seekers thrive on misery, illness, crisis, martyrdom. Often addicted since childhood.

Distress-avoiders thrive on health, contentment, activity, and do all they can to avoid and reduce distress.

Distress-provoking/reducing

Distress provokers thrive intentionally or unintentionally on creating misery, disharmony, illness and upset for others.

Distress reducers thrive on doing all possible to promote health, happiness, and growth in those whose lives they touch.

These patterns of thought and action often are set in motion during childhood through the *life script,* a concept to be explained in detail later. The pattern is perpetuated through the *repetition compulsion,* which brings us to the topic of barriers to change.

BARRIERS TO CHANGE

John's stress build-up was a result of both internal and external influences which blindly locked him into old, destructive patterns. Internally, he was impelled forward by his own repetition compulsion, that is, by his inner drive to do and be that which is familiar. The repetition compulsion is among the most powerful influences on human behavior. We repeat behavior because it is familiar, even if painful. We tend to avoid the new because it is unfamiliar and uncomfortable. When John finally decided something had to be done, he faced the need to overcome his repetition compulsion through awareness, inner strength, rational planning, and support from others. In the same way you can recognize and confront the enormous inertia of your own force of habit.

John also was faced with breaking out of his *lifestyle trap* — that set of obligations, roles and duties to which he felt bound to respond. To be sure, he had created this trap himself over many years. On any one day, however, the responsibilities could not easily be avoided. Tremendous dedication and insight were needed to alter his harmful patterns of living and coping. Similarly, you may need to break out of your lifestyle trap in managing stress more effectively, whether the trap entails harmful overload or underload, leading to overstress or understress.

John was fortunate. His race, cultural background, and education gave him options for turning his life in a more positive direction. The vast majority of the world's population and a sizable minority of the American population are not so fortunate. Their distress is not self-imposed. The impulse of the more fortunate usually is to "blame the victim," while ignoring economic, political, and educational realities which impose untold distress upon so many.[7]

A recent *Life* magazine featured the grim story of famine in Somalia — a trap not of these unfortunate people's own making.[8] Another recent news story told of the terrible difficulties experienced in a small, isolated black community in Louisiana in trying to obtain running water for the first time in its history from the all-white, family-controlled political machinery in the county.[9] A documentary movie describes the inhumane working conditions in a ring factory in New York, conditions which contribute to chronic ill health and demoralization among employees and their families.[10]

These are a few illustrations of the imposing external causes of distress from many people and the substantial pressures they face in seeking a more healthy, sane, and meaningful existence. Much distress throughout the world can be overcome only through changes in inhumane, social circumstances through increased educational opportunities, improved job chances, reduced discrimination in housing and employment, and better environmental conditions. It is important that we not only consider our own lives in isolation from others, but that we become more aware and engage in political and social action to improve life chances for others as well. Later in this book these steps are referred to as social approaches to managing stress.

For most who read this book, positive steps can be taken to improve management of stress in their own lives. This book presents a framework, guidelines, and techniques for doing so.

STRESS AND THE SEA PALM

I recently spent several hours on a cliff along the Pacific Coast passively watching the surf and occasionally reading. While there, I became intensely fascinated with sea palm colonies. Sea palms are seaweeds 12 to 18 inches tall and shaped like palm trees; they are found clinging to the rocks near the surf line. Several analogies between this hardy plant and humans struck me.

Like the sea palm, we are born with a strong desire to survive and grow to full potential. If external conditions such as light, water, or access to food are not right, sea palms and people cannot survive, much less grow to fullness. The sea palm does not avoid its stressors. Rather, it is destined to live where sea conditions are the most challenging, on the coastal rocks where waves pound the hardest. Similarly, we cannot realize our potentials by avoiding challenge. We need new demands and progressively higher goals. Otherwise we remain stunted, half-grown, potentially unrealized, rather than fulfilled, aware, and expanded.

If the sea palm is to survive and grow, it must be at once well-anchored on the rock and resilient. Similarly, we must be well-anchored to our values, our social support networks. We must care for our bodies to be strong, yet resilient. As the author of another book on stress has stated, we must know how "to bend without breaking."[11] Unlike the sea palm, however, you and I can help to determine the extent of fulfillment by the way in which we use two uniquely human qualities: awareness and choice. If we continue to grow in *awareness* of the self and the world around us, we are more likely to make stress work for us. And if we *choose* our actions wisely, we increase our chances of becoming winners rather than losers. For example, a loser might react to pressures of final examinations by getting drunk every night during final exam week. A winner reacts by planning carefully, studying hard, and finding time to relax and exercise each day during final exams.

Because you have the ability to exercise awareness and choice, you are well ahead of the sea palm. You need not be at the mercy of your surroundings. To a large extent, you can create your own future.

When awareness and choice are translated into *personal responsibility,* stress can be harnessed and directed effectively. Sometimes, of course, external circumstances are impossible to control or overcome. Often, however, people behave quite helplessly, blaming others rather than taking affirmative steps to change their circumstances or their reactions to them.

GOALS OF STRESS MANAGEMENT

This book is intended as a practical guide to stress management. Managing stress wisely depends on you — on your determination, patience, persistence, your willingness to learn and experiment with new patterns of behavior. In short, effective stress management, like effective preventive medicine, depends upon *self-care*.

There are few simple or quick answers to controlling stress, but this book can help you to trace modest steps toward the goals of good health and a higher quality of life. The book conveys information which can be useful as you pursue three goals: short-term, intermediate, and long-term.

Short-term Goals   To learn about the nature of stress, its causes and effects
To learn guidelines and techniques for managing stress more effectively

Intermediate Goals   To control the causes of distress
To recognize early warning signs of distress
To develop an effective lifestyle buffer
To perceive and appraise stressors positively
To control the emotional and physical stress responses
To regulate pace of life
To mobilize stress when needed
To cope constructively with mounting distress

Long-term Goals   To enjoy high-level wellness (good health, life satisfaction, maximum productivity, and expansion of abilities during future months and years)
To promote high-level wellness of others (to promote good health, life satisfaction, productivity, and expansion of those whose lives you touch)

These long-term goals represent high-level, perhaps even ultimate values. They are features of a quality life, too often eroded by stress. Understanding and managing stress effectively can promote them, and this book can assist you in this lifelong quest.

PERSPECTIVE AND PLAN OF THE BOOK

Throughout this book, a number of themes appear:

1. Stress is unavoidable, even helpful in moderate amounts. Distress is harmful, to be prevented and reduced whenever possible.

2. Prevention of distress and control of stress depends first and foremost on personal responsibility. The job cannot be given over to your doctor, minister, counselor, or spouse.

3. The stress experience is a whole-person experience involving mind, body, and behavior. Managing stress depends on attending to all three parts in an integrated, whole-person approach.

4. The stress experience is intricately interwoven with lifestyle. This includes, for example, pace of life, pace of change, beliefs and values, scope and quality of relationships, degree and types of involvement in the surrounding community, health habits, perceptions. Controlling stress depends on attending not just to attitude or relaxation techniques, but to a full web of situations and settings in which you spend your time.

5. Controlling stress and preventing distress depend upon:
    understanding stress
    monitoring stress
    managing stress.

Part I of the book focuses on the nature, sources, and effects of stress and distress — that is, on *understanding stress.* Chapter 2 focuses on the nature of the stress response and its opposite, the relaxation response. Chapter 3 deals with distress in some detail, including how moderate stress turns into harmful distress when you move outside your zone of positive stress. Also discussed are common distress symptoms, several distress-related illnesses. Common high-risk stressors, both internal and external, as well as the context of accelerating change within which they occur are dicussed in Chapter 4. Each chapter in Part I concludes with a series of questions for review and personal application of the topic covered.

Part II, which deals with *monitoring and managing stress,* builds upon facts and concepts in Part I to present an integrated, whole-person approach to controlling and reducing tension in your life. Chapter 5 sets forth the framework for Part II. Chapter 6 focuses on monitoring distress signals as you go about your daily affairs. We also will discuss ways of responding constructively to the signals you pick up from mind, body, and behavior. This chapter and those that follow include a series of practical and personal exercises, some for increasing awareness of past, present, or future, others suggesting specific steps for applying the techniques discussed.

Chapter 7 focuses on monitoring and managing stressors, ranging from overload to boredom, perfectionism, and daily hassles. Chapter 8 focuses on the lifestyle buffer — daily attitudes and actions which can help protect against potentially harmful stressors. Included are aerobic exercise, deep relaxation, nutrition, social support, and personal anchorages. In Chapter 9, we turn to how you perceive stressors. This is a vitally important chapter, since perception influences the nature and intensity of your mental and physical stress response, as well as what you do to cope with the stressor. Irrational beliefs and perceptions are also discussed.

Chapter 10 deals with monitoring and managing your mental and physical stress response, especially in the immediate situation in which arousal occurs. On-the-spot tension reducers are presented. Chapter 11 includes a variety of both negative and positive options for coping with stressors, that is how you interrelate with them. Special emphasis is placed on communication methods with people-stressors, since other people are common stressors of daily life.

Given your growing awareness of distress, how do you react to it? Do you deny, catastrophize, escape, or overeat? Or do you seek to identify the stress trigger and do something constructive about it and about your own distress? Chapter 12 focuses on these and other reactions to distress.

Chapter 13 goes beyond the individual and the stressor to look at the context in which stress occurs. To minimize distress you may need to change something in the environment around you or around the specific stress trigger. We focus on the workplace as an example of the context of stress. A number of suggestions are made for minimizing distress in the workplace. Chapter 14 builds on previous chapters, discussing steps for putting what has been learned into action. Included is a section on developing your own perspective toward stress management, as well as methods for self-reinforcement of change, and an opportunity to write down your plans for implementing what you have learned.

CHAPTER REVIEW AND PERSONAL APPLICATIONS

1. Applied to human stress, what does the following mean? "No man or woman is an island. No one stands alone."
2. Describe and illustrate five ways good "copers" differ from poor "copers."
   a. In which of these ways could you improve?
   b. Think of one person who stands out in your mind as an especially good coper with stress. Which of these five coping approaches are noteworthy in this person's life? Ask if necessary.
3. Distinguish between stressor and stress.
4. Identify three examples of internal stressors and three examples of external stressors in your own life during the past two days.
5. What are three advantages of the definition of stress used here?
6. Positive stress is:
7. Identify five ways stress has been beneficial to you during the past week.
8. Distress is:
9. True or False? "Distress can result from overload, but not underload." Explain.
10. What illnesses have you experienced which might well have been stress-related? Can you identify stressful experiences which preceded and perhaps contributed to these illnesses?
11. What is meant by this statement? "Distress symptoms are signs of disharmony." How might this apply to distress symptoms you have experienced recently?
12. What is the repetition compulsion? In what ways is it helpful? Harmful? How does it apply to you?
13. In what sense is lifestyle trap an external analog of the repetition compulsion?
14. What is meant by "blaming the victim?" What does it have to do with stress?
15. What can you learn from watching sea palms on the rocky coast about your own approach to managing stress?
16. What are short-term goals of stress management? Intermediate goals? Long-term goals?
17. Do you agree or disagree that long-term goals of stress management presented in this chapter are "high-level values?" Why or why not?
18. Do you agree or disagree that the ultimate goal of stress management is to eliminate stress? Why?
19. What is meant by a "lifestyle approach to stress management?"

20. Identify several ways you hope to benefit from reading and applying this book.
21. What is high-level wellness?

REFERENCES

1. Alvin Toffler, *Future Shock*. New York: Bantam Books, 1971, p. 365 (Originally published by Random House, 1970). This and all subsequent quotes from *Future Shock* are copyrighted by Alvin Toffler.

2. Karl Albrecht, *Stress and The Manager*. Englewood Cliffs, N.J.: Prentice Hall, Inc., 1979, p. 130.

3. Ibid., Chapter 2.

4. *Monthly Vital Statistics Report,* National Center for Health Statistics, Vol. 3, No. 2 (March 18, 1982), Table 6.

5. Adapted from John L. Roglieri, *Odds On Your Life*. New York: Seaview Books, 1980, p. 189.

6. Ibid., Chapter IX.

7. William Ryan, *Blaming the Victim*. New York: Pantheon Books, 1978.

8. *Life* (September, 1979), pp. 31-38.

9. *Time* (June 18, 1980), p. 68.

10. "The Factory," Verti Productions, New York, 1972.

11. Mary Ella Stuart, *To Bend Without Breaking*. Nashville, Tenn.: Abingdon, 1977.

THE STRESS RESPONSE AND THE RELAXATION RESPONSE

The fact is that a person can be intoxicated with his own stress hormones. I venture to say that this sort of drunkenness has caused much more harm to society than the alcoholic kind.[1]

Hans Selye

During a five-mile run in the canyon where I live, my easy rhythm was severely altered by the sudden, silent approach of a full-grown, teeth-baring Doberman Pinscher. Some months earlier the same dog had bitten my sixteen-year-old daughter, so I perceived him as a genuine threat. Already my heart had been beating at 130-140 beats/minute during the run. Suddenly it sped up, probably to 160-170 beats/minute. My breathing accelerated. My muscles tensed, my eyes dilated and opened wide. I could feel adrenalin pouring into my limbs.

My attention focused immediately on coping with this threat. I had two alternatives: fight or flee. Experience had taught me that fighting, or at least pretending readiness to fight, was the most effective. I yelled at the dog, reached for stones on the road, and threw two or three at the ground in front of him. The dog turned tail and vanished, but it took my body several minutes to "come down" from intense arousal to its previous normal condition associated with running at an easy eight-minute/mile pace.

This experience was unique in certain respects. I had never met this particular dog at this particular time of day or in this particular place. Yet in other ways, reactions in my body and mind were not at all unique. What I experienced was the stress response, a distinctive mental-neurological-muscular-hormonal reaction which I had known many times before. So has everyone. And so have animals other than humans.

My encounter with the dog was a genuine physical threat, eliciting an appropriate, useful response by my body. Arousal helped me cope. Most stressful situations, however, are social and psychological rather than physical. Hence, this physical arousal usually is quite useless. As we shall see, in fact, the stress response can be hazardous to well-being when chronic and unreleased. My stress response was *episodic* and intense, that is, *a maxi fight-or-flight response.* Normally, intense episodic arousal

43

does no harm, and in fact, may prove helpful. But the pressures of daily living too often result in a *chronic* stress response at too high a level. In short, chronic daily hassles often produce a continuous, erosive *mini fight-or-flight response*. Its damage is cumulative, often imperceptible, like a low-grade fever.

In this chapter you will learn more about the stress response and how it affects you. You also will read about its opposite, the relaxation response. This will provide an important base of understanding upon which to build attitudes and practices for managing stress effectively.

THE INTERPLAY OF MIND AND BODY

A fundamental assumption of our whole-person, lifestyle approach to stress is that mind, body, and behavior are closely intertwined. In fact, they are inseparable. Cause-effect arrows depicting the stress response run both ways as illustrated in Figure 2-1.

The examples used in Figure 2-1 refer to the maxi-stress-response. The same interconnectedness of mind, body, and behavior occur all day, every day, in smaller ways as you continually adjust to the demands of daily living. Physical wear and tear (body) often results from chronic mental strain (mind) associated with coping with (behavior) a difficult marriage or an unsatisfying job. Destructive distress often develops in precisely this way as mind, body, and behavior affect each other in an accelerating cycle of stress build-up. Later in this chapter you will read that mind, body, and behavior also interrelate during the opposite experience: the relaxation response. You will see that any of the three can be primary targets of stress management. Whichever is chosen, the other two will tend to follow. Throughout the book, you will see why an integrated lifestyle approach to harnessing stress is so vital to proper care of the whole person.

FIGURE 2-1

THE STRESS RESPONSE

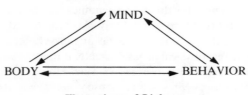

Illustrations of Linkages

1. Feeling of fear causes muscle tension (among other things).
2. Activation of the sympathetic nervous system leads to greater mental alertness.
3. Feeling of fear leads to avoidance behavior.
4. Avoidance behavior is followed by mental appraisal of the situation.
5. Physical arousal leads to stronger, faster behavior responses.
6. Persistent fighting-off of an attacker results in physical fatigue.

PHYSIOLOGY OF THE STRESS RESPONSE

The proper place to begin in understanding the stress response is with the stress trigger, or stressor (See Figure 2-2). In Chapter 4 you will read about the types of stressors most likely to cause distress, and you will be asked to monitor these in your own life for a designated period of time. Stress triggers may be intense (word of death of a relative) or mild (a child's dirty shoes upon entering the living room); pleasant (a daughter's high school graduation ceremony) or unpleasant (an unexpected medical bill). Whatever its nature, a stressor, once perceived, elicits a physical reaction and an associated mental response.

Perception of Stressors

Humans differ from lower animal forms in that, for us, the stressor-stress response link is not a direct stimulus-response connection. Intervening between the two is a distinctive, higher-level mental process: perception/interpretation/evaluation of the stressor. Humans are not unique in this regard. My dog sometimes pauses before responding to determine whether an approaching person is friend or foe. His behavior and physical response will vary markedly depending upon his assessment of the situation. Similarly, the nature and strength of a person's internal reactions are affected by whether a stressor is perceived at all, and, if so, how it is interpreted.

Whenever perception is aroused, the stress response is set in motion. In my work, the simple act of listening by one of my clients usually elicits an increased tone on a biofeedback monitor known as the galvanic skin response, which measures electrical conductions on the skin. A recent study reported that blood pressure usually rises while a person is talking and falls immediately afterward. These are two simple illustrations of the fact that almost any perception of a stimulus elicits the stress response. In relation to stress, the important questions are how intense, prolonged, and frequent the response is and what effects it has on the body. The important question for stress management is how this response can be contained. This book provides guidelines and techniques for managing the stress response.

FIGURE 2-2
THE STRESS RESPONSE

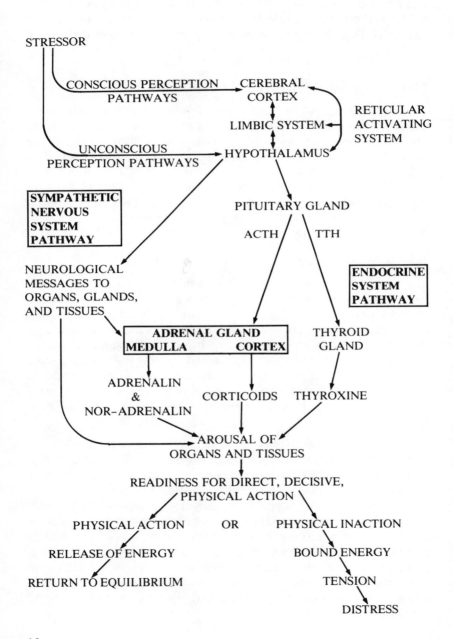

Sometimes arousal occurs through the *unconscious perception pathway*. For example, chronic arousal causing higher rates of mental and physical illness close to metropolitan airports probably occurs below the level of conscious awareness and perception. Here the stress trigger may enter directly into the sub-cortex, one of the two major divisions of the brain.

The second and more familiar pathway is the *conscious perception pathway,* which involves conscious perception, assessment, and interpretation. This is an important distinction, since it calls attention to the fact that stress can exist at a moderate or high chronic level, even in the absence of conscious arousal. Bringing these stressors into awareness can be a vital step to adapting constructively.

PERCEPTION AND THE BRAIN

When conscious appraisal occurs, the *cerebral cortex,* the second major division of the brain, becomes aware of, assesses, and interprets the stress trigger. The cerebral cortex is far more developed in humans than in other animals, and it allows for more thoughtful reactions to stress triggers.

> *The addition of the vast number of cortical cells (in humans) allowed the development and storage of analytical skills, verbal communication, some ability, empathy, fine motor control, additional emotion, memory, learning and rational thought, as well as more sophisticated problem-solving and musical ability...reactions could be more than reflex responses.* [2]

For better or worse, an individual's reality can be determined by his or her own perceptions. Behavior can be weighted against possible outcomes. Symbolism, goals, motivation, and anticipation become part of the functioning human being.

Human beings also are gifted with a more highly developed *limbic system* or mid-brain, which is part of the sub-cortex. This further removes us from a simple stimulus-response relationship to the world around us. Among other things, the limbic system attaches feelings to pieces of information in the cerebral cortex. These feelings may include fear, anxiety, anger, joy, or pleasure. Thus a continual interplay takes place between awareness and feeling as the cerebral cortex and limbic system exchange messages.

The *reticular activating system* (RAS) is a two-way pathway of nerve cells or neurons extending from the spinal cord up through the lower brain centers and mid-brain to the cerebral cortex. Its main function is to transmit messages and impulses among different parts of the brain. These messages may be specific or general. For example, the perception of an unusual sound is transmitted via the RAS to various lower- and mid-brain points, and this results in general attentiveness and arousal. Even before the cortex appraises the situation, the limbic system may produce a feeling of fear, and the hypothalamus, which regulates various body processes, may send messages to the body to prepare for action. This may include tensing muscles and increasing blood flow to the limbs.

An important feature of the RAS is that when it is turned on too frequently at too high a level, it will stay aroused. It essentially says, "If you are going to ask me to turn on like this so often, I will simply stay turned on continuously." Continuous arousal throughout the body can contribute to such stress-induced ailments as hypertension and insomnia.

A key link in the stress response is the *hypothalamus,* which though merely the size of a pea is a virtual dynamo of potency. When a stress trigger enters the brain through either the conscious or unconscious appraisal pathway, the hypothalamus is stimulated. Despite its small size, it is the control center regulating both the stress response and its opposite, the relaxation response.

As shown in Figure 2-2, the hypothalamus activates the body through two avenues, the sympathetic nervous system and the endocrine system. Let us first examine the sympathetic nervous system.

The Sympathetic Nervous System

When Sally Smith decides it is time to check the mail, she activates the voluntary nervous system, which controls striate, voluntary muscles throughout the body, controlling posture and movement. Along the way, she quickly dodges a falling digger pine cone, which can be quite lethal with its weight and dagger-like points. Here she activates her *autonomic nervous system,* which is often referred to as an involuntary system since it controls such internal processes as the circulatory, reproductive, and digestive systems.

In the past, these internal processes were thought to be involuntary. However, biofeedback monitoring has taught us that such internal activities as heart rate, blood pressure, brain waves, and temperature can be controlled through volition.[3] As Kenneth Pelletier has stated, "This discovery is one of the most profound discoveries of contemporary medicine, with far-reaching implications for the future of holistic, preventive health care."[4]

Most of the time, however, the autonomic nervous system does operate outside our conscious control. It is divided into two interconnected branches, the *sympathetic nervous system,* which arouses the body and the *parasympathetic nervous system* which quiets the body. When a stressor stimulates the brain, the sympathetic nervous system sends neurological messages to glands, organ, and tissues to arouse, to prepare for action. Our bodies cannot know what the stressor is and whether a physical reaction is indeed called for. It simply does what it is told by the sympathetic nervous system: prepare to react, to defend by fighting or fleeing. One important target of this activation is the *adrenal medulla.*

The adrenal glands are located just above the kidneys and are divided into two distinct parts — the adrenal medulla (inner part) and the *adrenal cortex* (larger, outer part). The medulla is stimulated during stress by the sympathetic nervous system. When this happens, the medulla secretes into the blood two hormones, *adrenalin* or *epinephrine* and *nor-adrenalin* or *nor-epinephrine.* Adrenalin acts upon the liver, which sends more glucose into the blood stream, assuring a quick source of energy. Adrenalin also increases carbohydrate metabolism, dilates arteries and capillaries throughout the body, accelerates pumping by the heart, elevates body temperature, increases the amount of blood sent out of the heart (stroke volume), and speeds up respiration. At the same time nor-adrenalin works with adrenalin in circulating free fatty acids, while also raising blood pressure and constricting certain blood vessels in the body.

The Endocrine System

Simultaneously, a part of the *endocrine* or *hormone system* is turned on to work in tandem with the sympathetic nervous system. A message is sent through a small network of blood vessels from the hypothalamus to the *pituitary gland,* which is next to the hypothalamus in the lower brain. The pituitary gland is the body's master gland, controlling the activities of all other glands in the body. The pituitary sends two chemicals into the blood stream. One, *thyrotropic hormone* (TTH) is designed to activate the *thyroid gland* when it reaches that destination. The thyroid, in turn, secretes *thyroxine* into the blood stream. Thyroxine increases the rate at which the body consumes fuel. During the stress response, metabolism is sped up in tissues and cells by thyroxine. Thyroxine also seems to make the body more sensitive and responsive to adrenalin.

The pituitary gland at the same time secretes *adreno-corticotropic hormone* (ACTH), which stimulates the outer part of the adrenal gland, the adrenal cortex. It is interesting to note that the greater the production of TTH and ACTH, the less the production of sex hormones. This probably accounts for the loss of interest in sex during stressful periods.

The adrenal cortex, in turn, secretes another important hormone, *gluco-corticoids,* which stimulates the liver to produce more blood sugar. More fats and proteins also are released into the blood for more energy. Release of too much protein for energy can reduce protein normally available for construction of white blood cells and other antibodies, thereby weakening the body's immune system over the long run. Release of too much fat, in turn, can promote atherosclerosis, build-up of plaque in arteries of the brain and heart. This may be one reason chronic "hurry sickness" dramatically increases the risk of heart attacks, as we shall see in Chapter 3.

Mineral corticoids, primarily aldosterone, are the other products of the adrenal cortex. This hormone, in turn, helps to dissipate heat and water generated by increased metabolism, as well as retain water and raise blood pressure and blood salinity through retention of sodium (salt). It also is a vital link in the body's mobilization of the immune response to fight infection.

Readiness for Physical Action

Through the sympathetic nervous system and endocrine system, the body is prepared for direct, decisive, physical action. Key observable or measurable signs of this preparedness are when:

pupils dilate
throat tightens
neck, upper back, and shoulders tighten
breathing quickens and becomes shallow
heart pumps faster
muscles and legs become taut, especially in front
skin cools
brain waves become shorter
blood pressure rises
blood shifts from abdomen to limbs
more glucose enters the blood stream
more white blood cells enter the blood stream
metabolism speeds up
cholesterol remains in blood stream longer
arteries and capillaries constrict.

As Pelletier notes, many of these internal changes have entered our common language.[5]

trembling with fear	a lump in my throat
cold feet	clammy hands
chills ran up and down my spine	a knot in my stomach
a racing heart	butterflies

Part of effective stress management is learning to monitor and recognize these and other warning signs of distress, especially when they become chronic.

Through these intricate pathways, then, the body is prepared for direct, decisive, physical action. In an extremely threatening situation, this is the maxi-stress response. In smaller ways, these changes occur constantly, resulting in chronic excitation of the mini-stress response.

When physical action occurs, this readiness, this pent-up energy is released. At one time in human history, such physical activity was constant, not necessarily at the moment of arousal, but certainly through the day as people worked, moved about, and played. In the past, too, more stress triggers were physical threats in which a physical stress response was appropriate.

However, three important changes have happened. First, the faster pace of life in this century has increased the number of stressors we face. Second, most stressors today are psychological and social, rather than physical. Third, we have become more sedentary, resulting in less release of energy build-up. Hence, an increase occurs in the *need* for physical action to release energy and tension at the very time physical action no longer is built into our daily lives. Thus, we find the build-up of *bound energy* and the rise of mental and physical tension. Stress-related disturbances and diseases often result.

Feelings, Thoughts and Actions in the Stress Response

At the beginning of this chapter we emphasized that body, mind, and behavior are all interconnected, yet thus far we have said little about behavior. What part does it play? As we have defined stress, behavior is not part of the stress response itself. Yet it is closely related in four ways:

Mental and physical arousal often are expressed in behavior.
Behavior such as exercise and self-disclosure, for example, can help

protect against out-of-control stress responses.
Behavior is used to cope or interact with stress triggers.
Behavior is used to react to distress, either constructively or destructively.

Emotional stress is closely interrelated with physical stress, as is intellectual stress. The interplay of these forms of stress will be discussed in more detail later. Here it is sufficient to recognize that thoughts and feelings may either trigger or reflect physical stress. However, thoughts and feelings do not exist apart from physical stress. This is important to note because altering the physical basis of stress through relaxation or exercise can alter troubling thoughts and feelings.

ADAPTATION TO STRESS

Many years ago, Dr. Hans Selye identified a universal pattern of physical stress known as the *general adaptation syndrome* (GAS) which helps us understand how the body handles stress over time and how physical stress sometimes gives way to distress.[6] The GAS also is useful in explaining the role of adaptation in managing stress effectively.

Whatever the stressor, the organism goes through a general non-specific response in addition to the localized stress response that may occur, for example, in reaction to a local infection or bruise. Selye points out that this local response constitutes "that part of the overall response to an agent (stressor) which we have to subtract in order to arrive at our stress syndrome. The features of the GAS (for instance, the increased production of adreno-corticoid hormones, the involution of the lymphatic organs, or the loss of weight) are the purely non-specific residue which remains after this subtraction".[7]

Selye's well-known definition of stress is "the non-specific response of the body to any demand made upon it."[8] This definition is very similar to the one we use in this book. The only differences are that the definition used here includes mental as well and physical reactions and introduces the somewhat more descriptive term "arousal." By including mental arousal, we include a much wider range of human experiences under the category of stress.

We may go through three phases as we seek to handle stress: an initial alarm reaction, sustaining resistance, and exhaustion. These phases, shown in Figure 2-3, can be seen most easily in the body's reaction to physical traumas such as fire or cold. But the same sequence occurs as you react to personal and social situations in daily life, such as a verbal attack, prolonged isolation, or chronic overload.

During the alarm reaction, the body is immediately prepared for direct decisive physical action (the fight-or-flight response), largely through instantaneous activation of the sympathetic nervous system, sometimes before the person is even aware of the stressor. Large amounts of glucose and oxygen are supplied to organs most active in warding off danger, such as the heart, the brain, and skeletal muscles. The curving line in Figure 2-3 falls below normal stress level because the body often is temporarily set back as it fights to restore internal balance.

As the body mobilizes additional resources, largely through arousal of the stress hormones, resistance increases. This is the stage of resistance. The body and mind cope with the difficulty in a sustained way, usually quite effectively. If the stressor is too intense for too long, however, the body's adaptive reserves begin to become depleted, at which time the stage of exhaustion begins. At this stage, wear and tear is progressive. Stress becomes distress, and illness is likely. Type of illness will be influenced by individual weaknesses.

FIGURE 2-3
THE GENERAL ADAPTATION SYNDROME[9]

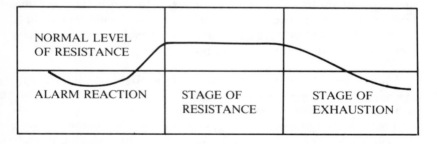

Selye demonstrated with laboratory rats that this sequence of adaptation occurs irrespective of the specific stressor, such as electric shock, cold, forced muscular work, drugs, injections.[10] He suggests that the same is true of humans. This discovery and Selye's resulting general adaptation syndrome has important implications for understanding how humans adapt to stress.

A remarkable feature of human beings is the ability to adapt — both to changing external circumstances and to internal stress levels. As you move from one place to another, change jobs, meet and lose friends, confront challenges in the classroom or on the athletic field, you may experience intense stress. Sometimes you wonder if you will make it. Yet you do. And you will again — because you do adapt to stressors and to stress. You get used to new situations.

Some years ago selected inmates from Oregon State Prison participated in Project New Gate, a college education program.[11] They attended classes inside the prison until a few months before parole or discharge. Their last several months as prisoners were spent at a halfway house at the University of Oregon campus. From the prison to the campus, the increase in stimulation level was enormous. Sometimes inmates found themselves overwhelmed by sounds, sights, choices, competition, dates, or the availability of drugs. A few inmate-students were so overwhelmed that they broke down, broke a rule, or simply asked to be returned to the "joint." Yet most adapted. Their zone of positive stress shifted upward. They learned to live with the higher stimulation of campus life. Their stress levels went down.

In track, swimming, and other sports, coaches deliberately control their athletes' adaptation to stress. The usual training program calls for practicing at a certain speed and distance for a designated period of time. During the first few days at a certain level of output, performance goes down while fatigue increases. After a few days, the athlete adapts to the new level of effort. The workouts, initially so demanding, become relatively easy within two or three weeks. In a systematic fashion, still more speed and distance are added until the athlete's body has adapted and a new level of performance has been reached.

In this incremental manner the athlete progresses to the point where maximum possible performance is attained. Performance limits may be set by mental barriers, by effort, or by breakdown in muscles, joints, or tendons. The athlete must adapt carefully to increasing levels of stress, while remaining just below the point of distress — that fine edge of injury, physical fatigue, or mental exhaustion.

You also have this capability to adapt, to adjust to different stresses as you move from one situation to another or as you take on new challenges. Adapting to stress is important if you are to achieve higher levels of self-fulfillment in the various facets of your life. What you need is *stress without distress.*[12]

An important word of caution is needed, however. We sometimes delude ourselves into believing we are adapting within our zone of positive stress. We become *comfortable* with a highly demanding job, fast pace of life, or bad marriage, for example. We assume we are adjusting within our own tolerance limits and that our health will not be adversely affected. Often, however, this apparent adjustment is not successful adaptation at all. Rather, we continue for a lengthy period in Selye's stage of resistance without returning to our optimum stress level.

In time, our bodies give way in one form or another, depending on the individual. It may be chronic colds, hypertension, a skin disorder, migraines, or even a sudden heart attack. All reflect wear and tear as we enter the stage of physical exhaustion. The aging process reflects such exhaustion.

Selye maintains that our deep adaptive reserves are limited and can be used up.[13] Disharmony exacts a toll in the long run.

In brief, adaptation to stress does not mean simply becoming comfortable with a stressor or set of stressors. True adaptation means adjustment of your spirit and your organism to those circumstances within the limits of your own, unique zone of positive stress. What is comfortable may not be healthful over the long haul.

THE RELAXATION RESPONSE AND HOMEOSTASIS

Just as the body possesses capabilities to arouse, it can recover and relax. The mind plays an equally important part in the relaxation response as in the stress response.

THE RELAXATION RESPONSE IS QUIETING OF MIND AND BODY

The human organism, like other animals, possesses a strong and persistent drive toward equilibrium or homeostasis. As Herbert Benson, author of *The Relaxation Response* states:

> *If the fight-or-flight response resides within animals and humans, is there an innate physiologic response that is dramatically different? The answer is yes. Each of us possesses a natural and innate protective mechanism against "overstress," which allows us to turn off harmful bodily effects, to counter the effects of the fight-or-flight response. This response against "overstress," brings on bodily*

changes that decrease heart rate, lower metabolism, decrease the rate of breathing, and brings the body back into what is probably a healthier balance. This is the RELAXATION RESPONSE.[14]

The relaxation response occurs naturally to some degree. Each time we are aroused, the body tends to restore itself to a more natural, lower level. This occurs through the parasympathetic nervous system, which counters the sympathetic nervous system, and through quieting of the endocrine system. Problems arise when the stress response is triggered too frequently or continuously without adequate recovery or when people do not know how to relax. Stress build-up results.

At the same time that physical exercise is needed to release bound energy and to prevent its accumulation, deliberate steps are needed to induce the relaxation response each day through mental and physical relaxation practices such as meditation or self-hypnosis.

In short, activity needs to be alternated with rest, arousal with relaxation, excitation with quiet. Research shows that 15-20 minutes set aside once or twice each day for *deep* relaxation, which takes body processes into a deeper quiet than the normal equilibrium level of daily living, can prove effective for both coping with distress already present and for preventing stress build-up from occurring in the first place. Later chapters will present techniques for releasing the relaxation response.

It is important here to note that popular notions of relaxation may be quite inaccurate. A non-work activity may be pleasant, but not necessarily relaxing in the sense that physical and mental quieting occurs. In fact the exact opposite may occur. The familiar coffee break may elevate the stress response through the stimulating effect of caffeine. A round of golf may arouse competitive urges, rather than quiet the hypothalamus, the pituitary gland, the adrenal cortex, the sympathetic nervous system. The same may happen with a do-it-yourself/home project. The activity may be beneficial by being a diversion, but may not be *relaxing.* Certainly it does not produce deep relaxation, so vital to counteracting chronic arousal of the stress response. Diversion and recreation may not be true relaxation.

PLEASANT AND UNPLEASANT STRESS

Stress may be pleasant or unpleasant. An example of pleasant physical stress might be the excitement of a close football game — even more pleasant if your team wins. The delight of a new intimate relationship is

56

an example of pleasant emotional stress, while the challenge of a debate or a writing assignment may bring pleasant intellectual distress. The surge of energy felt by a basketball player during the last two minutes of the game may be pleasant as well; it is stress, nevertheless. Unpleasant stresses are familiar: headache, depression, the pain of a minor burn, irritation of an abrasive noise, fatigue, anxiety.

All stresses cause some wear and tear. But, as Dr. Selye has noted,pleasant stress causes less harm to mind and body than does unpleasant stress, although the internal processes accounting for this difference are not fully understood.[15] Even so, pleasant stresses can build up to turn into physical or emotional upset. Examples are too many consecutive parties, a challenging series of work assignments, and a child playing too hard and too long in the hot sun.

ANTICIPATORY, CURRENT, AND RESIDUAL STRESS

Anticipatory stress is your response to expected stressors.[16] Mind and body prepare in advance for change, crisis, or challenge. Examples of this type of stress are numerous: tension before a test, "butterflies" before a race; apprehension about a parent's response to your breaking a rule; fear of an impending hurricane; dread of forced retirement. Anticipatory stress is useful in moderate amounts because it prepares your body and mind for events which are about to happen. Such stress increases sharpness and motivation. But it also can interfere with life in the present. This sometimes accompanies chronic overload as a person gives more attention to what may *happen* than what *is* happening. It also affects people who lack confidence or are seeking an escape from involvement in the present.

Dr. Elizabeth Kubler-Ross, a leading authority on death and dying, has studied the ultimate form of anticipatory stress: awareness of one's impending death.[17] She has identified five stages which such patients usually pass through:

Shock and denial
Anger
Bargaining for time
Depression
Acceptance

According to Dr. Kubler-Ross, individuals experience this sequence in different ways, but all five stages are common.

Current stress occurs during an experience: the body's extreme alarm during an auto accident; mental alertness in the midst of a debate; the surge of energy in the final 100 yards of a race. Current stress, if harnessed effectively, is vital for optimal performance.

Residual stress occurs after the experience has passed. The body remains in a state of alarm for some time after a near-collision on the highway. Athletes may have difficulty sleeping the night after a victory. Over-stimulation, whether pleasant or unpleasant, can have the same effect. A significant challenge in managing stress, then, is to develop ways of quickly returning the body and mind to normal levels of stress after challenges, crises, or changes. If normalcy is not regained relatively quickly a person is likely to experience some type of distress. "After-burn time" must follow intense experiences if a person is to return to normal. How much time is needed depends on both the event and the person.

STRESS FROM OVER- AND UNDER-STIMULATION

Stressors can be few or numerous with respect to a given time period. Similarly, stress can occur from under-stimulation or over-stimulation with the definition of "under" and "over" varying with the person.

Dr. Selye developed a chart (known as the "experience continuum") which illustrates the fact that stress shades into distress at either high or low extremes of stimulation.[18] In slightly modified form, the experience continuum is shown in Figure 2-4.[19]

FIGURE 2-4
THE EXPERIENCE CONTINUUM

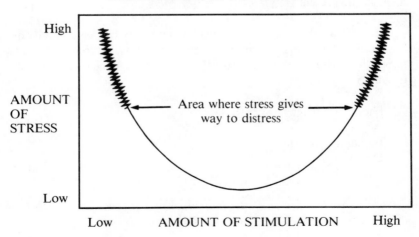

From this chart it can be seen that the amount of stress can increase at either extreme, over-stimulation or under-stimulation. But even in the middle range of stimulation, the experience line does not touch bottom, since the only time one reaches the point of no stress is at death. At all other times, some amount of stimulation is experienced. It is clear from this chart also that stress can turn into distress under conditions of either over-stimulation or under-stimulation.

This chart also can be used with pleasantness of the stress along the base: very pleasant at one extreme, very unpleasant at the other.

Let us examine stress and distress at the two extremes of stimulation. A number of laboratory experiments on "sensory deprivation" show that most people soon begin to experience disorientation, anxiety, depression, or other discomforts when deprived of light, touch, sound, and smell.[20] Sometimes these experiments are carried out in a tank of water where the submerged subject breathes through a mask but cannot experience even gravity. One journalist who volunteered for such a study in order to write a story acted confident and pleased immediately after leaving the tank. But toward the end of his interview with the scientist in charge, he said, "I honestly believe if you put a person in there, just kept him and fed him by vein, he would just flat die." He never wrote the story.[21]

Too little stimulation — "sensory deprivation" — can create serious mental and physical difficulties.[22] A less extreme form of under-stimulation is boredom. You probably have experienced the heaviness of mind or body, the feeling of depression, or the growing tension that sometimes accompanies too much stillness, too little to do. Prisoners-of-war have been known to break down after only a few days of total isolation.

At the opposite extreme are studies of people on the battlefield, in the workplace, or in school who simply have too much to do or to absorb in too short a time. Such people may become tense, anxious, fired up, hostile, upset, short-tempered, confused, unable to sleep. As in under-stimulation, too much stimulation generates an intricate network of changes in body, mind, and behavior. A vicious cycle often gets started in which a series of damaging reactions feed on one another. And, as research has shown, the chances of high blood pressure and heart attack increase markedly with chronic overload.

STRESS AND PERFORMANCE

As Mike mentally prepared during the last week for his moment in the State roller-skating championships, he recalled his ups and downs during that season. He had done very well several times, mediocre twice, and was definitely "off" at three meets. He had tried a number of different mental and physical techniques to prepare himself, sometimes entering the rink emotionally too high — pent-up, anxious, on edge — at others with a feeling of listlessness and lack of concentration. In looking back, it became clear to him that those meets in which he performed at his peak were instances where his stress level was in the middle, neither too high, nor too low. He realized in thinking further that the same had been true of his test performances at college, speeches he had given, even job interviews. He was struck by the vital importance of optimum stress in peak performances.

Mike's personal discovery was consistent with a principle observed by researchers in such diverse fields at athletics, drama, music, business management, and psychotherapy: peak performance occurs when arousal is neither too high nor too low, but in a person's middle range. This principle is shown graphically in Figure 2-5.

FIGURE 2-5
RANGE OF PEAK PERFORMANCE

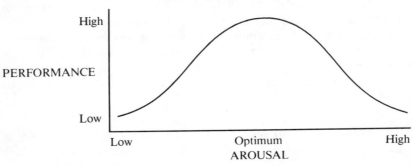

A personal challenge is to determine one's optimum arousal level. Another is to learn techniques, including an entire lifestyle, for creating and maintaining that optimum stress level.

A challenge facing managers, supervisors, teachers, and coaches is to learn techniques for creating the right stress level for those they influence, as well as to learn how to recognize when it is present. Forbes suggests the following as indicators of optimum stress among employees:

High energy
Mental alertness
High motivation
Calmness under pressure
Thorough analysis of problems
Improved memory and recall
Sharp perception
Optimistic outlook[23]

She suggests that managers might use these categories as checkpoints to assess stress levels at any given time among those supervised. Indicators of both under-stress or over-stress are:

Boredom
Apathy
High accident rate
Frequent grievances
Absenteeism
Negative outlook toward employer
Widespread fatigue
Insomnia
Change in appetite
Increased use of tobacco, drugs, or alcohol
Errors
Indecisiveness
Short-range attitude[24]

While these are difficult to objectify, they do bear noting, even informally, by the effective manager. Other suggestions are presented in Part II for mobilizing optimum stress in performance situations.

IMPLICATIONS FOR MANAGING STRESS

The description of stress above implies a number of ways to manage stress effectively.

Anticipate, monitor, and regulate stressors insofar as possible.

Be aware of and control perceptions of stressors.

Practice daily deep relaxation in order to balance chronic excitation of the stress response with recovery, as well as to keep arousal at a lower level most of the time.

Use mental and physical on-the-spot tension reducers to control mental and physical arousal when contronted with threatening stress triggers.

Practice daily exercise in order to regularly release tension and prevent stress build-up.

Recognize early warning signs of mental and physical distress.

Develop means of mobilizing and controlling stress in performance situations.

Use constructive reactions to distress when it does occur in order to reduce distress, rather than destructive reactions which heighten distress.

In Chapter 1 we noted that stress can be helpful for health, productivity, and satisfaction. This chapter showed how distress can result from too little or too much arousal — over-stress or under-stress. Between these two extremes is a zone of positive stress which is vital to learn to recognize in yourself and in those with whom you closely relate. In Chapter 3 we will see how this zone varies from one person to another and how a number of stress difficulties can turn moderate stress into damaging distress.

CHAPTER REVIEW AND PERSONAL APPLICATIONS

1. Distinguish between episodic and chronic stressors. Give two examples from your own experience of the past week.

2. Exactly what is meant by this statement? "Mind, body, and behavior are closely intertwined." Give two examples.

3. Describe the part played by each of the following in the stress response:
   a. Subconscious appraisal pathway
   b. Cerebral cortex
   c. Hypothalamus
   d. ACTH
   e. Adrenal medulla
   f. Thyroxine
   g. Bound energy
   h. Physical action

4. Describe six changes you can feel during a maxi-fight-or-flight response?

5. How might the three stages of the general adaptation syndrome correspond with stages of life?

6. True or False? "By definition, stress cannot be pleasant." Give two examples to support your position.

7. Identify one illustration from your own life during the past week when you have experienced noticeable stress arousal (not necessarily distress) of each of these types: anticipatory, current, residual. Exactly what stress symptoms were evident in each case?

8. Do you agree or disagree? "Stress always rises with increases in stimulation and falls with decreases in stimulation." Why? Explain with examples.

9. How might the discussion of stress and performance presented here apply to management behavior? Coaching? Test preparation?

10. Identify five ways in which the relaxation response is the physiological opposite to the stress response.

11. What does homeostasis have to do with stress and relaxation? Give two examples.

12. What does *deep* relaxation have to do with homeostasis?

REFERENCES

1. Hans Selye, *The Stress of Life.* New York: McGraw-Hill Book Co., 1976, p. 412.

2. Daniel A. Girdano and George S. Everly, Jr., *Controlling Stress and Tension.* Englewood Cliffs, N.J.: Prentice-Hall, Inc., 1979, p. 30.

3. Barbara B. Brown, *Stress and the Art of Biofeedback.* New York: Bantam Books, 1977.

4. Kenneth Pelletier, *Mind as Healer, Mind as Slayer. New York: Dell Publishing Co., 1977, p. 54.*

5. *Ibid.,* p. 55.

6. Selye, *op cit.,* Chapter 3.

7. *Ibid.,* p. 47.

8. *Ibid.,* Chapter 3.

9. *Ibid.,* p. 111.

10. *Ibid.,* Chapter 5.

11. Walt Schafer, *Stress, Distress, and Growth.* Davis, CA.: International Dialogue Press, 1978, p. 51.

12. Hans Selye, *Stress Without Distress.* Philadelphia; J.B. Lippincott, 1974.

13. Selye, *The Stress of Life, op cit.,* p. 307.

14. Herbert Benson, *The Relaxation Response.* New York: William Morrow and Company, 1975, p. 18.

15. Hans Selye, Remarks at conference on Stress Management, Concepts of Stress, San Francisco, October 2, 1977.

16. Schafer, *op cit.,* p. 43.

17. Elizabeth Kubler-Ross, *On Death and Dying.* New York: MacMillan, 1969.

18. Selye, *Stress Without Distress, op cit.,* p. 33.

19. Schafer, *op cit.,* p. 45.

20. Ogden Tanner, *Stress.* New York: Time-Life Books, 1976, p. 26.

21. *Ibid.,* p. 28.

22. Schafer, *op cit.,* p. 46.

23. Rosalind Forbes, *Corporate Stress.* Garden City, N.Y.: Doubleday and Co., Inc., 1979, p. 43.

24. John M. Ivancevich and Michael T. Matteson, *Stress and Work.* Glevisen, Ill.: Scott, Foreman and Company, 1980., p. 203.

CHAPTER 3

DISTRESS: OVER THE EDGE

In the previous two chapters, we saw that stress in moderate amounts can be pleasant, stimulating, and even helpful for meeting challegnes and emergencies. But distress from either over-stress or under-stress must be avoided whenever possible since it can be harmful to wellness as described in Chapter 1.

Occasional distress is unavoidable. For example, two or more people can live in arelationship only imperfectly. The physical environment is largely uncontrollable. Financial problems are bound to rise. Illness and death are inevitable. But the less distress the better.

In this chapter we will point out some of the ways moderate stress turns to harmful distress, resulting in stress-induced illnesses and in various forms of mental distress. At the outset, it will be useful to examine the notion of a "zone of positive stress."

ZONE OF POSITIVE STRESS

Allan had been accustomed to a fast pace of life since childhood. He thrived on challenge and productivity. Difficult work situations seldom threatened him. Rather, he attacked them with vigor and optimism. He did not seek out overload, yet his life seemed full most of the time. In short, he had high stress tolerance. He seldom missed work because of illness. He was productive and quite satisfied with his work and family life.

Fred felt continually awed by Allan's seemingly endless ability to tolerate challenge without showing signs of wear and tear. Fred by nature was more slow-going and required more time per work task. He tended to become flustered and ineffective when work piled up. He deliberately let others take on difficult confrontations with clients since he disliked the tension. Fred had considerably lower stress tolerance than Allan, to become emotionally and intellectually overloaded at a point where Allan thrived.

Each of us possesses a dintinctive zone of positive stress. A vital part of managing stress is to learn the range and limits of that zone. We must learn to recognize warning signs near its edges and to live within that zone most of the time.

ZONE OF POSITIVE STRESS: THE TOLERANCE RANGE OF STRESS WITHIN WHICH THE PERSON IS HEALTHY, PRODUCTIVE, AND SATISFIED

We can visualize the zone of positive stress better by means of Figure 3-1.

FIGURE 3-1

RANGE OF STRESS TOLERANCE

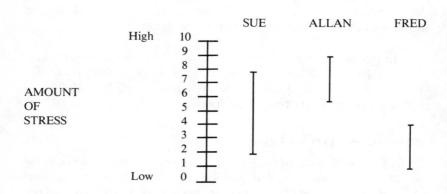

The scale on the left represents an objective range of stress tolerance which might be measured by physical indicators such as blood pressure, heart rate, muscle tension, or brain waves, or by indicators of emotional anxiety.

Three illustrative cases are listed in Figure 3-1. Sue, with a zone of positive stress from eight to two, is the most adaptable of the three, since she is comfortable, productive, and healthy at either a fast or slow pace, with high or low arousal. Her well-being is more independent of her environment than the other two in that she thrives within a wider range of stimulation and personal stress.

Allan's zone is narrower at a relatively high level. He is what Selye calls a "racehorse." He is bored and even experiences a bit of distress at point four or five on the scale, which is in Sue's mid-range. Allan generates a high activity level at home and work to keep his stress level high when his outside environment does not do it for him. He is a "sensation seeker."

Fred is a "turtle," with a narrow zone near the lower end of the scale. As noted above, he quite wisely avoids challenge and unfamiliar situations. He is somewhat of a plodder, yet he is dependable and effective in his work.

A common source of job stress is a misfit between the demands of the job and the zone of positive stress of the worker. A key challenge for managers and supervisors is to achieve an optimal job-personality fit among employees. Another is to fit employees together with relatively compatible tolerance zones whenever possible.

Another common problem is incompatible zones of positive stress between marriage partners. Let us hope that Allan's twin sister Eileen, who also is a racehorse, does not fall in love with and marry Fred, the turtle. Such a marriage would be destined for difficulty from the start because of the quite different paces of life.

Zones of positive stress are determined and shaped by a variety of influences: physical energy levels, background, personality, choice, demands of the home or work situation. Everyone's zone is changeable to some degree, of course. The decision to leave a life of relative leisure in order to return to law school brings with it a choice to raise the upper limit of one's zone. Entering a demanding new job also may require living with a higher stress level than before. Similarly, getting married or having a baby results in the need for greater tolerance than before. Each person has limits of adaptability. A great deal of ill health and unhappiness results from efforts to push one's limits too far — at either the upper or lower end of the scale.

Mental and physical distress can result from either too little or too much stress. Each person, then, possesses three zones — zone of positive stress, zone of overload distress, and zone of underload distress. Symptoms of the two types of distress may be similar or different (emotional anxiety, insomnia, irritability, for example).

Thus far, we have used one dimension (zero to ten) in describing the zone of positive stress. In order to enhance the usefulness of this model for understanding common stress difficulties, we will add a horizontal dimension as well.

A relatively distress-free day is represented in Figure 3-2. Note that stress level fluctuates throughout the day. In reality of course, blood pressure, brain waves, etc., vary throughout the day in much finer degrees than shown here. Larger swings, however, are shown. This individual stayed within her zone of positive stress most of the time, exceeding her upper limit only briefly. This is a desirable stress pattern.

FIGURE 3-2

STRESS LEVELS OVER TIME

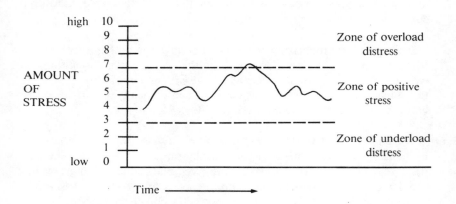

PERSONAL GROWTH THROUGH PUSHING YOUR LIMITS

If we stayed within our zones of positive stress constantly, however, personal growth might never take place. Substantial benefits can result from sometimes deliberately distressing ourselves for a time in pursuit of a meaningful goal or, to reach a higher level of performance than before, or to cope with an emergency. Marathon running, mountain climbing, studying very hard for a final examination, working very long hours on a project at work, missing sleep while caring for a loved one — all are examples of dedicated, meaningful efforts requiring pushing one's mental or physical limits.

If distance runners never entered physical distress, they would never approach physiological potential. Similarly, if you are never willing to work very, very hard in pursuit of a goal, you will remain half-developed. You may never know the trade-off of temporary emotional or physical pain for the joy of accomplishment and approaching potential.

Yet in daily life, a number of stress difficulties can arise in relation to zones of stress. We will now examine each of these difficulties.

EIGHT COMMON STRESS DIFFICULTIES

Figure 3-3 shows the same tolerance limits (between three and seven) as appeared in Figure 3-2. Here, however, are eight common stress difficulties. Each illustrates actual cases I have seen in the Stress and Health Center. No individual, in reality, would experience all eight in the same day — or even the same year. For graphic simplicity, I have drawn together a composite of separate persons and time periods into a single chart. Baseline stress level refers to hour-after-hour tension level when the individual is neither pressed nor experiencing deep relaxation. The following stress difficulties are illustrated in this figure.

FIGURE 3-3

COMMON STRESS DIFFICULTIES

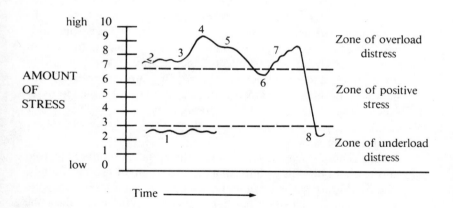

1. **Baseline stress level too low**
   Following retirement by her and her husband, Mildred was perpetually bored, with no personal goals, little social contact, and little meaning in her life. She had difficulty sleeping at night, yet was listless, devoid of energy, and irritable during the day.

71

2. **Baseline stress level too high**

   Jim, an ambitious young college professor, felt overwhelmed much of the time. He was constantly aware of a need to excel, to serve well on department committees, to show his best side to colleagues, and to receive good student ratings. He worked every night and most weekends. He also was a do-it-yourselfer at home, compelled to build, garden, and repair by himself. He had been a perfectionist since childhood, driven ever upward toward some illusory standard or goal with little satisfaction along the way. Jim had high blood pressure, free-floating anxiety, and frequent gastritis and insomnia.

3. **Hair-trigger stress reaction**

   John, an insurance agent whose baseline stress level also was too high, had virtually no tolerance for the noise or flippancy of his 11-year-old boy. In earlier years, they often joked and played together. Now, however, the slightest disturbance or demand of John after work produced an outburst of put-downs and discounts directed at the boy. He was often defensive with his wife, co-workers, and friends.

4. **Peak arousal too high**

   Sharon, a 38-year-old mother of four teenagers, decided last year to return to college after a 19-year lay-off. Understandably, her baseline stress level was too high much of the time, and she too was often over-reactive to high demands or deviations. In addition, she sometimes experienced debilitating test anxiety. She knew some anxiety helped her to prepare, but lately this arousal had gotten out of hand, resulting in serious mental blocks during tests. She also sometimes had angry outbursts at home, far out of proportion to the situation. Both the test anxiety and the displays of anger were instances where peak arousal was too high.

5. **Recovery too slow**

   Julie, a school teacher and mother of three, had been quite involved during recent months with the marriage break-up of her best friends, who lived nearby. She became the primary listener for both the man and woman, which often put her in a considerable bind, since she had to be careful what she said to whom. This involvement began to interfere with her own family life, especially as her concentration and attentiveness diminished at home. She found it difficult to put her friends' problems out of her mind as she tried to find possible solutions to suggest. Her sleep was frequently disturbed. In short, her recovery from tense emotions and involvements was too low.

6. Recovery not low enough

Ken, a 58-year-old bank manager, was hardly able to tolerate the thought that four years stood between him and retirement. The volume of his work was not only overwhelming, it had become meaningless to him. During a series of stress consultations, he became aware that he had no effective means of releasing tensions, of bringing his mental and physical stress level down to a more tolerable level in the evenings. Not only was his baseline stress level too high, his recovery too slow, but his recovery was not low enough. Although he had never exercised since his teens, he began a moderate program of walking and jogging after work, which served to get him out of the office earlier and to help him release built-up physical tension from the day, thereby bringing his emotional tension down to a reasonable level for the evening.

7. Stress build-up

Scott was a pleasant, kind, responsive, overweight elementary teacher of 41, who not only kept his family of seven in bread, butter, and shoes on a meager salary, but gave a great deal of time to the activities of his children. He car-pooled to scouting events, went camping often, built a swimming pool and deck for his family, went to church regularly. He also was a superb cook, especially for large banquets. Not surprisingly, he was asked often, usually as a volunteer, to cook for school or church events. He was a responsible and helpful teacher who took his job seriously. Thus, he was an easy target to organize special events or to take on difficult committee assignments. After several years of this, Scott became aware of a severe stress build-up. His easy-going manner became more tense, he snapped at others more often, he felt joyless, he put on weight, and had recurrent bouts with psoriasis, an uncomfortable and potentially dangerous skin disorder.

8. Recovery too low

George was a 23-year-old university student who decided to return to school after working three years as a gas station attendant. He studied hard to compensate for his limited activities and his three-year absence from book learning. At mid-term and final exam time, he would cram very hard, often long into the night, then resume studying in the morning. He would be emotionally up during these periods, but then would take a depressive nose-dive after exams were over. It sometimes took three to four weeks for him to recover his usual emotional level. In short, he experienced too low a recovery period. He was not seriously manic-depressive, but his pattern resembled manic-depression in its basic form.

These eight common stress difficulties can occur in combination or independently. When baseline stress level is too high, several other difficulties tend to follow: hair-trigger stress reaction, too high peak stress, too low recovery, recovery not low enough and too slow, and stress build-up. These illustrations underscore the fact that effective stress management does not rest on a single, simple solution, but on an integrated lifestyle approach involving control of time, release of physical tension, relaxation skills, altered relationships, and more.

These stress difficulties manifest themselves physically, emotionally, intellectually, and in behavior. We will now examine each of these forms of distress in more detail.

PHYSICAL DISTRESS SYMPTOMS
Below are illustrative physical distress signals which have been described to me by participants in my stress management workshops and groups during recent months.

Dryness of mouth or throat
General fatigue or heaviness
Trembling or nervous twitch
Pounding of heart
Diarrhea
Constipation
Frequent need to urinate
Upset stomach
Neck pain
Back pain
Dizzy spells
Decreased interest in sex
Loss of appetite
Increase of appetite
Chest pain
Heart palpitations
Tension throughout the body

Sometimes these occur in clusters, at other times singly. In many instances, they are only minor irritants, but sometimes they interfere with behavior and performance.

A fascinating form of physical distress is "network nerves" on TV talk shows. According to a Beverly Hills psychiatrist, network nerves usually includes "panic, stomach distress, flushed skin, tightness of the larynx, poor circulation, fast pulse, even vomiting."[1] He helps performers overcome their intense fear of on-camera blundering by suggesting pleasant, relaxing images they can call forth before their appearance.

Minor physical distress symptoms, when cumulative, do not remain minor. They often turn into full-blown stress illnesses. Whether or not this progression occurs depends on whether you respond adaptively or maladaptively to the early warning signs of distress, which is the topic of Chapter 12.

STRESS-RELATED ILLNESSES

The term "psychosomatic illness" often is popularly misused to refer to an illness which has no organic origin, but is "all in your head." To be sure, disease states often are imagined rather than real, as any practicing physician can attest. This may be why placebo pills are effective about one-third of the time.[2]

Psychosomatic illness properly refers to sickness in which the mind plays a causative part. Illnesses usually do not have one single origin, but rather result from the convergence of a number of factors: deficient nutrition, fatigue, exposure to germs, weakened immunity, and more. Through emotional and cognitive distress, the mind (and personal experience) sometimes contributes to illness in three ways:

Long-term wear and tear from excessive stress makes the body more *susceptible* to breakdown, such as peptic ulcers, colitis, cancer, migraines, or high blood pressure.

An acute episode of intense emotional stress can directly *precipitate* a physical ailment, heart attack, tension headache, or muscle spasm in the back.

High stress, chronic or acute, can *aggravate* an existing illness, such as angina, diabetes, arthritis, or hypertension.

Experts on stress and health estimate that between 60 and 90 percent of illnesses are stress-related in one of these ways. This is not to say that all such illnesses are unreal or imagined. But stresses helped induce or aggravate them in one or more of these three ways. More effective management of stress may be among the most effective means of reducing the soaring costs of health care (or sickness care) in this country.

In *The Doctor's Guide to Living With Stress,* Graham-Bonnalie listed the following illnesses as sometimes induced or aggravated by excessive stress:[3]

Acne	Eye conditions
Alcoholism	Fatigue
Allergies	Frigidity
Anorexia nervosa	Gout
Appendicitis	Headache and migraine
Asthma	Heart conditions,
Cancer	including hypertension
Colitis	Impotence
Constipation	Insomnia
Dermatitis and eczema	Obesity
Diabetes	Peptic ulcers
Diarrhea	Psoriasis
Eneuresis	Rheumatic fever
	Rheumatoid arthritis

Let us examine several prevalent stress-related illnesses in more detail.

HIGH BLOOD PRESSURE

Hypertension, or high blood pressure, is among the most lethal, wide-spread, and baffling ailments of our time.[4] One of five Americans suffers from it, with blacks exceeding whites by 50 to 100 percent. High blood pressure alone accounts for about 60,000 deaths per year, but if its indirect mortal impact through long-range effects on strokes, heart attacks, and kidney ailments are taken into account, it is a contributing factor in millions of deaths each year.

Hypertension is excessive pressure against walls of blood vessels throughout the body. It is a direct result of constriction of the size of those blood vessels through chronic contraction of small muscles in the blood vessel walls.

Blood pressure is measured with two numbers, systolic and diastolic. Systolic blood pressure, the numerator and larger number, refers to millimeters of mercury raised on a scale at the moment of contraction of the heart. Diastolic blood pressure, the denominator and smaller number, refers to millimeters of mercury raised on a scale at the moment between beats, when the ventricles (pumps) of the heart are refilling with blood and less pressure is exerted against blood vessel walls.

While glandular and other disorders contribute to hypertension in some cases, most cases are unexplained. One recent textbook on internal medicine stated that "...a specific cause for the increase in peripheral resistance which is responsible for the elevated arterial pressure cannot be defined in approximately 90 percent of patients with hypertension disease."[5]

Herbert Bensen and other experts contend that a substantial proportion of this "essential" (or unexplained) hypertension may result from prolonged, unreleased chronic excitation of the stress response.[6] This also may result from the lingering, residual effects of such excitation in the past. Numerous studies lend credibility to this position. For example, hypertension is a major problem for black Americans, a fact which may be less due to genetic disposition than to the greater life stresses of blacks.[7] A study of blacks residing in middle-class neighborhoods showed they had a rate of hypertension only about one-half that of blacks residing in ghetto environments for whom crime, unstable neighborhoods, pollution, and over-crowding are likely to create much more daily tension.[8]

Another study shows that air traffic controllers have a rate of hypertension about five times greater than comparable work groups, probably because of the intensely demanding pressures in the air traffic tower.[9] At the same time, other studies show that both exercise and meditation are effective in reducing blood pressure.[10]

In short, hypertension may be a severe health hazard resulting from the stresses of late twentieth-century existence, especially for certain population groups. In the long run, understanding and minimizing stress may be more potent means of containing this epidemic than even the most effective medications.

CORONARY HEART DISEASE

The coronary arteries wrap around the heart to furnish the heart muscle with newly oxygenated blood. If the continuous flow of blood through the arteries is cut off, death to heart tissue results. This is a heart attack.

Beginning early in life and continuing into adulthood, the inner lining of the coronary arteries develops tiny lesions or breaks. Little is known about why this occurs or why people differ in the number and severity of lesions. Fortunately, the body is equipped to repair these minor internal injuries, just as it can repair a minor external wound. Through a complex series of messages from the brain, blood clots and scar tissues emerge. New cells develop and the tiny wound is repaired. But as this happens, the size of the passageway through the coronary artery is narrowed slightly. The scar tissue continues to build up on new lesions along the coronary arteries or in old scar tissue.

Scars increase not only in number but also in size, partly because of continued clotting and partly because fat-like substances get stuck in tiny openings in the scar tissue. After a time, the scar tissue contains much of these fatty substances. The most dangerous of these is cholesterol.

More lesions, more clotting and scarring, more closure, less blood flow, more lesions — on the cycle goes. Finally a blood clot may break away, blocking the line at a narrow spot. Or arteries narrowed from high blood pressure may cause a complete closing off of blood flow, or the rhythmic pumping of the heart goes awry and stops altogether. The part of the heart deprived of blood soon dies and nearby cells are severely weakened. The heart can no longer pump blood to the lungs or throughout the body. If enough muscle dies from lack of oxygen, the result is death.

The term *coronary artery disease* refers to a partial closing of the coronary arteries. A *heart attack* or *myocardial infarction* occurs when a coronary blockage causes a complete cessation of blood to an area of the heart. The result is death of heart tissue. *Arrhythmia* refers to uncontrolled beating of the heart. It often causes death.

The emergence of heart attacks as a major cause of death has stimulated scientists to devote substantial time and energy to studying causes. While much remains to be learned, a number of fairly definite "risk factors" have been identified.[11] For example, you are more likely to succumb to heart attack if you are male or if you have high blood pressure (hypertension) or unstable sugar diabetes. You also are at risk if your diet is high in cholesterol, if you smoke cigarettes, if you are physically inactive, if there is a history of heart disease in your family, or if you are significantly overweight.

Researchers continue to study how much and in what ways each of these factors increases the chances of heart attack. Most scientists agree that these causes do not explain all heart attacks. Some believe they account for less than one-half. In recent years, heart researchers have turned their attention to entirely different potential causes, including how people live.

Significant progress in this area has been made by two San Francisco cardiologists, Dr. Meyer Friedman and Dr. Ray Rosenman.[12] They have established that the chances of heart attack rise considerably if an individual exhibits a "Type A" behavior pattern — that is, if he or she is chronically overloaded, working against the clock to get more and more done in less and less time. In short, heart disease seems to be caused in part by too much stress.

Friedman and Rosenman formally define Type A behavior as:

*...a characteristic action-emotion complex which is exhibited by those individuals who are engaged in a relatively **chronic struggle** to obtain an **unlimited** number of **poorly defined** things from their environment in **the shortest period of time** and, if necessary, against the opposing effects of other things or persons in this same environment.*[13]

The Type A syndrome then, is marked by intense drive, a struggle to get ahead, a continuing battle with the clock (and other people if necessary) in order to succeed. A person living a Type A life usually feels behind schedule with never enough time to get everything done. Because intimacy is another obstacle to "success," the Type A pattern seldom allows for warmth or emotional sensitivity. In fact, aggressiveness and hostility usually accompany the struggle against time. Other people represent demands on already scarce time. And they are convenient targets for pent-up frustration. This is especially true if a person does not learn to return to normal after intense stress.

How do you know if you are Type A — if you suffer from "hurry sickness?" Friedman and Rosenman explain that you exhibit Type A behavior if you consistently display most of the following traits:

Rush your speech
Hurry other people's speech
Hurry when you eat
Hate to wait in line

Never seem to catch up
Schedule more activities than time available
Detest "wasting" time
Drive too fast most of the time
Often try to do several things at once
Become impatient if others are too slow
Have little time for relaxation, intimacy, or enjoying
your environment.[14]

Type B behavior is the opposite of Type A. While a person who exhibits Type B behavior may be ambitious and successful, he or she is calmer, more patient, less hurried. Actually Friedman and Rosenman have identified a number of gradations within each behavior type. While there are many hard-core Type A or Type B individuals, most of us go back and forth between Type A and Type B as our activities and pressures vary from one day or week to the next. Friedman and Rosenman have concluded from their research that about 80 percent of urban Americans exhibit Type A behavior most of the time. They also note that many of the organizations in which we work or study virtually require us to succumb to hurry sickness. Certainly, the typical American definition of success encourages the Type A behavior pattern. Figure 3-4 contains a useful listing of Type A and Type B characteristics.

An incessantly fast and harried pace of life is a stressful life, and stress is correlated with heart attacks. To describe how hurry sickness leads to heart attacks, we must refer to the stress response described in Chapter 2. Type A's experience a higher continuous stress level than Type B's because of two distinctive characteristics:

1. Type A's are more likely to be stress-seekers, thereby exposing themselves to more challenges than Type B's.

2. Type A's put out more nor-epinephrine in response to challenge.

While Type A's are not necessarily at a higher level of arousal than B's at rest, A's are less often at rest. When engaged in challenge, the nor-epinephrine response of A's and B's differ as shown in Figure 3-5.[15]

FIGURE 3-4
TYPE A AND TYPE B CHARACTERISTICS*

	Type A	Type B
Time sense	"Hurry Sickness:" time-conscious, punctual, sense of urgency, impatience	Realistic time concerned
Time frame	Short-term	Longer view
Speech	Fast, emphatic, interrupting	Slower, softer
Attitude toward future	Worry	Relaxed
Personality	Driving, aggressive	Relaxed
Typical work	Sales	Decision-making position
Relax	With guilt	Without guilt
Natural work pace	Stressful	Nonstressful
Emphasis	Having; preoccupation with numbers (e.g., $)	Being
Reaction to stress symptoms	Ignore	Recognize and reduce
Temper	Easily angered	Slow to anger
Career pattern	Early success, early peak, burn-out	Slower, steady, sustained success
Work/play style	Anxious to lead, competition	Team player, fun, relaxation

FIGURE 3-4 (Con't)

	Type A	Type B
Habits	Smoke, drink, over-eat, drive fast, sleep poorly, take pills, little relaxation	Moderate, exercise rest, relaxation, recreation
Social	Anxious for advancement and recognition	Casual
Patience	Little	Average
Activity	Fast; several simultaneous activities	Normal; one thing at a time

*John L. Roglieri, M.D. *Odds on Your Life* New York: Seaview Books, 1980

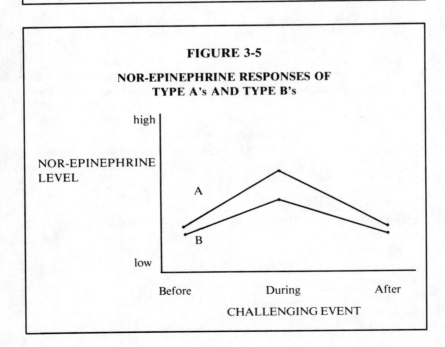

FIGURE 3-5

NOR-EPINEPHRINE RESPONSES OF TYPE A's AND TYPE B's

NOR-EPINEPHRINE LEVEL

high

A

B

low

Before   During   After

CHALLENGING EVENT

As a result of their enhanced nor-epinephrine response to challenge, Type A's more often expose themselves to an elevated heart rate, which in turn can cause continuous overwork and damage to the heart muscle. After many years, the heart may be less able to handle crises or to hold up under oxygen shortage from partial closing of a coronary artery.

Since part of the stress response is elevated blood pressure caused by nor-epinephrine discharge, Type A's are more likely to experience more frequent episodes throughout the day of temporary hypertension. More often than Type B's, then, Type A's expose their coronary arteries to further narrowing, greater wear and tear, and gradual loss of elasticity. High blood pressure also forces more cholesterol into existing plaque. Type A's not only experience more frequent temporary hypertension, they also are more prone to chronic hypertension.

At the same time, the more frequent stress response of Type A's results in more frequent discharges of insulin into the bloodstream. Insulin plays a key role in conversion of blood sugar to insulin. But it has the unfortunate side effect of causing further deterioration of the arterial walls, enhancing plaque build-up.

Finally, under high stress the body has *difficulty assimilating cholesterol*. More cholesterol stays in the blood stream. Friedman and Rosenman found that accountants have abnormally high blood cholesterol counts during two intensely stressful periods: in January when they close out their client's books, and in March and early April when they are preparing tax returns.[16] During those times, accountants are especially prone to heart attack. More cholesterol in the blood stream means more cholesterol in the coronary arteries (already narrower than normal because of hypertension). A build-up of arterial scars occurs as cholesterol gets trapped in nooks and crannies along the way.

In short, the high stress of Type A behavior increases secretion of nor-epinephrine into the blood stream, which in turn contributes to a higher heart rate, hypertension, insulin-induced damage to coronary artery walls, and excessive cholesterol flow in the blood. These physical processes occur in subtle, silent ways. Heart attack victims have little advance warning, although pain in or tightening of the chest is a warning in many cases. If you also smoke, do not exercise, are overweight, have a history of heart disease in your family, and eat too many high-cholesterol foods, your chances of heart attack are very high indeed.

A study in Canada recently showed that Type A managers are also more likely to be high in other risk factors: smoking, lack of exercise, overweight.[17] Thus, Type A behavior may exert both a direct and an indirect causal effect on coronary heart disease.

Research by Friedman and Rosenman, as well as by others around the world, strongly suggests that Type A behavior doubles the risk of heart attack, independent of other risk factors. The heart attacks of Type A's are two times more likely to be fatal than heart attacks of Type B's. And Type A's are five times more likely to have a repeat heart attack within a few years than Type B's.[18] In Chaper 6 we will discuss ways of avoiding and altering Type A behavior.

MIGRAINE HEADACHES

Migraine headache is a very painful condition associated with alternating constriction and dilation of one or both of the carotid arteries in the neck which supply blood to the head.[19] During the first stage (prodrome) arteries constrict. Subjective signs of the prodrome include dizziness, flushness, visual static, a familiar sense of uneasiness. Little or no pain may be felt at this stage. The second stage is the intense, usually one-sided pain associated with dilation of the carotid artery. Migraines can be devastating, often leading to nausea and to complete debilitation. Women suffer from them more often than men.

A curious feature of migraines is that they do not usually occur simultaneously with intense stress, but afterwards. Sundays and vacations are notorious migraine days, as if internal permission finally can be given to let down.

Migraines resemble heart attacks in that both are vascular problems. In many respects, the migraine sufferer also resembles the coronary-prone individual. Both tend to be rigid perfectionists, for example. But whereas Type A's are likely to be aggressive, controlling, and hostile in efforts to master their environment, the so-called migraine personality is characterized by self-sacrifice, compliance, and inability to delegate. Research on migraine patients many years ago by Harold Wolff, still considered definitive, suggest that the typical migraine sufferer is at bottom insecure.[20] As McQuade and Aikman have stated:

What he really wants is to be loved, but he will settle for being admired, or simply approved of: anything to still his gnawing sense of worthlessness. It is for this reason that he drives himself so hard, selflessly taking on thankless chores, burdening himself with ever-increasing responsibilities, conscious, rigid, somewhat fanatical. It is not surprising, then, that when leisure finally does catch up with him, he cracks. [21]

Another consistent behavior pattern often preceding onset of the migraine is withdrawing emotional energy from another person. Emotion is stopped from flowing outward. Anger and resentment are contained — turned inward where they boil and fester. At this point, the patient often will report a cold clammy feeling in feet and hands, sometimes contributing to sleep-onset insomnia. Through awareness, autogenic relaxation, and biofeedback, the individual often can learn to arrest progression of the migraine at the point of the prodrome by learning to divert blood to the extremities and away from the head area. One stress specialist reports that "85 percent of migraine patients I work with respond positively to stress reduction practices."[22] He also reports:

The people who do not get better usually are not practicing consistently because, for their own reasons, they are not quite ready to give up their migraines and discover a headache-free existence. I strongly recommend that migraine sufferers study the secondary gains they get from migraines and evaluate their lives to determine what needs are not being met appropriately. [23]

CANCER

A hazard in discussing stress and cancer is that readers with cancer may conclude that they induced their own illness in a direct cause-effect fashion. Cancer is not that simple. No one knows for sure why cancer appears when and where it does. A number of factors may contribute: diet, carcinogens in the environment, viruses, emotions, the immune system, and others. While stress and personality probably do not cause cancer in a straightforward fashion, they may well play a part. Therefore, it is important to understand how they sometimes interrelate.

Everyone's body conducts its own continuous surveillance for outside invaders and internal imperfections, including cell mutations. Cell mutations, unpredictable changes in hereditary material, usually are recognized immediately and the deviant cell is quickly destroyed before it can multiply and turn into a wayward, uncontrolled tumor. But in rare instances, the mutant cells escape destruction, gradually multiply, and become a runaway tumor, sometimes consuming normal tissue and organs as they grow. If not stopped, the tumor can cause death as it impedes normal functioning of key body parts. In other instances, cancer can metastesize, a part breaking away to take up residence and multiply at another location in the body. This process of growth and metastesis can occur within a few weeks or over many years. Tragically, many cancers are not diagnosed and treated with radiation, chemotherapy, or surgery until too late.

Stress sometimes contributes to cancer by weakening the body's surveillance or immune system. McQuade and Aikman have stated:

> *Stress helps to cause cancer because it depresses the immune response, the body's only real means of defending itself against malignant cells. It does this through the action of the adrenal cortex hormones, which partly effect t-lymphocytes. Searching out foreign antigens in the body is one of the tasks of the t-lymphocytes, and significantly they measure at low levels in the tissues of most cancer patients.* [24]

Other studies have shown t-cells to be lower in mice which have been exposed to stressful experiences as well as humans following a clustering of multiple life changes.

What kinds of emotional patterns or experiences have been linked with increased risk of cancer? There are no simple answers since mind-body interplay here is quite complex and varied. Several studies, however, are suggestive. In a well-known study of 455 cancer patients, LeShan found four common elements:

1. *A childhood marked by loneliness, guilt and self-condemnation, usually because of painful, troubled relations with parents and siblings. Often this is accentuated by specific events such as divorce, death of parent or sibling.*

2. *During late adolescence or early adulthood, the individual perceived a chance to come out of this deep loneliness by developing a "safe" relationship — usually with a spouse, child, or career. Feelings of isolation and loneliness greatly diminished though never completely disappeared. A great deal of emotional investment was poured into this new linkage, which lasted anywhere from one to over forty years.*

3. *Then the safe world collapsed — retirement, death of spouse, children leaving home, divorce. On the surface, the person "ad-*

justed," going about daily business as usual. But underneath, despair and hopelessness had returned. "Nothing gave them real satisfaction. It seemed to them as though the thing they had expected and feared all their lives — utter isolation and rejection — was now their eternal doom..."

4. *Helplessness and hopelessness followed. Meaning and zest went out of life. Energy declined. The fantasy from childhood that something was basically wrong with them returned. At some time between six and eighteen months later, the cancer appeared.*[25]

This scenario does not lead inevitably to cancer. Rather, LeShan's work suggests an increased probability or risk, given such a sequence of events.

A study of experimental mice by Vernon Riley of the Fred Hutchinson Research Center in Seattle also is highly suggestive. [26] Laboratory mice born to mothers with a known mammory tumor virus were exposed to a variety of environmental stressors, including isolation and severe crowding. Rice demonstrated that mammary tumor occurrences in these already vulnerable offspring increased up to 90 percent under stress, but remained at 7 percent in a protected stress-free environment. A generalization from experimental mice to humans cannot be made without extreme caution, yet this study is consistent with the position that stress may play a part in cancer. In *Getting Well Again,* Simonton, Simonton and Creighton cite two other important studies.[27]

Drs. A. H. Schmale and H. Iker observed in their female cancer patients a particular kind of giving-up, a sense of hopeless frustration surrounding a conflict for which there was no resolution.[28] *Often this conflict occurred approximately six months prior to the cancer diagnosis. Schmale and Iker then studied a group of healthy women who were considered biologically predisposed to cancer of the cervix.*

Using psychological measures that allowed them to identify a "helplessness-prone personality," Schmale and Iker predicted which women in this group would develop cancer and they were accurate 73.6 percent of the time.[29] *The researchers pointed out that this does not mean that feelings of helplessness cause cancer — these women appeared to have some predisposition to cervical cancer but that the helplessness seemed to be an important element.*

Over a period of fifteen years, Dr. W. A. Greene studied the psychological and social experiences of patients who developed leukemia and lymphoma. He too observed that the loss of an important relationship was a significant element in the patient's life history. For both men and women, Greene said, the greatest loss was the death or threat of death of a mother; or for men, a "mother figure," such as a wife. Other significant emotional events for women were menopause or a change of home; and for men, the loss or threat of loss of job, and retirement or the threat of retirement.

RHEUMATOID ARTHRITIS

Rheumatoid arthritis usually starts during young adulthood, continues into old age, and affects women three times more often than men.[30] This illness manifests itself through swelling and soreness in joints throughout the body. Stress often appears to play a part in the course and perhaps in its inception.

Like ulcerative colitis and perhaps cancer, rheumatoid arthritis is a disease of the immune system. Specifically, it is an auto-immune illness in which antibodies become directed against the body's own cells, thereby inflicting tissue damage. Usually the immune system has little difficulty distinguishing self and non-self. For reasons not entirely understood, this discriminating ability breaks down in rheumatoid arthritis patients, resulting in chronic joint inflammation usually in shoulders, elbows, hips, wrists, fingers, knees, ankles, and feet. Ultimately, cells of the synovial joint multiply at an abnormally fast rate, contributing to the swelling and finally filling up the joint space itself and eroding the cartilage and bone ends. Scar tissue may form, resulting in deformation and extreme pain.

Rheumatoid arthritis, like other illnesses, is multi-causal. For example, heredity seems sometimes to play a part through a blood protein called the "rheumatoid factor," which is found in about one-half of rheumatoid arthritics. The factor increases susceptibility, but does not always cause rheumatoid arthritis.

Research has not yet produced definitive conclusions as to why rheumatoid arthritis develops when it does in specific people. However, certain personality traits seem to be associated in most cases. According to Mason,

The following are typical: shy, inhibited, masochistic, self-sacrificing, anxious, depressed, resentful, and repressed anger. Peo-

*ple who possess these characteristics along with the rheumatoid factor are the most likely to be candidates for this disease; **people who have a healthy psychological balance and the risk factor rarely suffer from this disease.***[31]

My experience working with a handful of rheumatoid arthritic patients is consistent with references by a number of writers to a common pattern: emotional tension significantly worsens the symptons. A 48 year-old woman, for example, had developed the disease soon after marrying at age 18 while pregnant. The swelling and pain had plagued her off and on since then. Three years prior to her entering our 12-week stress control program, her husband had left her after a bitter series of feuds in which she felt discounted and unloved. For several months after the split, she was almost totally bed-ridden with pain and swelling. Gradually, she made her way back to independence and strength, though still very vulnerable and emotionally unstable. During and after our work together, she enrolled in a community college, began to swim daily, and practiced deep relaxation. Her symptoms subsided in harmony with the increase in her physical fitness, confidence, and optimistic outlook toward the future.

Like other stress-induced or stress-aggravated illnesses, rheumatoid arthritis often can be contained, if not diminished, through an integrated program of stress management.

ULCERS

Among the most common and clearly understood stress-related maladies are peptic and duodenol ulcers.[32] Peptic ulcers result from excessive gastric acid secretions in the stomach. Ultimately a lesion or open sore develops, which causes pain and sometimes bleeding. Duodenal ulcers, which are similar lesions in the small intestine just beyond the stomach, usually take longer to heal because of the constant flow of food and gastric juices through that area.

Clear evidence suggests that elevation of the stress response elicits greater secretion of digestive acids. This was observed directly for a number of years by Dr. Stewart Wolf in a patient who was forced to live with an opening in his stomach because of an unusual injury in his esophagus. Wolf found that whenever his patient became more emotional, greater amounts of stomach acids were secreted.[33]

Selye, who began his research on ulcers in rats more than 40 years ago, has summarized the link between stress and ulcers as follows:

The gastro-intestinal tract is particularly sensitive to general stress.
Loss of appetite is one of the first symptoms in the great "syndrome
of just being sick," and this may be accompanied by vomiting, diar-
rhea, or constipation. Signs of **irritation and upset of the digestive**
organs *may occur in any type of emotional stress. This is well known*
not only in soldiers who experience it during the tense excitation of
battle, but even to students who pace the floor before my door
awaiting their turn in oral examinations. [34]

Ulcer-prone people usually are driven "go-getters" who strive very hard in pursuit of ever-receding career goals. Underlying hostility often is present, but seldom is expressed. An even stronger unconscious urge to be accepted and loved similarly is repressed. Men with ulcers have a high incidence of unhappy marriage. Curiously, one study found that wives with rheumatoid arthritis often have husbands with peptic ulcers. Such women tend to possess strong drives to achieve public recognition and esteem, something the traditional husband cannot accept or understand. The husband is driven by his own success need, yet also craves emotional support, something the wife does nôt offer because of her resentment. "So the wife's bones and the husband's digestive tract ache to a common beat." [35]

Physical exercise, controlling pace of life, containing the drive to prove oneself, deep relaxation, and support from a warm, accepting partner — all are likely to help reduce emotional pressures toward ulcers.

INSOMNIA

Among self-observable signs of stress, Selye lists "insomnia, which is usually a consequence of being keyed-up." [36] He also notes, "muscular activity or mental work which leads to a definite solution prepares you for rest and sleep, but intellectual efforts which set up self-maintaining tensions keep you awake." [37]

Difficulty sleeping takes two forms: inability to fall asleep (onset insomnia) and inability to sleep through the night. Onset insomnia usually results from being keyed-up or excessively aroused throughout the day and especially during the evening. The mind fails in quieting itself and the body. Even though physical fatigue may be very great, continuing excitation of the stress response makes quieting of brain waves into the delta zone, which is needed for sleep, difficult or impossible.

Either type of insomnia can result from excessive residual or anticipatory stress — inability to leave events, thoughts, and feelings from the previous day or mental preoccupation with events anticipated for the next day. In either case, the challenge is to control the mind, which in turn can exert control over bodily tension.

It is important to accept occasional insomnia without too much concern. A "high" from an intimate encounter, worry over something left unsaid or undone the previous day, excitement or worry about a challenge the next day — all will result in occasional sleeplessness, even for the healthy, well-balanced person. Missing part or even all of a night's sleep will have little effect on one's performance. Sometimes it is even useful to get up during the night to read, write, study, think, or work on some other project. This is one way to turn a potential problem, lack of sleep, into an opportunity.

Quite a different matter is chronic insomnia, which can contribute to wear and tear and to stress build-up over days and weeks.[38] Unfortunately, loss of sleep, worry and tension often reinforce each other in a frustrating cycle, as shown in Figure 3-6.

FIGURE 3-6

SLEEP AND STRESS

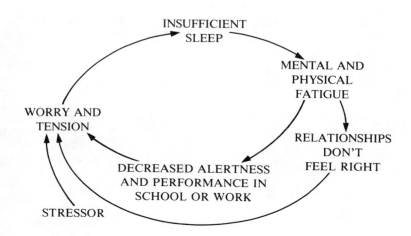

The key questions with chronic insomnia are: Where is the disharmony creating chronic off-balance, tension, arousal? What needs to be done to resolve it? Meanwhile a number of steps can be taken to facilitate sleep: regular daily exercise, daily deep relaxation, deliberate steps to taper off activity during the evening, avoiding caffeine late in the day, practice of specific techniques of relaxation just before and after going to bed. Such techniques will be discussed later in this book.

SUDDEN DEATH

Stress can not only contribute to illness; it can contribute to sudden death. George Engel has investigated the circumstances surrounding the unexplained sudden deaths of a large number of persons who died unexpectedly. Most were healthy at the time of their demise.

Engel discovered four categories of stressful life events that precipitated sudden death.[39]

The most common (135 deaths) was an exceptionally traumatic disruption of a close human relationship or the anniversary of the loss of a loved one. The second category (103 deaths) involved situations of danger, struggle, or attack. Loss of status, self-esteem, or valued possessions, as well as disappointment, failure, defeat, or humiliation, accounted for the third group of deaths (21 in all). And the fourth category (16 deaths) consisted of people who died suddenly at moments of triumph, public recognition, reunion, or "happy ending." Fifty-seven deaths in the first category were immediately preceded by the collapse or death — often abrupt — of a loved one. Some survivors were reported to have cried out that they could not go on without the deceased. Many were in the midst of some frantic activity — attempting to revive the loved one, get help, or rush the person to the hospital — when they, too, collapsed and died.

One common denominator emerges from the medical literature and the 275 press reports on sudden death. For the most part, the victims are confronted with events which are impossible to ignore, either because of their abrupt, unexpected, or dramatic quality or because of their intensity, irreversibility, or persistence. The individual experiences or is threatened with overwhelming excitation.

Implicit, also, is the idea that he no longer has, or no longer believes that he has, mastery or control over the situation or himself, or fears that he may lose what control he has.

Engel suggests these sudden deaths often can be explained by "derangement of cardiac rhythm" in response either to overwhelming discharge of catecholomines or to breakdown from rapid shifts between excitatory and withdrawal responses. Homeostatic balance within the organism is lost.

While such incidents are rare, they illustrate the intricate mind-body connection and the extremes to which this linkage can go awry.

We have reviewed how stress can contribute to hypertension, coronary heart disease, migraine, cancer, rheumatoid arthritis, ulcers, insomnia, and sudden death. All have in common some type of direct or indirect difficulty with the stress response, a part of human experience so useful, yet potentially so harmful. A balanced lifestyle with personal health promotion as a central focus can help prevent and sometimes even cure these and other stress-related diseases.

Thus far we have focused on physical distress. We now will examine certain forms of emotional and intellectual distress.

EMOTIONAL DISTRESS

Soldiers react to the extreme stressors of battle in a variety of ways. Some are relatively calm and confident. Most react at some time with emotional distress of one type or another. Similar reactions occur among refugees and among victims of natural disasters.[40] Toffler has pointed out that different types of people show striking parallels in their reactions to over-stimulation.

First, we find the same evidence of confusion, disorientation, or distortion of reality.

Second, there are the same signs of fatigue, anxiety, tenseness or extreme irritability.

Third, in all cases there appears to be a point of no return — a point at which apathy and emotional withdrawal set in. In short, the available evidence suggests that over-stimulation may lead to bizarre and anti-adaptive behavior.[41]

The stressors facing soldiers, refugees, and victims of disaster are much more intense than those generally faced in daily life. Yet each time you move, change jobs, go away to school, or in some other way

93

drastically alter your daily patterns of living, you run the risk of becoming emotionally upset — depressed, angry, fearful. When you live so fast that you experience the chronic overload of micro-stressors, mild emotional stress ("nervousness" or "tension") may give way to severe depression, anxiety, or disorientation. Similar results may accompany a chaotic life with little routine.

Emotional and physical distress often feed on one another, as illustrated by the following all-too-common tragedy.

Mrs. Loren was a 76-year-old grandmother who had lived alone since her husband of 52 years died. She had been a faithful wife and looked after her husband, children, home and garden with great care and pride throughout her life. She had never been sickly, although her general condition had weakened somewhat in recent years. After her husband's death she took a serious nose-dive, emotionally and physically. She seemed lost, lonely, and unable to find meaning. Last month she died of a lethal stroke. [42]

Traumatic as the death of a long-time spouse may be, most surviving mates do not experience such a severe downturn in health and spirit. This suggests that there must be more effective ways of adapting to such crises. Yet the fact remains that the death rate is very high for surviving spouses during the year after a mate's death.

Let us look more closely at six of the most common distress emotions: anxiety, depression, anger, fear, sadness and frustration.

Anxiety in moderate amounts is a normal part of living. Research shows that in sports, optimal performance is achieved when pre-contest anxiety is in the middle range, neither too high nor too low. The same is true of occupational or academic performance.

Anxiety can become a stress problem in two ways. One is when arousal before or during a critical event is debilitating or otherwise interferes with performance. Earlier in this chapter we referred to this stress difficulty as too high peak arousal. Difficulty speaking in front of a group, disoriented thinking because of panic during a test, profuse sweating, the intense fear before a job interview — all are examples of out-of-control situational anxiety.

The second type of anxiety problem is chronic anxiety, sometimes referred to as anxiety neurosis. As Mason notes,

A person suffering from anxiety neurosis may exhibit certain physical symptoms: palpitations, chest pain, cold and sweaty extremities, band-like pressure around the head, constriction of the throat, fatigue, lack of appetite, vomiting and diarrhea. [43]

Thus, anxiety is not just an emotional state, it is intellectual, physical and behavioral as well.

Depression, the second primary stress emotion, also is multi-faceted, as reflected in the following list of symptoms:

Emotional . . . . . . *a dull, tired, empty, sad, numb feeling with little or no pleasure from ordinarily enjoyable activities and people.*

Behavioral . . . . . . *irritability, excessive complaining about small annoyances or minor problems, impaired memory, inability to concentrate, difficulty making decisions, loss of sexual desires, inability to get going in the morning, slowed reaction time, crying or screaming, excessive guilt feelings.*

Physical . . . . *loss of appetite, weight loss, constipation, insomnia or restless sleep, impotence, headache, dizziness, indigestion, and abnormal heart rate.* [44]

Specific combinations of symptoms vary from one person to the next. All sufferers tend to have the following in common: reduced energy level, withdrawal from interactions with others, gloomy and dark affect, self-criticism, and a sense of helplessness.

Like anxiety, depression is a common and expected reaction to events that temporarily seem overwhelming or negative in other ways. Short-run bouts are little to be concerned about. But depression which lasts for weeks or months is cause for concern and may require positive, aggressive steps. Sometimes such experiences are the result of inability to adjust to a traumatic loss, such as death of spouse. Other times depression may result from accumulated fatigue, and in still other instances, it can accompany a profound sense of disharmony with work or marriage.

While medications may help in the short-run, lifestyle modification may be called for. As we shall see, running has been shown to be very effective in reducing depression, partly by helping to overcome the helplessness so often inherent in depression.

Anger, the third distress emotion, may be apparent as mild irritation, hostility, or intense aggressiveness. Often anger results from blaming others. As Parrino states,

> *The angered individual is intent on placing blame and leveling punishment for some misgiving. The angry self-dialogue often includes statements such as "you should not have done that to me." "It is your fault, and you should be punished." "If it weren't for you, I wouldn't be in this situation." "I'll get you for that."*[45]

Anger brings with it physical arousal much like anxiety. When unexpressed and unresolved, it can lead to clear damage to tissues and organs. A recent study by researchers at the University of Michigan reported that blood pressure was highest among people who resolved anger by repressing it, next highest among those who explode with it, and lowest among those who discuss it.[46] A fourth alternative which may be even more effective, especially in combination with discussion, is daily aerobic exercise and deep relaxation. For these practices are likely to reduce anger as an emotional and physical state through dissolving or releasing it. The challenge still remains, of course, to look behind the immediate anger at the patterns of perception and responses that produce anger in the first place.

Fear, the fourth distress emotion, involves a mild to severe feeling of apprehension about some perceived threat. Fear may be residual (consequence of something that has already happened), current (an immediate physical threat), or anticipatory (something believed likely to happen). Fear is based on conscious or unconscious appraisal of a threat. This appraisal may or may not be based on reality. Someone once said that the letters in the word fear stand for "faulty evaluation of actual reality," which often is true, especially among phobic, paranoid, or other persons simply lacking in confidence. Fear can elicit a very powerful and immediate stress response.

Sadness, the fifth primary distress emotion, is the dreary, dark feeling associated with a real, imagined, or anticipated loss. This loss may be a thing, achievement, expectation, illusion, limb, or whatever. The result is a gap in internal reality. Physical consequences through either elevation or depression of the physical stress response may include, for example, insomnia, chest pain, upset stomach, fatigue, or loss of appetite.

Behavior may become withdrawn, thought processes may become fuzzy and characterized by loss of concentration.

Frustration, the sixth primary distress emotion, is the sense of irritation, anger, or outrage at being blocked from something you want to have, experience, or do. It is familiar to all, since part of living with others is to compromise, giving up bits and pieces of what you would like for yourself. The key issue is your reactivity to frustration. Very disturbed or deranged persons are hyper-reactive, often becoming violent when they do not get what they want. Handling frustration calmly is a continuing challenge, especially when you are blocked from something you very much want. High internal reactivity without expression is perhaps the most dangerous of all to health, since it may result in chronic excitation of the stress response. Essential (unexplained) hypertension often is the result of this pattern.

"Mental illness" is a term often applied to stress-related emotional difficulties.[47] Application of this label however, sometimes leads to feelings of hopelessness and helplessness. The "mentally ill" are often stigmatized by neighbors and friends. Emotional strains sometimes are better understood and handled if they are seen for what they are — acute stress, too much stress for too long, or a harmful reaction to stress — rather than as "mental illness."

"Nervous breakdown" is another term often mistakenly applied to stress-related emotional and behavioral difficulties. A "nervous breakdown" has nothing to do with a breakdown of nerves or the nervous system. Usually it refers to a feeling of helplessness, loss of control, or confusion in a temporary crisis. People who feel they are about to break down or to lose control may need the help of family, clergy, or mental health specialists in getting through a crisis. But his sense of helplessness usually passes as the stressful circumstances are overcome.

People differ, of course, with respect to the point at which mild stress gives way to harmful distress.

INTELLECTUAL DISTRESS

Stressful situations sometimes produce a lack of concentration, poor memory, fuzzy or illogical thinking, confusion. Students who have not paced themselves properly often find their head "jammed up" in the middle of final exam week — they are unable to think clearly or remember very well. Young people who feel caught between pressures from their parents and those from their friends, or between the tugs and pulls of divorced parents, often find they cannot concentrate in class, complete assignments on time, or perform well on tests. These are examples of intellectual distress from overload — too many stressors in too short a time.

Toffler has pointed out that overload can lead to three forms of intellectual distress.[48] First, too much stimulation at the point of sensory intake can distort and twist perceptions of reality. Second, overload can lead to disturbances in the processing of information — how you remember, reason, or solve problems. Third, over-stimulation can cause the decision-making function to become irrational, blocked, out of control. In an accelerating society with many leading faster and faster lives, these three types of intellectual distress seem to be on the rise.

At the other extreme, assembly-line workers often become bored, dull, and intellectually stifled after many years on the job. This also happens to isolated retirees, to housewives, and to students who find school unchallenging. Such people also are victims of intellectual distress, but from under-stimulation rather than overload.

SECONDARY GAINS FROM DISTRESS

People may experience a variety of gains from distress, some negative and some positive.

Negative Gains

Many people become distressed because doing so meets one or several psychological needs.

Fulfills lifescript image of self
Opportunity to be excused from a troublesome problem or situation
Results in attention, care, and nurturing
Opportunity to be disqualified from living up to own or others' expectations
Way of proving to others you are not responsible, capable, dependable

These effects may be positive to the person in the short run, although perpetual ill health or emotional trauma can only lower the quality of life in the long run.

Positive Gains

A number of genuinely positive gains result from distress, if put in proper perspective.

An ulcer can stimulate a decision to slow down

A heart attack can draw attention to controlling risk factors

Pain of divorce can lead to reappraisal of communication skills

A major illness can lead to greater appreciation of loved ones, the beauty in daily life, and life itself

An unexpected bout with depression can bring loved ones together

The fear brought on by a number of closely linked distress symptoms can heighten personal awareness

Distress can clarify values, increase commitments, bolster self-support, lead to greater depth of experience, and promote closeness to others. Many people have found that their lives increase in depth and meaning after a crisis. Whether distress brings despair or spawns new life depends largely on the wisdom, courage, and creativity of the individual's responses.

WHO IS THE MOST VULNERABLE TO DISTRESS?

Research shows that all types of people sometimes experience distress. No one is immune. Yet there also is evidence that members of certain categories and groups are especially likely to encounter distress. For example:

Rates of coronary heart disease, cancer, and suicide are higher for divorced persons than married people.[49]

Unhappily married people suffer more stress-related illness than people who are happily re-married.[50]

All married groups — men and women, over 30 and under 30, with and without children — report higher satisfaction, general good feelings, and less stress than all unmarried groups — single, divorced, or widowed.[51]

Widows and widowers are more likely than others their age to become ill and die (especially after the death of their spouse).[52]

More wives than husbands have felt they were about to have a nervous breakdown, have experienced more intense anxiety, and report feelings of inadequacy, depression, and phobia.[53]

Compared with non-employed housewives, working wives are happier, communicate better with their husbands, report feeling better physically and mentally, and are more satisfied with their marriages and life in general.[54]

Compared with husbands of non-employed wives, husbands of working wives are less happy, experiencing greater job pressures, poorer health, and more dissatisfaction with their jobs and marriages.[55]

Depression is up to twice as common among women as men.[56]

Migrants from another country and from the farm to the city are more likely to experience stress-related illness and death than are non-migrants.[57]

Families that move a great deal are especially likely to experience suicide, ulcers, divorce, and emotional breakdown.

The unemployed are more likely than the employed to experience suicide, ulcers, divorce, and emotional breakdown.[59]

The ages of greatest stress-related ailments are 15-30 and 55-65.[60]

The poor are more likely to experience all types of distress than middle-income or wealthy persons.[61]

Black men experience higher rates of hypertension than white men.[62]

Teenagers with high-achievement pressures from parents are especially likely to be hypertensive.[63]

Urban dwellers have more stress-related illnesses than rural dwellers.[64]

Parents with young children report more feelings of pressure and stress than any other age or marital-status group.[65]

Blue-collar workers experience more boredom, stress-related illness, and job dissatisfaction than white-collar workers.[66]

100

Top corporate executives have lower mortality rates than do second-level executives.[67]

Sedentary workers have more heart attacks and die younger than those whose work requires physical effort.[68]

Older bachelors report more psychological problems than do older never-married women.[69]

In this chapter we began by pointing out that individuals differ in zone of positive stress, that is, in their range of tolerance for arousal. We noted eight common stress difficulties related to the zone of positive stress. These difficulties lead to relatively minor physicial and mental distress symptoms. Frequently, however, such symptoms transform into stress illnesses, several of which were discussed. We also reviewed the most commmon types of distress emotions, and some negative and positive gains from distress. Finally, we presented a number of research findings that suggest who is most vulnerable to various types of distress.

Chapter 4 will focus on the kinds of experiences that increase the likelihood of distress. These experiences tend to occur at some point in all of our lives.

CHAPTER REVIEW AND PERSONAL APPLICATION

1. Define "zone of positive stress."

2. Compare and contrast your own zone of positive stress with at least one other person.

3. What are your early warning signs of overload? Underload?

4. What did Selye mean by "racehorses?" "Turtles?" Do you know anyone who illustrates each type?

5. In your opinion, how changeable is the zone of positive stress? Under what conditions might it change?

6. How might a job supervisor make use of the idea of zone of positive stress in his or her management practices?

7. Describe and illustrate each of the following common stress difficulties, with respect to mind, then body, then behavior;

   a. Baseline stress level too low
   b. Baseline stress level too high
   c. Hair-trigger stress reaction
   d. Peak arousal too high
   e. Recovery too slow
   f. Recovery not low enough
   g. Stress build-up
   h. Recovery too low

8. Which of the above stress difficulties have you experienced during the past day? Week? Month? Six months?

9. Which of these stress difficulties might apply to "network nerves?"

10. Describe and illustrate three ways stress can contribute to illness.

11. What is hypertension? How can the stress response, described in Chapter 2, contribute to "essential" hypertension?

12. What is coronary heart disease? Heart attack? Risk Factor?

13. Draw a picture describing your image of Type A behavior.

14. How does Type A behavior contribute to coronary heart disease?

15. How does the "migraine personality" differ from the Type A personality?

16. What do T-lymphocytes have to do with possible linkages between stress and cancer?

17. True or False? "The 'rheumatoid factor' is the sole determinant of rheumatoid arthritis. Stress has nothing to do with it, according to available research." Explain.

18. True or False? "The greater the stress response, the greater the secretion of gastric acids." Explain, including how your answer relates to ulcers.

19. What are the six key stress emotions? What part does the stress response play in each?

20. Identify a recent situation in which you experienced intellectual distress. What events contributed to this experience? How was your behavior affected?

REFERENCES

1. "Network Nerves on the Talk Shows," *San Francisco Chronicle,* February 7, 1977.

2. Norman Cousins, *Anatomy of An Illness.* New York: Bantam Books, 1979, Chapter 2.

3. F. E. Graham-Bonnalie, *The Doctor's Guide to Living With Stress.* New York: Drake Publishers, 1972, p. 102.

4. Kenneth R. Pelletier, *Holistic Medicine: From Stress to Optimum Health.* New York: Delacourte Press, 1979; Kenneth Pelletier, *Mind as Healer, Mind as Slayer.* New York: Dell Publishing Company, 1977; Walter McQuade and Ann Aikman, *Stress.* New York: Bantam Books, 1974; L. Gatton, *The Silent Disease: Hypertension.* New York: Signet, 1973.

5. Kurt Isselbacher, *Harrison's Principles of Internal Medicine.* New York: McGraw-Hill Publishers, 1981.

6. Herbert Benson, *The Relaxation Response.* New York: William Morrow Publishers, 1975.

7. *Ibid.,* p. 43.

8. Sheldon F. Greenberg and Peter J. Valletutti, *Stress and the Helping Professions.* Baltimore: Paul H. Brooks Publisher, 1980, p. 58.

9. *Ibid.,* p. 58.

10. Benson, *Ibid.;* Kenneth Cooper, *The Aerobic Way.* New York: M. Evans, 1977.

11. John L. Roglieri, *Odds on Your Life.* New York: Seaview Books, 1980; John W. Farquhar, *The American Way of Life Need Not Be Hazardous to Your Health.* Stanford Alumni Association, 1978; David C. Glass, *Behavior Patterns, Stress and Coronary Disease.* Hillsdale, N.J.: Lawrence Erlbaum Associates, 1977.

12. Meyer Friedman and Ray H. Rosenman, *Type A Behavior and Your Heart.* New York: Fawcett Press, 1974.

13. Meyer Friedman, *Pathogenisis of Coronary Artery Disease.* New York: McGraw-Hill, 1969.

14. Walt Schafer, *Stress, Distress and Growth.* Davis, CA., International Dialogue Press, 1978, Chapter 6.

15. Remarks by Ray H. Rosenman at conference, The Healing Brain III, San Francisco, September, 1981.

16. M. Friedman, R. H. Rosenman and V. Carroll, "Changes in the serum cholesterol and blood clotting time in men subjected to cystic variation of occupational stress." *Circulation,* 1958, 18, 852-861.

17. John H. Howard, David A. Cunnington and Peter A. Rechnitzer, "Health Patterns Associated with Type A Behavior: a managerial population," *Journal of Human Stress,* Vol 2 (March, 1976), pp. 24-32.

18. Friedman and Rosenman, *op cit.*; Glass *op cit.,* The Review Panel on Coronary-prone Behavior and Coronary Heart disease, "Coronary-Prone Behavior and Coronary Heart Disease: A Critical Review," *Circulation* Vol. 603, No. 6 (June, 1981), pp 1199-1214; T. M. Dembroski, *et al.* (eds), *Coronary-Prone Behavior.* New York: Springer-Verlgs, 1973.

19. Pelletier, 1977, *op cit.,* pp. 169-173; McQuade and Aikman, *op cit.,* pp. 40-42.

20. McQuade and Aikman, *Ibid.,* p. 41.

21. *Ibid.,* p. 41.

22. L. John Mason, *Guide to Stress Reduction.* Culver City, CA.: Peace Press, Inc., p. 1.

23. *Ibid.,* p. 118.

24. McQuade and Aikman, *op cit.,* p.76.

25. *Ibid.,* p. 79.

26. Vernon Riley, "Mouse Mammary Tumors: Alterations of incidence as apparent function of stress." *Science,* 189 (1975): 465-67.

27. O. Carl Simonton, Stephanie Matthews-Simonton, and James L. Creighton, *Getting Well Again.* New York: Bantam Books, 1978, p. 55.

28. A. H. Schmale and H. Iker, "The Psychology setting of uterine cervical cancer," *Annals of the New York Academy of Sciences,* 1966, 125,807-13.

29. W. A. Green, "The psychological setting of the development of leukemia and lymphoma," *Annals of the New York Academy of Sciences,* 1966, 125-794-801.

30. Pelletier, 1977, *op cit.,* pp. 149-151, 181-184. McQuade and Aikman, *op cit.,* pp. 72-3.

31. Mason, *op cit.,* p. 128.

32. Pelletier, 1977, *op cit.,* pp. 72-73; McQuade and Aikman, *op cit.,* pp.48-51; Robert M. Rose and Molly A. Levin, "The Role of Stress in Peptic Ulcer Disease, *Journal of Human Stress,* Vol 5, (June, 1979), pp. 27-37.

33. McQuade and Aikman, *op cit.,* p. 49.

34. Hans Selye, *The Stress of Life.* New York: McGraw-Hill Book Company, 1976, P. 259.

35. McQuade and Aikman, *op cit.,* p. 49.

36. Selye, *op cit.,* p. 175.

37 *Ibid.,* p.423.

38. Schafer,*op cit.,* p. 176.

39. George Engel, "Emotional Stress and Sudden Death." *Psychology Today,* (November 1977), pp. 118 and 154-155.

40. James N. Logue and Holger Hansen, "A Case-Control Study of Hypertensive Women in a Post-Disaster Community: Wyoming Valley, Pennsylvania,*"Journal of Human Stress,* Vol. 6 June, 1980, pp. 34-38

41. Alvin Toffler, *Future Shock.* New York: Bantam Books, 1971, p. 348.

42. Schafer, *op cit.* p. 58.
43. Mason, op cit., p. 140.

44. "Depression: The Sickness of the 70's," *San Francisco Chronicle,* April 13, 1977.

45. John J. Parrino, *From Panic to Power,* New York: John Wiley & Sons, Inc., 1979, p. 124.

46. Cited in *Executive Fitness Newsletter.*

47. Schafer, op cit., p. 58.

48. Toffler, op cit., Chapter 16.

49. Joseph Eyer and Peter Sterling, "Stress Related Mortality and Social Organizations," *The Review of Radical Political Economics,* Vol. 9. No. 1 (Spring, 1977), pp. 1-44.

50. Jessie Bernard, *The Future of Marriage,* New York: Bantam Books, 1973.

51. Angus Campbell, "The American Way of Mating: Marriage Si, Children Only Maybe," *Psychology Today,* (May, 1975) pp. 37-43; Angus Campbell, Phillip E. Converse and Willard L. Rodgers, *The*

Quality of American Life, New York: Russell Sage Foundation, 1976.

52. Eyer and Sterling, op cit.

53. Bernard, op cit.

54. "The Most Unhappy Husbands," *San Francisco Chronicle,* December 27, 1976.

55. Ibid.

56. Bernard, op cit.

57. Vance Packard, *A Nation of Strangers,* New York: Pocket Books, 1974; Eyer and Sterling, op cit.; Lennard Levi and Lars Andersson, *Psychosocial Stress: Population, Environment and Quality of Life.* New York: Spectrum Publications, 1975.

58. Eyer and Sterling, op cit.

59. Ibid.

60. Ibid.

61. Ibid,; John Kosa, Aaron Antonovsky, and Irving Zola, *Poverty and Health: A Sociological Analysis.* Cambridge, Mass.; Harvard University Press, 1969.

62. Lawrence Galton, *The Silent Disease: Hypertension.* New York: Signet, 1973, pp. 88-90.

63. "A Growing Concern Over Teen Hypertension" *San Francisco Chronicle,* November 28, 1976.

64. Eyer and Sterling, *op. cit.;* John Helmer and Neil A. Eddington (eds.), *Urbanman: The Psychology of Urban Survival.* New York: The Free Press, 1973; Levi and Anderson, *op. cit.;* David C. Glass and Jerome E. Singer, *Urban Stress: Experiments on Noise and Social Stressors.* New York: Academic Press, 1972; Jonathan L. Freedman, *Crowding and Behavior.* New York: Viking Press, 1975.

65. Campbell, *op. cit.*

66. Eyer and Sterling, *op. cit.;* Special Task Force to the Secretary of Health, Education and Welfare, *Work in America.* Cambridge, Mass.: MIT Press, 1973, Chapter 2 and 3.

67. *Metropolitan Life Statistical Bulletin.* Vol. 55, No. 2 (February, 1975), pp. 3-5.

68. "Hard Workers Have Fewer Heart Attacks," *San Francisco Chronicle,* March 23, 1977. Also see Leon Belshin and Dean T. Mason, *Love Your Heart.* Davis, CA.: International Dialogue Press, 1982

69. Gerald Gurin, Joseph Veroff, and Sheila Feld, *Americans View Their Mental Health.* New York: Basic Books, 1960.

HIGH-RISK STRESSORS

Life is a constant process of responding to stimuli, pressures, and demands. The person does not live in a vacuum but is an "open system," continually exchanging energy, information, and feelings with the environment. We also place demands on ourselves. Thus, stressors may originate internally or externally.

In a later chapter, you will learn some practical steps for identifying, modifying, or avoiding stressors. In this chapter we will first list some of the ways stressors can vary, then we will show how rapid social change generates a high risk of distress. A number of other high-risk stressors, independent of the rate of change around us, will be noted.

VARIABILITY OF STRESSORS

Here are some of the key ways stressors may vary.[1] Examples given may or may not be "high risk," depending on the person.

1. **Origin**

   Internal stressors: a self-imposed time deadline, unrealistically high standards, a decision to compete in a race, guilt, out-of-date anger at a parent

   External stressors: Physical: rain, cold, heat, noise, a threatening animal

       Social: a crowded room, a dominating husband, role conflict, inflation, a company retirement age, people who create noise, a job interview

2. **Pleasantness**

   Pleasant: A new grandchild, a new job, food, sports victory, sex, paycheck

   Unpleasant: A drunk driver, death in the family, a stepchild who lies, divorce, own illness

3. Number

Few:
Slow pace during cabin vacation, emptiness of retirement, middle-aged mother with empty-nest syndrome

Many:
Final exam week for students, week after finals for professors, tax season for accountants, Saturday night for city police, geographic move for father and mother of six

4. Intensity

Micro-stressors:
Constant noise from nearby airport, commuting, three children under five, repetitious job, cost of gasoline

Macro-stressors:
Burning house, Republican (or Democratic) president, loneliness after move to city, pre-marital pregnancy, cancer

5. Duration

Episodic:
Auto accident, new boss, graduation, birth of child, child leaving home

Chronic:
Unhappy marriage, job overload, fluorescent lights, traffic noise on nearby street, sales quotas, inflation

6. Familiarity

New:
A new professor at beginning of semester, first child, entering job market, being laid off, being drafted

Familiar:
Preparing dinner after hard day at work, making ends meet, an oppressive supervisor, the assembly line

7. How Chosen

Voluntary:
A challenging golf match, a theater script, a difficult do-it-yourself project, a vacation to the San Juan Islands, writing this book

Involuntary:
High interest rates, the need for food and shelter, urban growth, urban crime, being assaulted, forced retirement

8. Changeability

Easy to change:
A flat tire, a cool room, a mistaken purchase, sleepiness, hunger

Difficult but possible to change:
A bad job-personality fit, a poor marriage, a disrespectful child, being too far in debt, a leaky roof, being unemployed

Impossible to change:
Disappearance of a favorite landmark, death of a loved one, weather, eruption of Mt. St. Helens

9. Change Agent

Changeable by self:
Fatigue, job dissatisfaction, overweight, overspending

Changeable by others:
A too-loud stereo next door, autocratic supervision, taxes

Changeable by both:
Sexual appetite, marital tension, work overload, household overload

Changeable by neither:
The need to make a living, a terminal illness, Oregon rain

Understanding these distinctions is vital to an effective integrated approach to stress management, since it can help sensitize you to where your difficult stressors originate, what their basic nature is, and what options are available for dealing with them (e.g., changing, avoiding, or adapting). In Chapter 6, we will return to analysis and application of these variabilities in your own current experience. We will now turn to the larger social context in which stressors occur.

FASTER SOCIAL CHANGE: THE CONTEXT OF PERSONAL STRESS

In order to understand the nature and sources of stress as the basis for taking constructive steps to manage it, it is important to step back to view the context in which we live and work. The dominant feature of that context is social change — in fact, accelerating change.

SOCIAL CHANGE: CHANGES IN THE SOCIAL WORLD SURROUNDING THE INDIVIDUAL

Note at the outset that *social* change refers to the world outside the person. *Personal* change refers to change in the individual's own life such as moving, changing jobs, getting older, becoming more assertive.

Perhaps the best description of the accelerating pace of social change is found in Alvin Toffler's *Future Shock*.[2] Toffler offers considerable evidence that things are moving faster than they did in the past, certainly faster than in our parents' or grandparents' time.

One reason for the increase in the pace of social change is rapid *population growth* around the world. The world's population is expected to double in about 35 years at its present growth rate. In many countries, population will double in only 25 years. Already we number about 4.4 billion people. An increase, of course, will mean more mouths to feed, more bodies to clothe, more houses to build, more goods and services to be produced, more crowding.

A second reason for the faster rate of change is *technology* — the increasing use of sophisticated mechanical and electronic devices to solve problems and produce goods. Our reliance on science, combined with the need for more goods and services and the need to keep ahead of competition, leads manufacturers to constantly produce new goods and devices. What used to take weeks, months, or even years now can be accomplished in seconds. Yet technology exists not only in factories and computer centers. It has rippled outward to affect entire communities. One look at a modern kitchen, compared with one in your grandparents' time, should be enough to convince you of the broad impact of technology.

114

As Toffler points out, if we think of technology as the great "engine of change," then knowledge is the fuel on which that engine runs."[3] The fantastic speed-up in generation of *new knowledge* is the third factor responsible for the faster rate of social change. The computer is partly responsible for this increase in knowledge, especially in the sciences. The number of new scientific books and articles is staggering — and still growing. A chemistry professor comments that he could pass few college examinations these days because so much has been discovered in recent years. Another professor notes that more than half of all knowledge has been developed in his own brief lifetime.

C. P. Snow, the novelist and scientist, has remarked that "until this century, social change was so slow that it would go unnoticed in one person's lifetime. That is no longer so. The rate of change has increased so much that our imaginations cannot keep up."[4] Signs of this speed-up are all around us — faster transportation, consumer fads, whole new skylines in big cities and the disappearance of old ones, new shopping centers, people moving from one place to another, a higher divorce rate.

Accelerating social change since the turn of the century has brought with it four major trends that bear on personal stress:

From rural living to urban living
From stationary to mobile
From self-sufficient to consuming
From physically active to sedentary

As these social changes have occurred — and continue — a speed-up in *personal* change also takes place. One way of understanding how social change affects the person is to think of daily life as consisting of situations, each of which is made up of five simple elements:

Things
Persons
Places
Organizations
Ideas

Each of these elements is more temporary than before, speeding up the "flow of situations."[5] *Things* are more and more transient. If you are like most people, you buy things, then discard them more quickly than your parents did. Consequently, you make and break emotional ties with things more often than people did 25 to 50 years ago. Each time you do, you must adjust.

115

Advertising is a prime reason for this faster turnover of things. We think we need new products partly because we are told that we do. Another reason is we move more often and cannot take all our possessions with us. Still another is we think we need to "keep up with the Jones'." If your friends or neighbors have a snowmobile, a new car, a swimming pool, or new skis, you may believe you need them too. So you adopt a "throw-away mentality." You come to expect more temporary connections with such things as clothing, cars, houses, toys, art, furniture.

With *places* too, we make and break ties more often. Think about place of residence, for example. Many Europeans are the ninth, tenth, or fifteenth generation in their communities. Many visit their nearby churchyard cemetery every Sunday to pay respects to their ancestors — and to reinforce their linkages with the past. In contrast, one of every four Americans — about 55 million — move each year. Place loses much of its emotional meaning as we come and go.

Our changing relationship with place also is affected on a daily basis. In times past, home and work were close together. Shop and farm were next to living quarters. But with the development of the large factory and the large store, people went away from home to work. Now the daily commute to work may take up to an hour or two each way. Or even more. A college professor travelled every Wednesday from Northern California to Salt Lake City to complete his graduate studies — returning in time for his full load of teaching duties the next day. A minister travelled from Phoenix to Chicago for studies every Tuesday, then returned to Phoenix for pastoral duties on weekends. Place is more fleeting than ever before.

People also are less permanent in your life than was true for your parents and grandparents. Because you move more often (and if you don't, your neighbors do), you must make and break relationships more often. In the college dormitory, for example, very close friendships develop during a school year. For many students these relationships are the most meaningful of their lives. Yet the year ends and the entire dorm social system for that year disappears. Some friendships remain steadfast; but most disappear. Each time you make and break ties, an adjustment must be made. Stress — and sometimes distress — results. And many people wonder why they should get involved, since they, their neighbors, or their friends probably will be leaving soon.

The *organizations* in which you work, play, worship, and study also flow through your experience more rapidly. This occurs in two ways. One is that organizations appear and disappear more often. The other is that organizations change more quickly. Whereas organizations once tended to be rigid bureaucracies, resistant to change, many now are much more fluid. More and more workers — and students — must adjust more often and more quickly to shifting organization environments. As a result, many people sink roots less deeply into their organizations and groups, just as they hesitate to get too attached to their neighborhoods and friends.

Finally, *ideas* and *information* come and go more quickly, requiring increasingly rapid turnover of images in your mind. The English language is changing constantly, as illustrated by the substitution of "black" for "Negro" and the rapid appearance and disappearance of such words as teach-in, sit-in, hassle, psychedelic, fast-back, wash-and-wear. Toffler points out that if William Shakespeare were alive today, he would be virtually illiterate since so many English words are new. Faster change also occurs in intellectual fads, best-selling books, trends in art and music. Referring to the rapid pace at which we must change our conception of reality and our mental images of the world, Toffler raises the question: "How fast and how continuously can the individual revise his inner images before he smashes up against these limits?" No one knows for sure. But we may be approaching those limits.

In a rapidly changing world more and faster adjustments are needed. More stress sets in. One way of looking at this is to think of the individual as a channel through which a multitude of experiences flow — as diagrammed in Figure 4-1.

FIGURE 4-1

FASTER FLOW OF EXPERIENCES

In the 1980s all of us must process more elements of the situation than did people in the 1920s, 1940s, or even the 1960s.

In short, you must face a greater number, variety and intensity of stressors than people did in earlier times. While you can and do learn to adjust to this faster tempo, there is a greater chance of distress. Not only do individuals risk illness, intellectual and emotional distress, or behavioral difficulties, our entire society may be showing symptoms of too rapid change:

> *The malaise, mass neurosis, irrationality, and free-floating violence already apparent in contemporary life are merely a foretaste of what may be ahead unless we come to understand and treat this illness... unless man quickly learns to control the rate of change in his personal affairs as well as society at large, we are doomed to massive adaptational breakdown.*

One way of illustrating how faster social change causes stress and distress is shown in Figure 4-2.

FIGURE 4-2

SOCIAL CHANGE AND STRESS

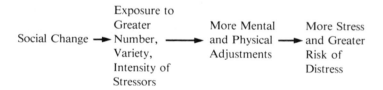

We will now examine the key types of stressors which require more adjustment by the typical American, beginning with *external stressors* such as: overchoice, overload in life pace, transitions, clustering of life events, environmental factors, role conflicts, and role ambiguity, understimulation, isolation, financial uncertainty, and daily "hassles." Internal stressors will be taken up in the final sections of the chapter.

OVERCHOICE

As Toffler points out, an important by-product of rapid change is a vast increase in options:

Ironically, the people of the future may suffer not from an absence of choice, but from a paralizing surfeit of it. They may turn out to be victims of that peculiarly super-industrial dilemma: choice. [6]

Many social critics have attacked the creeping standardization of modern life, believing we are all being pressured toward fewer choices — toward acting, thinking, and feeling the same. Their protest is symbolized by the computer card, which they see as a tool for making everyone alike. But they probably are wrong. For the real problem seems to be too much choice, too many options. Many Americans feel overwhelmed by the choices they must make: what to do, how to live, what to believe, what to buy, where to move, how to look, what to wear. Overchoice adds to stress and distress, since every option is a stressor.

One aspect of overchoice is the tremendous increase in the variety of consumer goods. Some people feel uncomfortable in the supermarket; they are numbed by so many options on the shelves. Toffler points out that two economic factors account for this trend toward diversification of goods:

...first, consumers have more money to lavish on their specialized wants; second, and even more important, as technology becomes more sophisticated, the cost of introducing declines.

This is the point that our social critics — most of whom are technologically naive — fail to understand: it is only primitive technology that imposes standardization. Automation, in contrast, frees the path to endless, blinding, mind-numbing diversity." [7]

Automobiles are a good example: the number of options can be staggering. In Toffler's words:

Thus the beautiful and spectacular Mustang is promoted by Ford as the "one you design yourself," because as critic Reyner Banham explains, "there isn't a dung-regular Mustang anymore, just a stockpile of options to meld in combinations of 3 (bodies) x 4 (engines) x 3 (transmissions) x 4 (basic sets of high performance engine modifications) — 1 (rock-bottom six cylinder car to which these modifications don't apply) x 2 (Shelby Grand Roaring and Racing setups applying to only one body shell and not all engines/transmission combinations)." This does not even take into account the possible variations in color, upholstery and optional equipment. [8]

119

The same kind of diversification — and overchoice — has taken place in movies, magazines, television sets, soaps, houses, clothing, arts, and illegal drugs.

The material goods of the future will be many things; but they will not be standardized. We are, in fact, racing toward "overchoice" — the point at which the advantage of diversity and individualization are cancelled by the complexity of the buyer's decision-making process. [9]

Another aspect of overchoice is the increase in *lifestyle* options. Should you live in the country or in the city? If in the country, should you live in the mountains, on the coast, in the forest, in the desert? What size city? What type of house — ranch-style, modular, suburban cardboard, corner duplex? And with whom should you spend your time — with drug users, hot-rodders, Jesus converts, Zen Buddhists? With vegetarians, meditators, executives, scientists, gays, athletes? To consider all possible options — or even a few of them — is to be bombarded by choices. The mind boggles. Subcultures are everywhere. Which to join? None? Try a few, one at a time? Which ones? Why?

Meanwhile what happens to you? Are you still there? Or are you simply whatever you are *doing,* whichever group you are with, wherever you live this year, this month, this week? This is the third aspect of overchoice: more frequent *identity crises,* especially among young people. Identity crisis refers to uncertainty — and sometimes intense anxiety — over these questions: Who am I? What kind of a person am I? Do I want to be? Can I not be? Can I be? In a stable, slow-moving society such questions do not arise. A person's position in life, beliefs, and identity are given. There is little choice. In our society, at least for many of us, there is too much.

The level of personality disorder, neurosis, and just plain psychological distress in our society suggests that it is already difficult for many individuals to create a sensible, integrated, and reasonably stable personal style. Yet there is every evidence that the thrust toward social diversity, paralleling that of the level of goods and culture is just beginning. We face a tempting and terrifying extension of freedom. [10]

In the face of overchoice, you must be centered and self-directed in order to retain your sanity, dignity, and self-control. Otherwise you risk being overwhelmed by too many options.

OVERLOAD IN DAILY PACE OF LIFE

Consider this: experts estimate that the average American is exposed to 65,000 more stimuli *per day* than our ancestors a mere 100 years ago.[11] This means we live a much faster daily pace of life.

PACE OF LIFE: THE NUMBER, VARIETY AND INTENSITY OF STRESSORS, PER DAY, WEEK, OR YEAR

Variations in pace of life can be visualized as in Figure 4-3.

FIGURE 4-3
PACE OF LIFE[12]

SLOWER
PACE OF LIFE   O ! X ! ! X O O X ! X O ! ! X X O O ! ! O

MODERATE
PACE OF LIFE   ! *O!X*⁶!XO/*ˢ*!*O**!/!!**X!XOO/!*

FASTER
PACE OF LIFE   NXX X O OX*! *O*X!X/!*!O*O*Y!*X*O !*X X !

It is likely that the average American can be described by the faster pace depicted. We process more situations, we cram more into an hour, a day, a week. If you live at a faster pace, you probably experience the following:

A greater number of stressors
A greater variety of stressors
A higher proportion of new, unfamiliar stressors
A greater number of intense stressors
Faster movement from one stressor to the next, with frequent overlap
More demands for adaptation or adjustment
A greater amount or intensity of stress
Higher chances of distress because of the greater amount and intensity of stress

In Chapter 3 we noted that Type A behavior is a major risk factor in heart disease. Type A behavior almost invariably breeds a faster pace of life since such a person is driven to accomplish as much as possible in the shortest possible time, chronically impatient with "wasted" time, as well as with others' slower pace. Many work organizations actively promote Type A behavior, especially if the management at the top is Type A and if the other organization is rapidly growing. Some families also promote it, as shown in a number of recent studies of how Type A behavior and a fast-paced pattern are taught to children in certain types of families.[13]

Friedman and Rosenman point out that American culture places high value on a fast pace.[14] Speed, numbers, accomplishment, competitive success, incessant upward climbing — all are held up as elements of the American ideal of the "good life" and the "successful" man or woman. Urban living, with its crowding, commuting, and rush, reinforces this pattern, especially among the middle and upper classes.

Faster and slower paces of life theoretically are measurable, assuming separate actions could be recorded, counted, and weighted in terms of the stressfulness to the person. In that sense, pace of life is quantifiable in the abstract. Practically, of course, this is virtually impossible. However, it is worth noting that analytically, a faster pace of life may or may not breed distress. It depends entirely upon the upper limit of the individual's zone of positive stress. "Racehorses" thrive on a pace that would overwhelm a "turtle." Often, however, Type A persons and others delude themselves into believing they are racehorses by nature. At the onset of physical breakdown, such as a heart attack, persistent dizziness, or chronic trembling, they begin for the first time to realize they have overestimated their tolerance for a fast pace. An important point of the book is that an effective lifestyle buffer probably can increase our tolerance of fast pace, thereby increasing the amount of potential productivity and other experiences with less hazard to health and emotional life.

Associated with any activity are two necessary time periods — lead-time and afterburn. Consider, for example, a student facing an examination in history, an especially important one because she needs a "B" to qualify for a scholarship to college. Lead-time is the period of emotional and intellectual preparation she needs the day before and on the morning of the examination. Afterburn is the time needed after the exam to think about how she did, feel it, talk to her friends, set it to rest. If she has neither enough time to prepare nor enough time afterward to "come down" — to relieve the pressures of the exam — she will feel slightly off-balance, a bit tense. No single instance is terribly significant. But ignoring the need for adequate lead-in and after-burn time thousands of times during a lifetime can create an enormous build-up of many small tensions and stress.

A fast pace of life, especially for someone who needs quite a bit of lead-in and afterburn time, can be a significant source of tension, stress, and distress. Various ailments — colds, asthma, chest pains, high blood pressure, sore back — often result if too many activities are crammed into too short a span of time.

In a recent study of Type A behavior among runners, 572 members of six Northern California running clubs completed a pencil-paper version of the Type A test.[15] They also provided other information about their health patterns, including stress and running injuries. The results were striking and significant: the higher the Type A behavior, the greater the distress symptoms, the higher the perceived stress level during the past three months, the more the running injuries, the greater the number of running days missed or reduced because of injury, the greater the number of health-care appointments because of running injuries, the more the days of work missed because of illness, and the greater the number of health-care appointments for illness other than injuries. Runners are like-ly to be protected to some degree from ill effects of Type A behavior. Even so, the greater the Type A behavior, the more adverse the effects on stress and health.

Research on role overload on the job further supports the notion that a fast daily pace may be hazardous to health. Work overload may be of two types: quantitative and qualitative.

When employees perceive that they have too much work to do, too many different things to do, or insufficient time to complete assigned work, a condition of **quantitative** *overload exists.* **Qualitative** *overload, on the other hand, occurs when employees feel they lack the ability to complete their jobs or that performance standards are too high regardless of how much time they have. An engineer asked to design a containment system for a new nuclear power plant within three months may feel that, given the other projects he/she is already responsible for, three months is insufficient time. This is quantitative overload. The same assignment given to a non-engineer may cause qualitative overload, since the individual may lack the necessary skills to complete the project.*

An electrical system that is unable to handle all of the electricity introduced to it is overloaded. In most instances, a fuse blows or a cir-

123

cuit breaker is tipped, stopping the input and preventing damage to the system. When an individual is unable to handle all the input, that person may become overloaded. Unfortunately, unlike the electrical system, people do not have an automatic safety device, and the overload condition can lead to physical, mental, and job performance problems. [16]

Among the adverse effects of job overload are elevated cholesterol, increased incidence of heart attacks and hypertension, lowered confidence, decreased work motivation, increased absenteeism, sharply reduced numbers of suggestions contributed, and increased drinking behavior. Clearly, too fast a pace of life on or off the job, especially when it results in overload, is dangerous when it becomes a chronic condition.

TRANSITIONS

Another type of experience which frequently causes distress is transition — from one set of habits to another, from one place to another, from one social setting to another. In a fast-paced society, you probably experience less permanence than your parents or grandparents did. You make and break ties to the world around you more often. You more frequently change how you live and what you do. Each change requires a transition. Each transition requires an adjustment. Stress always results, distress sometimes follows.

Geographic mobility — moving from one community or neighborhood to another — is a type of transition experienced by millions of Americans each year. When a family moves, each member must pass through a host of transitions — from familiar to unfamiliar places, from one set of friends to another, from one school or work setting to another, from old routines to new ones. Research has shown that the stresses of moving are especially painful for children between the ages of two and four and for teenagers, for whom the trauma of leaving their home towns and their friends may be extreme. Research also has shown that a variety of illnesses, including coronary heart disease, occur more frequently among uprooted adults.

Role transition also can create substantial stress. Promotions, demotions, marriage, divorce, remarriage, becoming a parent, a job transfer, becoming a high-school or college student causing stress, and sometimes distress. A distress reaction is especially likely under certain conditions: if the transition is from a high to a low-stimulation environment (or vice versa); if the transition is involuntary; or if several role transitions occur

124

simultaneously. When a person's new role requires behavior that falls outside his or her comfort zone, the chances of distress will be heightened.

A lifestyle change also can be highly stressful, yet thousands of Americans undergo changes in lifestyle each year. Part of the problem with such transitions is the in-between space — the void, the search, the uncertainty, the absence of anchorage.

Severe stress symptoms are common during such transitions. Yet they do not always show up in the short run.[17] A 19-year-old youth once described his experiences of the previous four years as follows: In the ninth grade, he was into athletics. Finding that world unsatisfying, he took up with a motorcycle gang in the tenth grade. The following summer, he became involved with heavy drug use. A year later — his senior year — he was "rescued" from that lifestyle by the "Jesus people." In a discussion group that included a 75-year-old woman who had lived on the same ranch for 50 years, he later commented: "It took me a whole month to get over that one." There were few immediate signs of stress or distress in this case, yet one wonders about the outcome over the long run.

A serious loss is a wrenching transition.[18] Death of a family member is almost always traumatic. So is loss of a home through fire, separation and divorce, termination of a professional career, involuntary retirement, theft of a valued personal possession, disappearance of a family pet, loss of an arm. In each case, one must "say goodbye" and adjust to life without the lost object or person. Whatever the loss, people pass through remarkably similar steps of mourning. As described by Horowitz, these steps are shown in Figure 4-4.[19]

FIGURE 4-4

STAGES IN REACTION TO LOSS[19]

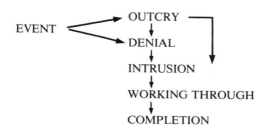

125

Horowitz points out that individual differences affect the order of entry into phases, how long is spent in each phase, and the signs of stress or distress which occur in each phase. But in general, people tend to follow this pattern. Let us focus, for example on the loss of a spouse.

Outcry is an almost automatic emotional response that may take varied forms — weeping, screaming, panic, or fainting. For example, a woman told that her husband has just died in an accident may cry out in anguish: "No, no, it can't be true!"

Denial refers to a numbing avoidance of the reality of the loss. For example, relatives of the widow just described might come to help out and provide comfort. Since they are less deeply affected by the loss, they may already have entered the intrusive phase. For example, they are likely to think of the deceased constantly, to cry, and to express intense sadness. The widow in contrast, may be numb, busy with planning and "entertaining," giving the appearance of strength. But she only appears to be "doing very well."

Intrusion, which follows denial and/or outcry, is a preoccupation with the lost spouse through dreams, recurrent reminders of past events, even visual images of the deceased. This phase may not begin until after the relatives have left. Weeks or months later, "she might begin to oscillate between periods of denial and numbing episodes in which she experiences waves of search grief, ideas about the emptiness of her life, and even an hallucinatory sense of the 'presence' of her lost husband."

Working through is gradually coming to terms with the reality of the loss and adjusting to life without the spouse. In most cases of death of a family member, this requires six months to one year of emotional adjustment, decisions and planning, and changing daily routines.

Completion is reached when the person is able to get on with a new stage of life without denial or serious intrusion of the loss.

People always have had to cope with the expected and the unexpected. Even for our ancient ancestors, the uncertainties of climate, food supplies, and relations with neighboring tribes made life a continuing process of adaptation. In contemporary times, change is inherent in the life cycle itself. One writer refers to these predictable life cycle events as "marker events."[20] Marker events begin early. The five-year-old entering kindergarten experiences a dramatic confrontation with the unfamiliar — new faces, new routines, new expectations, new challenges. To some extent, this is repeated every time a student enters the next level of school. The move from high school to college can be especially stressful because of the need for greater self-reliance, increased financial concerns, keener competition, and new social demands. Marriage is another stressful "passage," pleasurable as it may be. Having children, especially if several are closely spaced, creates stress on each parent and on the marriage. So does the child-rearing process and, later on, the departure of children from the home. Retirement is a difficult, and sometimes, lethal, adjustment. Death of the spouse is the last major change for many people.

Throughout the life cycle, a number of intense personal adjustments must be made, regardless of the pace of social change. But rapid social change and a faster pace of life bring a number of additional life changes. These are relatively new in human history, at least on such a mass scale. Among the most important of these are divorce, remarriage, and geographic mobility.

CLUSTERING OF LIFE EVENTS

In the preceding section, we focused on stressful single life transitions. Emphasis here is on the high risk to health, life satisfaction, and productivity of the accumulation of too many life changes in too short a time.

When referred to the Stress and Health Center by her physician, Carolyn, 55-years-old, suffered from diarrhea, insomnia, hemorrhoids, hypertension, and swings between severe anxiety and depression. The symptoms had appeared within a few short months quite unexpectedly to Carolyn, who had been emotionally stable and free of illness throughout most of her adult life. An interview and paper-pencil test revealed a clustering of the following events in her life during the preceding nine months:

> *She retired after 32 years of elementary teaching.*
> *Her husband sold his hardware business and retired.*
> *They decided to move to a retirement community in another part of the state.*
> *They sold their home.*
> *They left their neighborhood, church, and extended family.*
> *They bought a new home.*
> *They adapted to a new climate.*
> *They developed a new friendship group and entered a new church.*

They readjusted their marriage to both being home.
They adjusted to a 50 percent reduction in income.
She deliberately lost 50 pounds, which seemed a good idea at
*   this transition time.*
She and her new doctor decided it was time to stop hormone
*   treatments prescribed earlier for menopause.*
Their only daughter filed for divorce.
Their 15-year-old cat died.

Clearly, this woman faced an enormous number of virtually simultaneous adjustments in mind, body, and behavior. She was overwhelmed. Her body and spirit began to break. She felt near a "nervous breakdown."

Fortunately, greater awareness of why she was experiencing these difficulties, together with proper temporary medications, daily deep relaxation, and daily brisk walking, brought her out of this intense period of worry and frustration. Our program, combined with medical treatment, restored her health and emotions to a normal level after a few brief months.

Carolyn is but one illustration of a common pattern among highly stressed patients referred to the Center by physicians: too much change in too short a time. Her experience is consistent with a growing number of studies showing that the greater the clustering of life events, the greater the chances of becoming ill.

One study, for example, examined the illness rates of 2,500 sailors at sea for six months.[21] Just before embarking, the sailors were given a long checklist of life changes to determine how many they had experienced the previous year. These ranged from apparently insignificant changes in daily habits to dramatic, wrenching changes.

The questionnaire went on to probe such issues as the number of times he moved to a new home. Had he been in trouble with the law over traffic violations or other minor infractions? Had he spent a lot of time away from his wife as the result of job-related travel or marital difficulties? Had he changed jobs? Won awards or promotions? Had his living conditions changed as a consequence of home remodeling, or the deterioration of his neighborhood? Had his wife started or stopped working? Had he taken out a loan or mortgage? How many times had he taken a vacation? Was there any major change in his relations with his parents as the result of death, divorce, marriage, etc.?[22]

The questionnaire did not ask whether the sailor thought the change was pleasant or unpleasant, good or bad, but simply whether or not it had happened. Results showed that "life-change scores" for the previous year were correlated with illness rates while at sea. The greater the number of life changes the greater the chances of illness. And the more significant or serious the changes the more serious the illness. A more recent modification of this scale is presented in Chapter 6.

Another scale recently was developed by a professor at the University of Kentucky. This scale includes stressful life changes likely to affect young people. Recent research on students entering college revealed much higher average life-change scores than previously found for adults. The professor noted: "We had a population that had a risk for hurting themselves or someone else."[23]

Many studies now have documented the contribution of individual life changes to physical and psychological distress.[24] While technical and scientific questions still remain about some of these studies, the overall pattern of findings is clear: the greater the number, clustering, and intensity of life changes, the greater the chances of illness, injury, or psychological problems. Two scientists recently summarized these findings as follows:

> *In both retrospective and prospective investigations, modest but statistically significant relationships have been found between mounting life change and the occurrence or onset of sudden cardiac death, myocardial infarctions, accidents, athletic injuries, tuberculosis, leukemia, multiple sclerosis, diabetes, and the entire gamut of minor medical complaints. High scores on checklist of life events have also been repeatedly associated with psychiatric symptoms and disorders, and such scores have been found to differ between psychiatric and other samples.*[25]

Mental and physical illness is not inevitable, by any means, during or after clustering of life changes. But the chances jump, dramatically. The key question is: What can I do to protect myself, to reduce the chance of distress from clustered change? The lifestyle approach to managing stress presented in this book, and especially, a good lifestyle buffer, can help add mental and physical resistance against distress from too much change. In Part II, you will be given an opportunity to assess your own life-change score, as well as to plan for dealing with changes more effectively.

PHYSICAL ENVIRONMENT

Noise is perhaps the most troublesome — and common — of all stressors in the physical environment.[26] Girdano and Everly point out that noise can produce the stress response in three ways:

1. By causing physiological reactions; that is, by stimulating the sympathetic nervous system.
2. By being annoying and subjectively displeasing.
3. By disrupting ongoing activities.[27]

When sound enters the ear, it activates two parts of the brain. One pathway ends in the auditory cortex, where the sound is interpreted. The other ends in the reticular activating system, which switches on the sympathetic nervous system, and the entire stress response. When elevated sounds are chronic, as in a factory or near a freeway or airport, the RAS does not increase and decrease in excitation with each sound, but remains turned on, with consequent chronic stress arousal. While stress adaptation can result in tolerance to noise, adaptation is never complete.

This continuous stress response occurs anywhere in excess of 85 DBA (decibels on the A audiometric scale), which is comparable to heavy freeway traffic, household appliances, a bus ride, or a 10 HP outboard motor at fifty feet.[28] If noise exceeds 120 DBA continuously, tissue damage can occur. Noise at this level can be generated by a rock concert, jet take-offs, emergency vehicle sirens at 100 feet, or an air drill at five feet.

Beyond these direct physiological links to the stress response, noise can have a serious indirect effect by arousing negative emotions such as resentment or fear, which in turn elicit physiological arousal — unwanted music from next door, nearby whispering while studying in the library, construction down the block. Of course, what is annoying and unpleasant to one person (e.g., a parent) may be quite pleasant, even soothing to the next (e.g., a 16-year-old daughter).

Studies of the adverse effects of noise are numerous. Moderate to high unexpected noise has been found to impede circulation to arms, hands, legs, and feet. Chronic high noise can elevate blood pressure, as well as stress hormones in the blood. Rates of miscarriage, physical illness, and admission to mental hospitals have been demonstrated to increase the closer one lives to major airports.[28] Another study of the effects of factory noise in Mexico City found that high noise levels resulted in greater job tension, abnormal weight loss, heart attacks, and loss of sexual desire.[29] Finally, children living on the lower floors of multi-story apartment buildings next to a twelve-lane freeway in New York City scored lower than children living on upper floors on tests requiring them to distinguish between words which sound similar, such as gear and hear, cope and coke, guile and dial. Since the ability to make such distinctions importantly determines reading ability, children from lower floors scored significantly lower on standardized reading tests.[30] Clearly, excess noise, especially when perceived as unpleasant, can elicit the stress response and, when chronic, can affect behavior, health, emotions, and thinking. Even when our bodies and minds adapt, there may be long-term costs, since adaptation of this type itself can wear and tear, depleting energy reserves.

Another distressing stressor in the physical environment may be improper *lighting*.[31] Adverse emotional and physical effects such as frustration and tension can result from inadequate light, as well as from too much glare, or from certain types of lighting, such as fluorescent lamps. Whether or not a particular lighting pattern is stressful may depend on such factors as the task (e.g., detail work may require more), how continuously a person is exposed, other aspects of the physical environment, or individual differences in perception and preference.

Temperature at either extreme also can have direct and indirect effects on stress.[32] For example, excess heat drains energy, lowers resistance, requires greater oxygen, blood flow, and heart rate, and can quickly result in emotional distress such as irritability, especially without breaks and fluid intake. Crimes occur during periods of high temperature and fall off again as temperatures drop. Extreme cold can be deleterious as well, both emotionally and physically, resulting in marked alterations in behavior.

Other physical stressors with potential harmful effects are *vibration, motion,* and *polluted air.*

ROLE CONFLICT

A role is the cluster of expectations associated with a social position such as teacher, student, husband, neighbor. As a social being, your life is a continual process of adjusting to the behaviors and expectations of other people. As you do, you seek to balance what you want with what you think others want. But your own desires sometimes conflict with what others want or expect from you. And you may not always perceive accurately what others expect. In short, you may experience role conflict.

In a rapidly changing society such as ours, role conflicts are more common than in a stable, slowly changing society. Such conflicts exist in several forms. One type occurs as *personal desires conflict with the expectations of others.* You may find yourself unable or unwilling to do what others expect because you want something different or because your skills do not fit the situation.

In a poor job-person fit, Pamela believed she should go out of her way to be friendly, warm, and personable and to do everything she could to accommodate the wishes of customers. This was her definition of responsibilities on the job — which was consistent with her outgoing personality. But she was reprimanded repeatedly by her boss and finally was fired because he expected her to spend less time with each customer. She argued that more clerks were needed. He maintained that customers could be served adequately with present staff if less time were devoted to each customer. Her wants and needs conflicted with his expectations of her. He won; she lost. [33]

A second form of role conflict occurs when *expectations associated with one role conflict with expectations asssociated with another.* Each of us plays a multitude of roles. When time demands do not conflict and when the expectations placed upon us are consistent with each other, we face little difficulty in performing multiple roles. But role demands often bump into one another. What is expected of us in one role may be inconsistent with what is expected in another.

Jane Dougall is a college junior who occupies several roles: student, roommate, lover, daughter, employee. Usually others' expectations do not seriously conflict, but sometimes she does feel in a bind. On a recent Thursday, for example, her history professor and classmates expected her to present an oral report at their 12:00 class on the love life of Calvin Coolidge, her roommates wanted her to help clean the apartment all morning, her boyfriend wanted to have lunch with her, she felt pressured to answer her mother's letter of last week, and her boss called at 7:30 a.m. to ask her to substitute all day for a sick employee. [34]

Other examples of conflicting role expectations are common: mother versus employee, executive versus husband, friend versus father, supervisor versus fellow worker. Conflicting expectations almost always create stress. When too many role conflicts accumulate or when conflicting expectations are held by persons whose approval is especially important, stress may give way to distress — illness, emotional problems, confusion, or irritability.

A third type of role conflict occurs when *different expectations of a single role conflict with each other.* If you are a college student taking several classes, you have many conflicting demands on your time and energy: for example, from your biology, anthropology, mathematics, and history classes. Most of the time you probably can handle your various professors' expectations. But occasionally expectations will conflict: your biology professor expects you to complete a lab report on the same day that your anthropology professor expects a report on the reproduction habits of an Amazonian tribe — which happens to be the same day your mathematics professor plans a mid-term examination. By chance, this is the same day you are expected to present a report to the history class on causes of the Civil War.

A factory foreman is caught in a perpetual bind: he must please both labor and management. So is the school superintendent who must respond to a number of potentially conflicting role partners: the school board, parent groups, the teachers' union, other school administrators, and students. On delicate issues such as pay raises or student participation in decision-making, satisfying one group can mean automatically displeasing another. Stress results. And sometimes distress.

Research shows that the greater the role conflict on the job, the lower the job satisfaction, the greater the anxiety, the higher the blood pressure, the greater the incidence of heart attacks, the higher the cholesterol, the greater the obesity, the higher the heart rate, the greater the occurrence of abnormal EKGs, the greater the absenteeism, and the greater the worker turnover.

An effective school superintendent can seek to minimize conflict through compromise, satisfying one group this time, another group the next time, and a third group later on; or simply by doing what seems morally right, letting the chips fall where they may. People in jobs with perpetual conflict, like the foreman and the school superintendent, often survive through a kind of emotional insulation or numbness. This response may be useful in one respect (it does minimize stress and distress in times of role conflict), but it can have unfortunate side-effects — deadening all feeling on and off the job.

ROLE AMBIGUITY

Conflicting expectations are not the only stress-related problems associated with social roles. Roles sometimes lack clarity in what is expected. That is, the guideposts by which a person finds direction may be ambiguous. Young people today face role ambiguity in a host of ways.

Probably no society makes the transition from childhood to adulthood more difficult than we do in America. We have developed very few patterns that dramatize the "coming of age" of the adolescent. We have provided him with few guideposts by which to find directions. At adolescence, we expect the boy or girl to stop being a child, yet we do not expect him to be a man or woman. Any definitions he has of his changing age positions are quite inconsistent. He may drive an automobile at sixteen, leave school at eighteen, be subject to the draft at nineteen, and vote at twenty-one. He is told he is no longer a child, but he is treated like a dependent, supported by his parents, and mistrusted for the tragedies that befall some adolescents — auto accidents, juvenile delinquency, pre-marital pregnancies, and drug addiction. In a word, there are many situations in which he scarcely knows whether his is expected to act like an adult or a child. [35]

Another ambiguous role is the contemporary young mother. What is a "good mother?" Should she stay home full-time — and risk social isolation and stagnation? Should she work part-time and stay home part-time? Work full-time until the children are old enough to attend nursery school? And just how should children be raised these days? Permissively? Strictly? Some of both? Social guidelines are not at all clear on any of these matters. Each mother must search for her own way. Normal stresses of motherhood are compounded by role ambiguity.

Role ambiguities occur for several reasons. One is *rapid change.*

The contemporary South provides an illustration. Rapid industrialization and urbanization have occurred within the region in the past twenty-five years. Large numbers of individuals, both black and white, have been drawn from small towns and rural communities — from modified folk communities — and propelled into an urban, industrial world. Many have experienced an undermining of old rural values and life-ways and have found themselves isolated from many previous personal ties and roots. Considerable ambiguity has confronted them in their new settings. Where individuals have

few social anchorages to support them or standards to guide them,
they often become susceptible to influences that are offered. Social
movements are an important source of standards and guides and
thus have much appeal for individuals in such circumstances. [36]

Role ambiguities also may develop from emergence of *new roles*
such as paralegal advisor, community service worker, and ombudsman.
Lack of clear expectations associated with *passage from one life-cycle*
stage to another also can result in role ambiguity. Transition from
childhood into adolescence and from adolescence into adulthood are
classic examples. Less apparent, but sometimes just as stressful, is the
passage from mother with children at home to mother with no children at
home.

Another source of role ambiguity may be *inattentiveness by role*
partners to the need for clarity. This may be true, for example, of role expectations sent by parents to children, by teachers to students, by doctors
to nurses, by supervisors to employees.

Whatever the cause, role ambiguity can heighten distress and increase stress-related illness, emotional disturbance, and adverse behavior.
Research in the workplace, for example, shows the following negative effects of role ambiguity: more job dissatisfaction, more job-related tension, lower self-confidence, higher blood pressure, lower self-esteem,
greater depression, greater anxiety, and greater resentment. Living with
role ambiguity at home, school, or work can exact substantial costs. Suggestions are offered later in the book for modifying role ambiguity and
for adapting to it when necessary.

UNDER-STIMULATION

In Chapter 2 we pointed out that distress can result from too little as
well as too much arousal — from under-stimulation as well as over-
stimulation. Definitions of "too much" and "too little" vary with the individual, but anyone who has experienced either for extended periods
knows well the effects on morale and health.

Under-stimulation can result from a number of influences. One is a
sudden dropoff in stimuli when moving from a fast-paced environment
to a slow-paced environment. This is illustrated by teachers and students
who, after looking forward to the end of the academic year, nevertheless
go into a depressive nose-dive because of the rapid fall-off of activity.
Under-stimulation can result from under-use of one's abilities, as in a

135

poor job-person fit. Excessive repetition, as in assembly line work, can also contribute to under-stimulation, even if the worker is physically active. Lack of personal goals can also contribute to under-stimulation as can work that is meaningless (discussed later in this chapter).

Under-stimulation is especially prevalent among the poorly educated who have little opportunity to enter stimulating jobs, among retirees, housewives, students in standardized classrooms, and blue-collar workers in highly routinized lines of work.

The distressful effects of under-stimulation can range from depression and loss of motivation to irritability, anxiety, resentment, physical tension, high blood pressure, and various imagined ailments. Often under-stimulation is blamed on others in the environment, when helplessness within the person is a key cause.

ISOLATION

The devastating effects of extreme social isolation are illustrated by the case of Anna:

Anna's first five-and-one-half months after birth were complicated by frequent change of domicile. Various efforts at adoption failed and eventually Anna was returned to the home of her mother and grandfather. The mother maintained Anna physically over a period of years in an attic-like room, but neglected her to an extreme degree. When "discovered" and removed from these conditions, Anna could not talk, walk, or do anything that showed intelligence, and appeared extremely emaciated and undernourished. Although possessing normal reflexes, she was in most other respects an apathetic, vegetative creature. Anna was placed in the county home and later in a school for retarded children where she died of hemorrhagic jaundice at ten years of age.

In the four years following her discovery, Anna made progress toward becoming "human." She could bounce and catch a ball. Her food habits were normal except that she used a spoon as sole implement. Except for fastening her clothes, she was capable of dressing herself. She kept her clothing clean, habitually washed her hands and brushed her teeth, and used the toilet without fail. She could follow directions and would try to help other children. Although easily excited, she nevertheless had a pleasant disposition. And most remarkable of all, she finally acquired some speech; she talked most-

ly with phrases but would repeat words and attempt to carry on a conversation. By virtue of Anna's death, firm conclusions regarding the case are not possible. Further, it is necessary to entertain the hypothesis that she was mentally deficient. Nevertheless, her later development suggests that she was able to acquire various skills and capabilities that she never could have realized in her original condition of isolation. [37]

Anna's experience illustrates the damaging effects of social isolation on stress level as well as on the unfolding of human potential during childhood. It has long been known that adults tend to experience greater stress when they are isolated from meaningful, continuous human contact. Past research has shown isolation to be associated, for example, with higher rates of depression and other emotional problems, physical ailments, and suicide. An important recent study of nearly 7,000 Californians found that the ties that bind people together also help them to live longer. [38] Socially isolated men were about two and one-half times more likely to die during the nine-year period of the study than socially involved men. The most striking difference was observed in women between the ages of 30 and 49 — the mortality risks of those with few social ties were about four and one-half times higher than those of women with stronger social bonds.

It made little difference in this study whether the "social network" of those who stayed healthier was composed mainly of a spouse, a family, friends, or an organization of some type. Isolated persons who died succumbed to the same diseases that kill others in the population. Significantly, the adverse effect of social isolation was independent of other factors such as health at the start of the study, income level, and psychological factors such as satisfaction with life.

Social isolation can increase the chances of damaging stress in three ways. First, isolation itself can be a serious macro-stressor, directly resulting in depression, anxiety, or illness. While some persons have developed sufficient internal supports to fend off the stress of being alone, others — perhaps most people — are adversely affected over a period of time. Second, social isolation makes a person more vulnerable to other stressors. Being alone most of the time weakens one's lifestyle buffer, so that changes, crises, or even the usual stressors of daily life are more apt to exact a toll in high stress. Isolation means less support and caring, more repressed feelings, less advice and feedback. Third, socially isolated individuals are more likely to use destructive reactions to distress. According to the California study, for example, isolated persons are more likely to eat too much, drink too much, and miss sleep.

In combination, then, these three reasons combine to increase the chances that social isolation will contribute to some type of distress or even to premature death. Unfortunately, the number of isolated people goes up each year with increasing geographic mobility, more divorces, break-up of the extended family, decline in church attendance, and the disappearance of neighborhood integration.

FINANCIAL UNCERTAINTY

Another potentially distressing stressor is financial uncertainty, especially for heads of households. Low-income people face a unique lifestyle trap. Their trap has less to do with pace of life than with *quality* of life: limited money for basic needs, limited job opportunities, poor community services, sub-standard schools, inadequate health care, poor housing. Children in poor families often grow up amidst insecurity, despair, anger — and high stress. Poverty happens among ethnic minorities more often than among whites.

Whether white or black, rural or urban, young or old, most poor people face an array of stressors. Predictably, rates of stress-related illness, psychological disturbance, violence, and crime are higher among low-income people than others. For example, black men have very high rates of hypertension in the United States, although the black-white difference disappears when economic status is the same. Crime rates are highest in big-city ghettos.

In a recent report to the Congressional Joint Economic Committee, Professor M. Harvey Bremer identified seven indicators of social stress as statistically related to unemployment in the United States between 1940 and 1973.[39] These indicators were homicide, suicide, deaths from cardio-vascular disease and kidney disease, deaths from cirrhosis of the liver, total deaths, number of people sent to jail, and admissions to mental hospitals.

This study suggests that the stressors of economic uncertainty do not affect only those who are poverty-stricken or members of a minority group. They may affect anyone faced with high taxes, inflation, the threat of job loss or job transfer, or simply the need to make ends meet. This is especially true of those on fixed incomes as the disabled and the elderly.

Stress from economic uncertainty may never be completely overcome. However, effective stress management practices such as those suggested in Part II of this book may be useful for softening the impact of financial hard-times and uncertainty.

DAILY HASSLES

A recent exploratory study by Richard Lazarus of the University of California suggests that, while major life events adversely affect health and emotional well-being, it may be the minor irritating daily hassles that do the most damage of all.[40] According to Lazarus,

> *Hassles, as I define them, are the irritating, frustrating, or distressing incidents that occur in our everyday transactions with the environment. They can take the form of disagreements, disappointments, accidents, or unpleasant surprises. They range from getting stopped in traffic jams to losing a wallet; from an argument with a teen-age son to a dispute with a superior or a subordinate at work.*[41]

The ten most frequent hassles among 100 middle-aged respondents in Alameda County, California, were:

1. Concern about weight
2. Health of a family member
3. Rising prices of common goods
4. Home maintenance
5. Too many things to do
6. Misplacing or losing things
7. Yard work or outside home maintenance
8. Property, investments or taxes
9. Crime
10. Physical appearance

Other hassles no doubt would appear on the lists of different age or ethnic groups in different locations (rural, small town, big city, for example).

The more frequent and intense the hassles reported during the year of the study, the lower the overall mental and physical health at the end of the year. This was a much better predictor than a measure of life changes. The two may not be unrelated, however. That is, "the effects major events do have may occur through daily hassles they provoke," for example, a divorce will set in motion a great number of minor, day-today adjustments or difficulties. It might, for example, "force a man inexperienced at such tasks to make his own meals, do the laundry, or clean the house; it might force a woman to handle household finances or repair a leaky faucet for the first time." In Chapter 6 you will have the opportunity to monitor your own daily hassles. Similar micro-adjustments will be caused by death of a close relative, a job change, or a geographic move. Much will depend, of course, on the person's perception of such major events and on his or her ways of coping with them.

The implications of this research are significant. The daily hassles we create for ourselves through absence of routine, poor time planning, poor financial planning, unresolved bad feelings, rancorous relationships with family members, poor health care — these are the features of *lifestyle* which can erode wellness and lead to dangerous distress. Thoughtful regulation of daily life thus becomes vitally important to effective stress management.

We will now take a look at some *internal stressors* with a potential for causing distress: absence of meaning, banal and tragic life scripts, perceived gap between ideals and reality, unresolved emotions from the past, perfectionism, and fear of failure or success.

ABSENCE OF MEANING

A requisite for a life of optimum health is a sense of direction, meaning, importance. Its absence breeds malaise, demoralization, loss of zest for life. Absence of meaning often is part of a broader pattern of depression. Nothing seems very important or worthwhile. Helplessness and meaninglessness are familiar twins.

Meaninglessness also can result from internal disharmony of a different sort, namely lack of "centeredness." By this I mean lack of harmony between one's external life (job, relationships, lifestyle) with one's innermost desires and needs. Often this disharmony is a by-product of bringing into full awareness what one wants or needs. Each of us possesses what the Quakers call an "inner light" or "inner voice." Some believe it to be the Godness within everyone. Meaninglessness can result from not listening to this inner light or from making life choices which contradict it.

Absence of meaning can be caused by a lack of clear values and therefore often occurs during periods of personal transition. Or it can result from values or beliefs having changed, while one's objective position in life, such as job, is out of synchrony with these new values.

The term "boredom" has many popular meanings.[42] Its proper meaning is "disinterest." The risk of boredom is increased when one or more of the following exist:

Meaninglessness
Isolation
Excessive routine
Under-stimulation from too little challenge

The greater the number of these factors present, and the more intense each one, the greater the risk of boredom and its multiple negative side-effects.

Absence of meaning is a key disharmony which can produce distress signals. Depression, anxiety, insomnia, and a variety of stress ailments can follow. Close examination of the fit between values and circumstances, between inside and outside, may be needed.

BANAL AND TRAGIC LIFE SCRIPTS

Eric Berne, the founder of transactional analysis, contended that nearly everyone emerges from adolescence with a *life script* — a blueprint for thinking, feeling, and living.[43] As an actor follows a stage script, people spend their lives blindly living out their own life script. Included in the script are directions related to such matters as:

How to be masculine or feminine
How to get love and attention
How to feel about oneself
How to feel about others
How to cope with stress
How to spend time
Whether and how to succeed or fail

Your life script emerges during childhood and adolescence out of early messages from parents and other adults and early decisions you make. Early messages — given through example, reward and punishment, and direct instruction — include attribution (you are, you aren't) and injunctions (you should, you shouldn't, you must, you must not). Because you have the power of choice, you are not merely a passive receiver of these messages. Choice is possible — acceptance, rejection, or modification of early messages. Many people raised in destructive homes are exposed to "losing" or violent messages yet turn out well, because they choose their own life plan.

Life scripts are inherently limited, since they stifle authenticity and spontaneity. By definition, they are harmful. But they are damaging in another way as well — they often lead to distress. Life scripts can cause distress in several ways.

1. By directly calling for a life of unhappiness, failure, pity, half-effort, depression, boredom, illness, or loneliness. These are *banal life scripts.*

2. By directly calling for tragedy — suicide, a life in prison, premature death through alcoholism, accident, or heart attack. These are *tragic life scripts.*

3. By indirectly calling for either a banal or a tragic life through inept or harmful coping responses — violence toward others, drugs, schizophrenia, impulsive spending, or compulsive overeating.

Life scripts reflect in part the norms and values of the surrounding culture and subculture. Yet each script is unique in many ways. Scripts maintain their lifelong hold over a person through the *repetition compulsion* — the drive to be and do what is familiar. This drive probably is stronger than the "pleasure principle." Doing and feeling what is familiar often takes priority even over enjoying life — not out of choice, but out of habit. A tragic illustration of power of the repetition compulsion is the fact that as many as 90 percent of parents who abuse their children are repeating their own histories of abuse by their parents — a pattern currently scarring the lives of as many as 2.2 million children between the ages of 3 and 17 in the United States.

Not everyone has a life script. A small minority of people are raised by parents to be *self*-directed, to make up their *own* minds about what to believe and how to live — rather than to be controlled by a script from childhood. Yet most people are bound by their script, spending their lives blindly following it or struggling somehow to break free. Many adults succeed — attaining genuine authenticity, autonomy, and self-direction. Through awareness, effort, and support from others, life scripts can be left behind or at least rewritten in major ways. Full development of potential depends on script-free living.

PERCEIVED GAP BETWEEN IDEALS AND REALITY

If a person's perception of what *is* fails far short of what he or she thinks *should be,* distress can result. The teenage girl sometimes sees herself falling short of her ideal of how to look or act with boys. Boys in turn feel a gap between how they view themselves and their idealized image of the jock, the tough guy, the intellectual, or the lady's man. Equally intense stress can occur in the case of the college student who berates herself for not getting all A's, the mother who feels she is failing to live up to her ideal of motherhood, the father-husband who believes he is failing to keep up to get ahead. An ideal-reality gap can occur at many different points throughout the life cycle.

If the gap between how you view reality and the way you wish things could be becomes too extreme, intense unhappiness can result, along with the physical illness and behavioral maladjustment. You may feel constantly off-balance, discontent, down on yourself (if you blame yourself) or on those around you (if you blame others). In moderate amounts, however, the stress created by such a gap is healthy because it mobilizes you to improve yourself. It contributes to self-development. The key is to adopt personal goals that are not impossible to reach; to live with imperfection; to accept yourself as "not there yet," while continually striving for improvement at a moderate pace.

For ethnic minorities, women and poor people, the gap between ideals and perceived reality often is based on fact. They grow up believing that opportunities are unlimited, that if they try hard enough, they will get ahead. Too often, their hopes turn sour. They do not get ahead — partly because of overt discrimination, poor education, or behavior patterns which do not fit the demands of school or job. The result is anger, frustration, despair. High rates of crime, delinquency, hypertension, and marital discord among these groups are testimony of the stress produced by such experiences.

In this case, personal approaches to reducing stress through lowering personal goals or "trying harder" are not enough. Also needed are social reforms that will open up educational and job opportunities for minorities and the poor and a welfare system that provides a decent standard of living for those who cannot work — single mothers with small children, the disabled, the handicapped, the elderly.

143

UNRESOLVED EMOTIONS FROM THE PAST

Many psychologists maintain that another internal stressor, which creates a great deal of physical and emotional distress and blocking potential, is the presence of unfinished emotions from the past, even from childhood. Arthur Janov refers to a "pool of pain" that often is created in children who are abused by parents and are not allowed to express their hurt or fear.[44] As they grow, their energies are blocked by pain. Janov contends that the only way the person can be freed from this burden is to regress through therapy to hurtful "early scenes," under the guidance of a trained therapist, to finish expressing the hurt, anger, or fear that was never fully expressed at the time.

Other psychologists maintain that Janov may well be right in principle, although he places too much emphasis on his methods of releasing these feelings. They agree that unexpressed emotions of hurt, fear, anger, resentment, or rejection may linger and create a chronically elevated stress response, doing long-term damage to the person. Such unexpressed feelings may arise from recent as well as more distant experiences.

Figure 4-5 illustrates the different effects of expressing feelings fully and immediately and delaying or only partly expressing them.[45] The solid line represents the way emotional stress occurs when feelings are expressed fully as soon as they develop: stress is somewhat higher, but it returns quickly to normal. The broken line, on the other hand, depicts the lingering wear and tear which occurs when expression of feelings is incomplete or delayed. In the latter case, emotional stress remains for a longer time. Good health, good feelings, good relationships, and effective performance all may suffer.

FIGURE 4-5

EXPRESSION OF FEELINGS AND STRESS

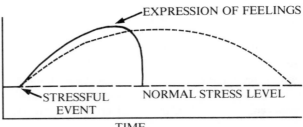

Feelings from the past can be dissolved by means other than direct expression: for example, awareness of them and simply deciding to leave them behind. Two facts importantly determine whether a method of expressing feelings is effective. Does it release your own energy flow? Does it promote the well-being of others, or does it harm them? Staying "cleared out" can help you to ease the impact of stressors on your mind and body.

PERFECTIONISM

Life is never easy and seldom enjoyable for a perfectionist.[46] There is nothing wrong, of course, with high standards. Genuine pleasure often derives from healthy pursuit of excellence. As a recent report on perfectionism stated, "without concern for quality, life would seem shallow and true accomplishment would be rare." This writer, a therapist who frequently works with perfectionism at the University of Pennsylvania Mood Clinic, makes an important distinction between those who strive for realistically high standards and true perfectionists.

> *The perfectionists I am talking about are those whose standards are high beyond reach or reason, people who strain compulsively and unremittingly toward impossible goals and who measure their own worth entirely in terms of productivity and accomplishment. For these people, the drive to excel can only be self-defeating.*

> *Evidence is mounting that the price this kind of perfectionism pays for the habit includes not only decreased productivity, but also impaired health, poor self-control, troubled personal relationships, and low self-esteem. The perfectionist also appears to be vulnerable to a number of potentially serious mood disorders, including depression, performance anxiety, test anxiety, social anxiety, writer's block, and obsessive compulsive illness.[47]*

Perfectionists suffer under their burden of unrealistic pressures for a number of reasons. They engage in all-or-nothing thinking, seeing things as all black or all white. For a student perfectionist a "B" is a catastrophe. The perfectionist fears mistakes and tends to overreact to them. He is also perpetually at odds with others around him who "in their shades of grayness" seldom meet his standards. The perfectionist over-generalizes, fearing, for example, that a single negative performance will set in motion a downward drive toward inevitable failure. "I never do anything right." He or she is beset and preoccupied with "shoulds" in relation to both self and others. "They harangue themselves, saying, 'I *shouldn't* have goofed up.' I *ought* to do better! I *mustn't* do that again!'' Self-punishment rather than self-reward prevails with predictably depressing effects.

Perfectionists also fear self-disclosure because of their fear of appearing foolish or inadequate. They are greatly concerned with maintaining an outward image of doing everything "right." Not surprisingly, perfectionists usually are lonely and isolated. Because of their vulnerability to rejection or disapproval, they tend to react defensively to harmless and even helpful criticism. They keep their distance, missing out on the warmth which would provide the very assurance and comfort they so badly want and need.

Perfectionism is a common, high-risk, internal stressor, especially among active, striving middle-class students and professionals. In Chapter 6, we will suggest several steps for monitoring this harmful, distressing pattern of thought and behavior.

FEAR OF FAILURE AND FEAR OF SUCCESS

Fear of failure is common to most of us. To fall short of our own or others' expectations in school, job, athletics or any other activity is to risk both external and internal costs: disapproval, rejection, humiliation, guilt, chagrin, a blow to self-esteem. Fear of failure, then, is a perfectly natural, even positive part of everyday life. Without it, we would be less motivated to strive for high ideals.

Sometimes, however, fear of failure becomes so extreme that it creates unnecessary emotional and physical distress. Ellen is a college sophomore who carries an intense fear of failing from early childhood when her parents humiliated her several times in front of friends for having gotten C's on tests. This lingering memory continues to create intense anxiety every time this student faces a test. Ellen is intensely afraid she will "fail" again, thereby "ensuring" rejection by others. While she is almost always well prepared, she often underperforms because her fear creates "static" in her thinking process during exams. Moreover, she deliberately avoids challenging situations whenever possible because of this fear of failure. For Ellen, a normal desire to perform well and to avoid a poor showing has turned into an irrational, nearly debilitating fear of failure which creates much unhappiness and threatens to stunt her continued academic and occupational progress.

Less common is fear of success. To succeed is to convey the message to others that you are capable, bright and dependable. The natural result is that others will expect you to succeed again in the future. This is a frightening prospect for persons so lacking in self-confidence and so fearful of rejection that they don't want anyone to expect anything of them, now or tomorrow. The solution is to avoid succeeding.

Since such persons also fear failure because of the rejection that would result, they cannot risk total failure in school, job, athletic, or community situations either. Two alternatives present themselves: either avoid performance situations altogether or be sure to perform in a mediocre fashion, neither clearly succeeding nor failing. Hovering continually somewhere between these two extremes is not very rewarding, to be sure, but safe from rejection from either failing now or falling short of others. Those who fear success, then, usually destine themselves to a lifetime of banality, neither realizing performance potential nor enjoying the rewards of accomplishment.

Figure 4-6 shows the growing gap through time between actual performance and perception of others' expectations. The consequence is evermounting anxiety, despite or because of rising performance. The solution for some persons, though usually not a conscious choice, is to fail dramatically, as in not answering any of the test questions at all, being totally unprepared for an important job meeting, going to work drunk, or oversleeping for a conference with the boss. Figure 4-6 shows that such failure quickly brings others' expectations down to a low level again. Anxiety thereby is reduced again to a tolerable level, while low self-esteem again is reconfirmed. For others, the answer is to hover between success and failure, never really trying.

FIGURE 4-6

PERFORMANCE AND PERCEIVED EXPECTATIONS

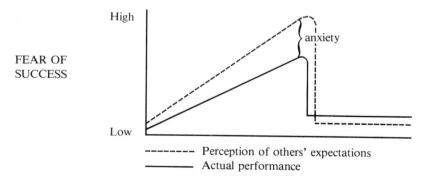

-------- Perception of others' expectations
———— Actual performance

NEED FOR A LIFESTYLE BUFFER

In this chapter, we have discussed a number of stressors that are potentially distressing for each of us. The stressors discussed are categories or types, but the reader can apply these categories to specific circumstances of his or her life. For example, role conflict is a category or type of experience. What specific events and situations from your daily experience fall within this category?

Whether or not each of these types of stressors impose moderate, even helpful, stress or harmful, and damaging distress depends on a number of factors. In formal, academic language, these are "conditioning variables:"

Other difficult stressors the person may currently be coping with
Physical energy as influenced by biological constitution
Enduring personality qualities such as open- or closed-
    mindedness, assertiveness, rigidity, and self-esteem
How the stressor is perceived and interpreted.
Kind of lifestyle the individual maintains — the degree of vulner-
    ability and protection it offers

The last of these points is perhaps the most important of all — because, like perception, it is something you can do something constructive about.

LIFESTYLE BUFFER: ATTITUDES AND ACTIONS WHICH CAN ADD TO A PERSON'S RESISTANCE AGAINST DISTRESS

Components of an effective lifestyle buffer are regular aerobic exercise, good nutrition, social support, daily practice of relaxation, and personal anchorages. In Chapter 7 we will look at the components of a good lifestyle buffer and consider how you can take concrete steps to strengthen your own.

CHAPTER REVIEW AND PERSONAL APPLICATION

1. Describe and give examples of how stressors can vary in each of the following ways:

Origin	Familiarity
Pleasantness	How chosen
Number	Changeability
Intensity	Change agent
Duration	

2. Distinguish between social and personal change and give an example of each.

3. What is meant by "flow of situations?" How is it accelerating? Give examples.

4. Draw a simple diagram showing how faster social change increases stress and the chances of distress.

5. Identify three examples of overchoice for you during the past month.

6. What do lead-time and afterburn have to do with pace of life? Give examples from your own experience.

7. In what sense are human reactions to overload different from an overloaded electrical system?

8. What is a marker event? Give three examples.

9. How much noise has been found to stimulate a dangerous level of stress? In what three ways can stress occur?

10. Describe and illustrate from personal experience three types of role conflict.

11. True or False? "Role ambiguity is one form of role conflict." Explain with examples.

12. List three ways social isolation can contribute to distress.

13. What predictions would you offer as to the effects throughout the population of widespread unemployment? What might individuals and families, schools and governments do to reduce the harmful distress from unemployment?

14. What is boredom? What "risk factors" increase chances of boredom?

15. What is the difference between banal and tragic life scripts? How can each cause distress?

16. True or False? "The opposite of perfectionism is mediocrity." Explain.

17. What does "pool of pain" have to do with the stress response? Give two examples.

18. Why are perfectionists likely to be perpetually discontented and to experience frequent distress symptoms? List four reasons.

19. Identify several factors that help to determine whether a particular stressor is or is not distressing for a particular person.

20. What is meant by lifestyle buffer? In what sense does it intervene between stressors and the stress response?

REFERENCES

1. Walt Schafer, *Stress, Distress and Growth.* Davis, CA.: International Dialogue Press, 1978.

2. Alvin Toffler, *Future Shock.* New York: Bantam Books, 1971.

3. *Ibid.,* Chapter 3.

4. *Ibid.,* p. 22.

5. *Ibid.,* p. 33.

6. *Ibid.,* p. 264.

7. *Ibid.,* p. 265.

8. *Ibid.,* p. 267-8.

9. *Ibid.,* p. 269.

10. *Ibid.,* p. 299.

11. Marilyn Ferguson, *The Aquarian Conspiracy.* Los Angeles: J. P. Tarcher, Inc., 1980, p. 300.

12. Schafer, *op. cit.,* p. 117.

13. David C. Glass, *Behavior Patterns, Stress, and Coronary Disease.* Hillsdale, N.J.: Lawrence Erlbaum Associate, 1977, Chapter 11.

14. Meyer Friedman and Ray H. Rosenman, *Type A Behavior and Your Heart.* New York: Fawcett Crest, 1974, Chapter 13.

15. Walt Schafer and John McKenna, "Hurry Sickness, Stress and Running Injuries," *Running and Fitness,* Jan/Feb 1983.

16. John M. Ivancevich and Michael T. Matteson, *Stress and Work.* Glenview, Ill.: Scott, Foreman and Company, 1980, p. 113.

17. Schafer, *op. cit.,* p. 78.

18. Peter Marris, *Loss and Change.* Garden City, N.Y.: Park Book, 1974; William Bridges, *Transitions.* Reading, Mass.: Addison-Wesley Publishing Company, 1980.

19. Mardi J. Horowitz, *Stress Response Syndrome.* New York: Jason Aronson, Inc., 1976, p. 56.

20. Gail Sheehy, *Passages: Predictable Crises of Adult Life.* New York: E.P. Dutton and Company, 1976, pp. 20-21.

21. Richard H. Rahe, "Life-Change Measurement as a Predictor of Illness." *Proceedings of the Royal Society of Medicine,* 1968, p. 61, 1124-1126.

22. Toffler, *op. cit.,* p. 331.

23. M.B. Marx, T.F. Garrity, and F.R. Bowers, "The Influence of Recent Life Experience on the Health of College Freshman," *Journal of Psychosomatic Research,* Vol. 19 (1975), pp. 87-98; T.F. Garrity, M.B. Marx, and G. Somes, "Personality Factors in Resistance to Illness After Recent Life Changes," *Journal of Psychosomatic Research,* Vol. 21 (1977), pp. 23-32; T.F. Garrity, G. Somes, and M.B. Marx, "The Relationship of Personality, Life Change, Psychophysiological Strain and Health Status in a College Population," *Social Science and Medicine,* Vol. 11, (1977), pp. 257-263.

24. For reviews of this research see, for example, Barbara Dohrenwend and Bruce Dohrenwend, editors, *Stressful Life Events: Their Nature and Effects*. New York: John Wiley and Sons, Inc., 1974; Richard A. Rahe, "Life Change Events and Mental Illness: An Overview," *Journal of Human Stress*, Vol 5 (September 1979), pp. 2-10; Richard H. Rahe, David H. Ryman and Harold W. Ward, "Simplified Scaling for Life Change Events," *Journal of Human Stress*, Vol. 6 (December 1980), pp. 22-27; Barbara Dohrenwend and Bruce Dohrenwend (eds.), *Stress Life Events and Their Contexts*. New York: Neale Watson Academic Publications, 1981.

25. Judith G. Rabkin and Elmer L. Struening, "Life Events, Stress and Illness," *Science*, Vol. 194 (December 3, 1976), pp. 1013-1020.

26. Sheldon Cohen, "Sound Effects on Behavior," *Psychology Today*, October, 1981, pp. 38-49.

27. Daniel A. Girdano and George S. Everly, Jr. *Controlling Stress and Tension*. Englewood Cliffs, N.J.: Prentice-Hall, Inc., 1979, pp. 100-101.

28. *Ibid.*, p. 101.

29. *San Francisco Chronicle*, November 1, 1977.

30. Ogden Tanner, *Stress*. New York: Time-Life Books, 1976, p. 60.

31. Ivancevich and Matteson, *op. cit.*, p. 105.

32. *Ibid.*, p. 107.

33. Schafer, *op. cit.*, p. 73.

34. *Ibid.*, p. 74.

35. James W. Vander Zanden, *Sociology: A Systematic Approach*, Third Edition. Copyright, 1975. The Ronald Press Company, New York.

36. *Ibid.*, p 105.

37. *Ibid.*, p 207.

38. L. F. Berkman and S. L. Syme, "Social Class, Susceptibility and Sickness," *American Journal of Epidemiology,* 104: 1-8, 1976.

39. "Health Dangers Linked to High Unemployment," *Sacramento Bee,* October 31, 1976; Charles Piller, "The Plague of Unemployment," *Medical Self-Care,* Number 17 (Summer 1982), pp. 30-31.

40. Richard S. Lazarus, "Little Hassles Can Be Hazardous To Health," *Psychology Today,* July, 1981, pp. 58-62.

41. *Ibid.,* p. 61.

42. Sam Keen, "Chasing the Blahs Away: Boredom and How To Beat It," *Psychology Today,* (May, 1977), pp. 78-84; Estelle Ramsey, "Boredom: The Most Prevalent American Disease," *Harpers,* (November, 1974), pp. 12-22; Victor Frankl, *Man's Search for Meaning.* Boston: Beacon Press, 1962.

43. Eric Berne, *Games People Play,* New York: Grove Press, 1964; Eric Berne, *What Do You Say After You Say Hello?* New York: Grove Press, 1972; Eric Berne, *Beyond Games and Scripts.* New York: Grove Press, 1976; Claude Steiner, *Scripts People Live.* New York: Grove Press, 1974.

44. Arthur Janov, *The Primal Scream.* New York: Dell Publishing Company, 1970; Arthur Janov, *The Primal Revolution.* New York: Touchstone, 1972.

45. Schafer, *op. cit.,* p. 159.

46. David D. Burns, *Feeling Good: The New Mood Therapy.* New York: Signet, 1980, Chapter 14.

47. David D. Burns, "The Perfectionist's Script for Self-Defeat," *Psychology Today,* November, 1980, p. 34.

PART II

MONITORING AND MANAGING STRESS

CHAPTER 5

A LIFESTYLE APPROACH TO STRESS MANAGEMENT

This chapter is an important transition between Part I and the chapters that follow. Building on the understanding about stress developed in the preceding four chapters, we will focus here first on dispelling false myths about stress and stress management. Next, we will discuss goals of an effective stress management program, what such an approach must do for the person, principles that must guide an effective stress management plan, and the content of a coherent, integrated lifestyle model of stress and stress management. Based on this model, we will identify targets of stress management.

FALSE MYTHS ABOUT STRESS

Many false beliefs about stress exist in the minds of people who know they have too much distress and are searching for what to do about it. If these beliefs remain simply beliefs, little concern need exist. However, too often they are translated into action — action that is destructive at worst and ineffective at best in handling stress. Therefore, it is important to identify and dispel the following myths, drawing upon the facts described in Part I.

1. **All stress is bad.**
   Stress can be helpful as well as harmful. Positive stress can provide zest and enjoyment, as well as attentiveness and energy for meeting deadlines, entering new situations, coping with emergencies, achieving maximum performance, meeting new challenges. In moderate amounts, stress is useful. Even in large doses, it is often appropriate and vital.

2. **The goal of stress management should be to eliminate stress.**
   Stress cannot and should not be eliminated. As Hans Selye has stated, only the dead are free of stress. Arousal is part of life. The goal of stress management should be to control stress so it turns into harmful distress as infrequently and as briefly as possible.

3. **The "good life" should be free of stressors.**
   Stressors, demands on mind and body, are an ever-present part of existence, just like stress. It is vital, insofar as possible, to con-

trol stressors and your perception of them so they are not over-burdening in intensity or number. But fulfillment of human potential, in fact life itself, depends on exposure to appropriate kinds of stressors.

4. **The less stress, the better.**
   Not nessarily. The more the arousal the better when facing the challenges or emergencies, up to a certain point. Stress mobilizes for action, shapes perception, heightens attention. The less distress, the better, since by definition distress is harmful.

5. **A person can always successfully adapt to difficult cir-cumstances if he or she tries hard enough.** This myth is false on two counts. First, each person has limits of adaptability. If physical, social, or psychological pressures exceed your upper stress limit for an extended period, wear and tear will lead to eventual breakdown. The stage of resistance will give way to the stage of exhaustion. Second, "trying harder" is not always the answer to distress. The opposite may be true, in that activity needs to be alternated with rest and recovery.

6. **Some people are destined by their heritage to be highly stressed.**
   It is true that genetic and social background can affect resistance and vulnerability to pressures to some degree. But environmen-tal and biological inheritance sets only very broad limits, except in cases of severe mental or physical handicap. Whatever the background, most people can take constructive steps which can dramatically increase ability to handle and reduce stress.

7. **Distress has only harmful effects.**
   By definition, mental and physical distress is harmful to self and others. However, even intense distress can have positive side ef-fects — new learning about self or others, a new beginning, a deeper relationship with someone, for example.

8. **Physical exercise drains energy that otherwise might be used to cope with stress.**
   Moderate, progressive physical exercise increases energy through the body's marvelous adaptive process. The claim, "I don't have enough energy to exercise, I need to save it to meet emergencies" is a hollow excuse without foundation in the reality of exercise physiology. The only exception is when a very hard work-out might leave one temporarily too tired to cope well.

160

9. **Meditation is cultish, anti-Christian nonsense.**
   Some forms of meditation are indeed associated with gurus and cults. But meditation itself is a highly effective method of controlling stress by means of quieting the body (releasing the relaxation response) with a repeated mental focus, such as a silent sound, word, or thought. Research clearly shows that deep relaxation through meditation is effective in preventing and reducing stress-related illnesses. It is important to assess meditation as a method separately from any persons or organizations that might promote it.

10. **Stress affects only adults.**
    Stress is part of everyone's life, young or old. Children, adolescents, and youth experience the same responses as adults and run the same risks of distress illnesses. Therefore, the guidelines and techniques presented in this book apply equally to persons of all ages.

BENEFITS OF EFFECTIVE STRESS MANAGEMENT

In Chapter 1 we stated that managing stress effectively can help promote several long-term goals. Stated differently, a high quality of life includes the following, which distress can erode and wise stress management can promote:

1. High-level wellness, which includes:

   Good Health: The common medical and popular definition of is absence of disease. Implied here is that if you are not sick, you are well. High-level wellness includes something more — maximum mental and physical energy for daily living. Physical fitness and vitality are important parts of good health. Poor stress management can erode good health and effective stress management can promote it.

   Life Satisfaction: A reasonable expectation of "the good life" is basic enjoyment of daily life — work, family, community, leisure, aloneness. Distress obviously implies less satisfaction; effective stress management contributes to satisfaction.

   Productivity: Stress management is not intended to promote mediocrity or withdrawal from responsibility, much less

161

avoidance of challenge. Rather, it can help increase performance. Distress erodes productivity.

> **Self Development:** A worthwhile value, in fact an essential component of a high-quality life, is becoming more complete, more effective, more developed in the various sectors of one's life. This is becoming more fully human. Distress stagnates. Good stress management promotes unfolding of potential.

2. Promotion of others' high-level wellness.

> **Distress harms others as well as the self.** Managing one's own stress effectively can help in promoting others' high-level wellness, satisfaction, productivity, and self-development. Effective stress management by individuals, then, can contribute to the collective good as well.

Whatever philosophical, religious, or political framework you bring to reading this book, you probably will agree that the above values are important and worthwhile. Poor handling of stress erodes them, and stress management can move you closer to them. My hope is your application of the guidelines and techniques suggested in Part II will yield these long-term benefits.

ASSUMPTIONS ABOUT STRESS MANAGEMENT

The lifestyle approach to stress management presented in the following chapters is based on several guiding assumptions.

1. **Personal Responsibility.** Effective management of stress can be accomplished only by you. Your doctor, counselor, spouse, or minister cannot do it for you. They can help. You will need them as partners from time to time. But self-care rather than dependence on others is a keystone in the chapters that follow. The opposite to personal responsibility is helplessness, a bedfellow of distress.

2. **Holism.** There is no single magical way of controlling stress and minimizing distress. Regular running or swimming can help. So can improved diet, regular meditation, slowing down, expressing feelings, taking vacations, and a number of other activities. The approach presented in Part II involves the whole person and total lifestyle.

3. **Gradualism.** No one should adopt too many new stress management methods at once. If you try too hard or expect change too soon, you will be frustrated and overloaded. You must be patient. Introduce one or two new stress management methods at a time so you can concentrate and carry through. Change comes gradually, not overnight. Wholeness is a long-term ideal, gradualism the short-run way to get there.

4. **Balance.** As you search for the pace of life and daily habits that are best for managing your stress, you stand to gain from striving for balance between:

   — Self-interest and the well-being of others
   — Work and play
   — Intensity and ease
   — Thought and action
   — Risk and safety
   — Change and stability
   — Stimulation and quiet.

Only you can determine the balance that is right for you in each of these respects — and what is right for you can change over time. You must be continually alert to internal cues that tell you what balance your body and mind need for health and growth.

5. **Rhythm.** Stress and distress come and go in stages and rhythms, some of which are quite predictable. Perhaps the greatest contribution of Gail Sheehy's best-selling book, *Passages,* has been the message to millions of readers that many adult crises are predictable, that many people experience the same crises, and that these crises will pass. The same holds for the pre-adult years and for the later years.

   Knowing that distress ebbs and flows can be reassuring. Your inner drive toward health and growth can take you from the deepest valleys to new peaks of authenticity and self-expression.

   An important ingredient of wise stress management is conscious control of the rhythms of stress and distress. In daily life there inevitably are stressful periods of intensity and effort. If you are to manage stress wisely you must deliberately return your stress level to normal relatively quickly so you can handle

163

the next stressful event of the day. The same is true for weeks and seasons: extended periods of deliberately induced calm, relaxation, and recovery.

6. **Awareness.**This book has emphasized the key role of understanding stress and distress — what they are, what causes them, how they can play useful and harmful roles in your life, how you can handle them. Continually increasing your understanding of both can be useful in two ways. First, awareness can be directly useful. If, for example, you are aware that a particular mental or physical state is stress-related (and that you are not"going crazy"), your worry about it almost always will subside. Similarly, anticipating a crisis and the fact that it might produce illness or upset can lessen the tension. In short, understanding in itself can aid in handling stress.

Second, enhancing awareness can play an indirectly useful role, by leading to coping responses that are constructive rather than irrelevant or destructive. Knowing through experience, for example, that two long nights of sleep are vital for reducing accumulated tensions can aid you in coping with depression or intense anxiety. Conversely, the awareness that simply working harder may not help can encourage you to slow down or take a vacation. Awareness of stress often comes with *hindsight* — after-the-fact awareness. Next comes *midsight* — for example, awareness during a destructive coping response. Finally comes *foresight* — awareness before getting into severe distress or before a harmful coping response starts.

7. **Action.** Awareness by itself is only half the picture. the other half is paying attention to what you **do** as you seek to manage stress. How you spend your time, the actions you take, what you do in relation to others and your daily tasks — ultimately these will determine how well you manage stress. Both understanding and action are necessary, but neither is sufficient alone. Action guided by informed understanding — that is the necessary and sufficient combination required for handling stress well.

8. **Experiment of One.** People are different and the same approach will not work for everyone. Scientists can tell us what sometimes works to improve health or reduce tension for different kinds of people. But in the final analysis, you are unique. You have your own particular needs; you live your life in your own way; and

your social setting is not exactly like anyone else's. You need to test out what fits your own body, personality, and way of living. Through experimentation, you will discover your own methods for controlling stress and preventing distress. This means that you must adopt the perspective of a scientist toward yourself — testing, observing, drawing conclusions, repeating what works, discontinuing what doesn't, searching for new stress methods when needed. The artful application of wisdom gained in this manner is an exciting and continuing challenge.

9. **Lifelong Process.** Managing stress is not something you do once, and then forget. Rather, in my life as in yours, managing stress is an ongoing, never-ending, sometimes joyful and sometimes frustrating challenge. This underscores the vital importance of deeply internalizing the principles in this book, making them part of your everyday approach to time, your own body, people, daily activities.

A FRAMEWORK FOR POSITIVE ACTION

The analysis of the nature and effects of stress in Part I leads to formulation of a framework or "model" of stress and stress management summarized in Figure 5-1. Two main advantages are inherent in this framework. First, it puts into simple graphic form a number of complex concepts and ideas. By being able to picture your experience with stress in this way, you may be able to better understand where specific guidelines or actions fit into the total stress management picture. This is the "cognitive" advantage. The "action" advantage is that each of the elements of this framework is a target or focus for stress management.

Let us briefly examine the framework, part by part.

1. **Social and Physical Context.** Stressors do not impinge upon the person in a vacuum. Rather, they are part of a larger environment. For example, a manager's oppressive behavior toward employees is best seen as a part of the context of the larger organization. Similarly, the specific stressors on each employee and the way each person reacts to distress are embedded within and influenced by his or her surroundings, including the physical environment, the organizational climate, the work group, the family, the community, the society. It is sometimes vital, then, to focus stress management efforts on this surrounding context,

165

rather than simply on the individual experiencing stress or distress. Chapter 13 will address this topic, especially in the workplace.

2. **Stressor.** In Chapter 4, we identified a number of ways in which a number of "high risk" stressors can vary. A vital target for stress management is to monitor and manage stressors insofar as possible. This may mean avoiding, changing, or facing them — getting at the root of your stress. Chapter 7 will focus on monitoring and managing stressors.

3. **Lifestyle Buffer.** You are not destined by biological or social background to react to stress in a given way, as noted above in our discussion of false myths. By developing an effective lifestyle buffer, you can add physical or mental resistence to stressors. A good lifestyle buffer includes, for example, daily aerobic exercise, daily deep relaxation, good nutrition, a social support network and personal anchorages. Steps for strengthening these components of your lifestyle buffer are suggested in Chapter 8.

4. **Perception of Stressors.** Another vital link intervening between stressors and your mental, physical, and behavioral reactions to them is your perception of these stressors. For example, a change in job location or assignment can be perceived as a threat or an opportunity for growth. Perceptions and interpretations of stressors can be controlled. Chapter 9 will focus on means for doing so.

5. **Mental and Physical Stress Response.** In Chapter 2, you read in some detail about how the brain and the body receive and respond to perceptions of stressors through either the conscious or unconscious appraisal pathways. Learning to regulate and control these responses immediately prior to, during, or immediately after arousal is another important target of stress management and will be addressed in Chapter 10. This includes mobilizing stress needed for peak performance.

6. **Coping Response.** Note that vertical arrows interconnect mental, physical, and behavioral responses to stressors. Each is affected by the other. For example, feeling fearful of another person prepares the body for direct, physical action. Physical action such as fleeing, fighting, compromising, or freezing,

166

FIGURE 5-1
A LIFESTYLE FRAMEWORK OF STRESS AND STRESS MANAGEMENT

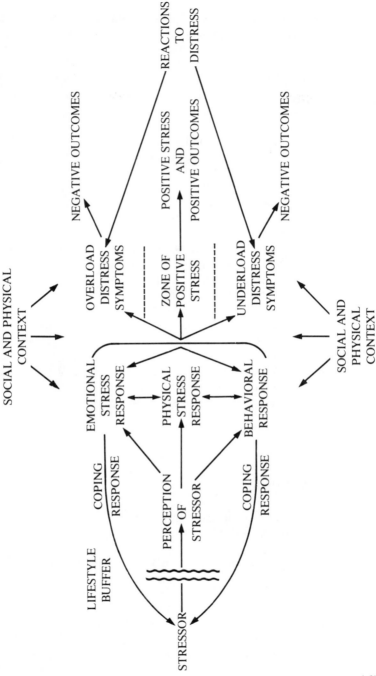

which in turn loop back on feelings and physiology, are important to monitor. What you *do* behaviorally in coping with stressors is represented in the chart by the coping response. Arrows return from behavioral and mental stress response back toward the stressor, reflecting the ways you think, act, and feel as you interact with the stimulus. Chapter 11 focuses on managing the coping response.

7. **Underload and overload distress symptoms.** If arousal takes your mind or body above or below your stress limits for any extended time, you leave your zone of positive stress and enter your zone of underload or overload distress. This can lead to negative outcomes such as described in Chapter 3. Recognizing your own distress symptoms is an important target of stress management, since these signals provide the basis for doing something constructive about the circumstances you are in, your perception of it, your reactions to it, your preparedness for similar situations next time. Monitoring and managing distress signals are the subject of Chapter 6.

8. **Reactions to Distress.** What you do or don't do to seek to reduce distress is the focus of Chapter 12. Unfortunately, a great proportion of stress problems result not from the original stress, but from ineffective or destructive steps for dealing with it. Chapter 12 will focus on steps for monitoring and managing both destructive and constructive reactions to distress.

CHAPTER REVIEW AND APPLICATIONS.

1. Can you describe in your own words at least six or eight of the false myths described in this chapter.

2. Which of these, if any, did you believe before reading this book?

3. What are the potential benefits of effective stress management?

4. What is "good health?"

5. Describe in your own words the assumptions underlying the

stress management approach set forth in Part II. Do you disagree with any of these assumptions? Why?

6. What is the difference between "coping response" and "reaction to distress?" Give examples from your own life.

7. See if you can reproduce the flow chart in Figure 5-1.

8. Define lifestyle buffer and give serveral illustrations from your own current life.

9. Why is the social and physical context of stress important to this framework?

10. True or False? Coping responses include behavior but not thoughts or feelings. Explain.

CHAPTER 6

MONITORING AND MANAGING STRESS SIGNALS

Recognizing distress signals at an early stage is a vital first step in preventing moderate, useful stress from turning into harmful, destructive distress. This chapter will assist you in tuning more closely into your physical, mental, and behavioral signals of mounting stress.

You will find a series of exercises in this chapter, like those that follow, for monitoring and managing different aspects of stress. You will be presented with more exercises than you can possibly use. Select those that seem most useful for you.

CAUTION: OVER-CONCERN WITH SYMPTOMS

A word of caution is needed as we begin this chapter. I am not advocating narcissism, "blissing out", disengaging from people or activities, or hypochondriasis. Carried to the extreme, suggestions in this chapter could readily be misunderstood and misused. Rather, I advocate continued awareness of what you are experiencing inwardly as you focus your energies and activities outward. Learning to self-monitor and regulate your life accordingly is intended to help you stay healthy, satisfied, and productive while engaged with the world around you.

This point is reinforced negatively by the fact that "neurotic" individuals, as well as many youthful drug-oriented drop-outs, often are so preoccupied with themselves they find it extremely difficult to see beyond their own eyelashes, much less engaged constructively with people or issues around them. For many who begin our stress and health management programs this is true. Certainly, I do not want to reinforce such inward fixation.

Research shows that "good copers" are highly committed to and involved in activities in the world around them. They engage life rather than hanging back on the fringes of it. This is the opposite of alienation and narcissistic preoccupation with subjective symptoms and signs of stress.

What I suggest, then, is an inward-outward perspective towards the self-in-action. This chapter is intended to sharpen your perception of stress signals and to help you understand how to use them as a basis for continually regulating your daily activities and personal care.

PHYSICAL DISTRESS SIGNALS

How you move and hold your body conveys a great deal about your internal tension. For example:

— Toe jiggling and foot tapping often reflect impatience and ir-ritability.

— Tight, hunched shoulders which often become chronically sore can signal anxiety, fear, or embarrassment.

— Tightly folded arms may signal disapproval, anger, apprehension, or the desire to be left alone.

— Tightly crossed or coiled legs can convey several messages — wanting to be left alone, anxiety, fearful anticipation.

— Sagging, sloping shoulders and back can reflect fatigue,temporary or cumulative, feeling burdened (or simply not knowing how to stand straight).

— Nail biting often conveys worry, tension, anxiety — and low self-esteem.

— A jutting jaw often shows apprehension and tension.

— Clinched fists or taut fingers reflect anxiety, usually of a current or anticipatory kind.

— Furrows and frowns in the forehead are another sign of worry, fatigue, or depression.

These are illustrations of a more extensive list of physical stress signals which also includes the following. The specific meaning and importance of these signals can best be determined by the person experiencing them:

— Dryness of mouth or throat from tension
— General fatigue or heaviness
— Slow recovery from a stressful event
— Diarrhea
— Trembling or nervous twitch
— Pounding of heart from tension
— Headache

174

— Chest pain
— Neck pain
— Back pain
— Upset stomach
— Loss of appetite
— Frequent need to urinate
— Increased appetite.

Recognizing these symptoms requires no great skill or insight. Understanding them as messages about stress does require greater attentiveness and awareness. Do they reflect positive, temporary arousal associated with an intense, but positively challenging situation? Or do they reflect more troublesome, ongoing distress? What can you learn from the following emotional signals?

EMOTIONAL DISTRESS SIGNALS

— Depressed feelings — blue, down, helpless, gloomy
— Emotional ups and downs
— Strong urge to cry
— Strong urge to "run away from it all"
— Strong urge to hurt someone
— Feelings of being "overwhelmed by it all"
— Feelings of being emotionally unstable
— Feelings of joylessness
— Feelings of anxiety
— Feelings of being "fed up"
— Feelings of sadness
— Fear of the future
— Fear of others' disapproval
— Fear of failing
— Fear that others are "out to get me"
— Difficulty falling asleep
— Difficulty sleeping through the night
— Decreased interest in sex
— More impatience than usual
— Struggling to get up to "face another day"
— Feeling that things are out of control
— Feelings of hopelessness.

As with physical distress symptoms, these signals may be temporary and even positive, reflecting for example, a temporary "high" from a thrilling challenge. Or they may be messages from your mind and body that arousal has been too high (or too low) for too long. Distress may be present or on the way. Positive steps to regulate inputs or your responses to them may be called for.

Closely related yet distinctly different are thinking stress signals, which can cause serious interference in relationships, problem-solving, and productivity.

THINKING DISTRESS SIGNALS

— Fuzzy, foggy thinking
— Forgetfulness
— Mental block
— Difficulty organizing thoughts
— Inability to concentrate
— Bizarre, disjointed thoughts
— Inward preoccupation interfering with listening
— Nightmares.

Disturbed thinking is closely intertwined with emotions, especially with emotions of fear, anxiety, depression, and anger. Disturbed thinking also may be associated with a distressed body. Observing your thought processes sometimes can cue you about other distress warning signals which otherwise might not be noticed.

For many people, signs of distress are more apparent in actions than in emotions, thoughts, or body.

BEHAVIORAL DISTRESS SIGNALS

— Irritability
— Compulsive, spur of the moment actions
— Talking faster than usual
— Easily startled
— Stuttering or stumbling in speech
— Grinding teeth
— Difficulty sitting still
— Verbal attack on someone
— Difficulty staying with one activity very long
— Significant interpersonal conflict
— Short-tempered
— Withdrawn
— Crying spells
— Lashing out at something or someone.

While the above usually are direct reflections of internal tension, the

176

following behaviors are indirect signals in that they reflect increased use of specific actions to release the physical and mental pain of distress. In other words, if these increase in frequency, they may reflect an increased level of distress to which they are a response.

— Increased smoking
— Increased alcohol consumption
— Increased use of prescribed medications to reduce tension
— Use of sleep as an escape
— Use of T.V. as an escape
— Increased use of over-the-counter aids for sleeping or relaxing
— Increased use of illegal drugs
— Increased consumption of coffee or colas
— Seeing medical doctor for tension or tension-related health problems
— Irrational spending sprees.

Exercise 6-1 — Schafer Distress Symptom Scale.

You are invited to complete the following inventory of your current distress signals, which includes many of the above items. While some of these items may reflect positive stress (for example, talking faster than usual or difficulty falling asleep), the scale as a whole is intended to measure distress. The fact that it correlates highly with a number of other stress-related scales suggests that it is a valid measure of distress symptoms. The most important thing for you is that it will give you a fairly vivid picture of what you are experiencing in mind, body, and behavior. When you are finished, add your score, using the numbers given at the top of the scale.

Please indicate which of these occurred during the past two weeks. Use the checks as follows:

    0 ____Did not occur
    1 ____Occurred once or twice
    5 ____Occurred several times
   10 ____Occurred almost constantly

____Irritability   ____Grinding teeth
____Depressed feelings   ____Difficulty sitting still
____Dryness of mouth or throat   ____Nightmares
    from tension   ____Diarrhea
____Impulsive, spur-of-the-moment   ____Verbal attack on someone
    actions

_____Emotional ups-and-downs
_____Strong urge to cry
_____Strong urge to "run away from it all"
_____Strong urge to hurt someone
_____Fuzzy, foggy thinking
_____Talking faster than usual
_____General fatigue or heaviness
_____Feelings of being "overwhelmed by it all"
_____Feelings of being emotionally unstable
_____Feelings of joylessness
_____Feelings of anxiety
_____Emotional tension
_____Easily startled
_____Hostility
_____Trembling or nervous twitch
_____Stuttering or stumbling in speech
_____Inability to concentrate
_____Difficulty organizing thoughts
_____Difficulty sleeping through the night

_____Mental block
_____Frequent need to urinate
_____Upset stomach
_____More impatience than usual
_____Headache
_____Neck pain
_____Pain in back
_____Loss of appetite
_____Decreased interest in sex
_____Increased appetite
_____Forgetful
_____Chest pain
_____Significant interpersonal conflict
_____Struggling to get up to "face" another day"
_____Feeling things are "out of control"
_____Feelings of hopelessness
_____Difficulty staying with one activity very long
_____Short-tempered
_____Withdrawn
_____Difficulty falling asleep
_____Slow recovery from a stressful event

Exercise 6-2 — Questions About the Schafer Distress Symptom Scale

1. Is your score higher than you would like?

2. What do you see that is new or surprising?

3. Underline the two or three items most troublesome to you during periods of overload.

4. Underline the two or three items most troublesome to you during periods of underload.

5. What can you learn about your zone of positive stress from the items you have underlined?

6. How do you suppose your mate, a close friend, or working partner would rate you on the scale? Ask him or her.

Exercise 6-3 — Comparing Your Schafer Distress Symptom Score

Compare your score with the scores of the following groups who have recently taken the same self-assessment.

Group Scores on Schafer Distress Symptom Scale

Group	Number of Respondents	Median Score	Percentage with Scores Higher than 100
Participants in weight loss clinic	26	36	15%
Employees of county housing authority	15	74	33%
Mothers of nursery school children	70	52	16%
Dental support staff	71	35	8%
Dentists	41	19	5%
Special education teachers	54	50	17%
Elementary school teachers	15	40	20%
Physicians	24	37	0%
College students (First week of classes)	63	53	8%
College students (Final exam week)	79	54	32%
Small town newspaper editors	48	41	8%
Certified Public Accountants (non-tax season)	52	34	5%
Certified Public Accountants (tax season)	52	45	19%
Realtors	29	22	7%
Pharmacists	40	27.5	10%

Members of secretarial Organization	78	40	11%
College Custodians	54	20	4%
College dept. secretaries	26	9	8%

Exercise 6-4 — Monitoring Distress Signals

Without becoming overly preoccupied, use this list of 50 distress signals as a guide to more closely monitoring messages from your mind, body, and behavior during the next two days. What can you learn? What stressors seem to lead to specific types of distress?

Exercise 6-5 — Distress Signals and Disharmony

When stress signals are not related to a perceived or actual positive stress, they probably indicate unwanted and potentially harmful distress, either current or unanticipated. As pointed out in Chapter 1, distress is a signal of disharmony somewhere in your life. Distress is, after all, internal disharmony — an equilibrium gone wrong, an imbalance between mind and body, or a conflict among different parts of yourself. If your score on the Schafer Distress Symptom Scale is higher than you think it ought to be, you are invited to complete the following exercise:

1. Given what you have learned thus far from this book, what is your best guess as to the disequilibrium or imbalance within your body? Between your mind and body? With what simple words would you describe this disequilibrium?

2. What is there about your life right now contributing to your high distress symptom score? In other words, where is the disharmony? Here are a few possibilities:

   — You are not getting something you want or need very much — love, affection, approval, food, money, recognition, advancement, for example.

   — Two feelings about someone or something are in conflict, doing battle. Examples might be: the desire to live together conflicts with wanting time alone, desire for more money conflicts with wanting to stay in my present job, I like certain things about him or her, but others I can't stand.

— Uncertainty about the future — job change, marriage, divorce, school, move.

— Something I am doing which I hate myself for — like smoking, overeating, being inaccessible to others, overspending, abusing my body in other ways.

— Conflict with someone else — boss, mate, friend, co-worker, neighbor.

— Disharmony between job requirements and my personality.

— Conflict between my need for slower pace and demands of my current situation.

— Others?

3. What constructive steps can you take, beginning this very day, to resolve this disharmony, whether it is purely internal in origin or in your relationship with your surrounding world?

4. Do it.

Exercise 6-6 — Bodily Symptoms — Trackdown on Deeper Meanings

We learn time and time again that illness, pain, and accident are manifestations of deeper needs which are going unmet. Perhaps this trackdown method will help you to get in touch with some of these needs.[1]

Symptom	Trackdown	Regina's Example	Your Example
e.g. tension headache	1. It feels like:	(a knife over my right eye)	
	2. It happens when:	(I've been pushing myself hard for several days)	
	3. It prevents:	(reading, feeling excited about life)	
	4. It encourages:	(more sleep, less work, admitting my weaknesses)	

5. It provides the reward:	(attention and help from Jere)
6. It may indicate the deeper need for:	(Jere's acceptance of me)
7. A more direct way to meet this need might be:	(expressing this to him; scheduling more special time with him)

Exercise 6-7 — Monitoring Heart Rate

A simple, fascinating, highly accessible means of monitoring what is happening inside your body is to take your own pulse rate. Use your wrist or carotid artery in your neck. Right now, count the number of beats for 15 seconds, multiply times four. This is your pulse rate per minute.

1. Take it for four days as follows, recording it each time.

Days One and Two
— Before getting out of bed
— At 10:00 A.M.
— After running up at least two flights of stairs
— At 3:00 P.M.
— At 7:00 P.M.
— Before getting into bed.

Days three and four
— Just before getting out of bed
— Just before exercising
— Immediately before dinner
— Immediately after deep relaxation
— During a stressful situation (no one will notice)
— Thirty minutes after a stressful situation

2. What did you learn? Discuss with a friend.

GETTING TO KNOW YOUR ZONE OF POSITIVE STRESS

You may recall from Chapter 3 that each person possesses his or her own zone of positive stress — the tolerance range of stress in which the person is healthy, productive, and satisfied. You may also recall this can be translated into a number scale ranging from, say 0 to 100. In order to get to know your zone of positive stress, you are invited to complete the following exercise.

182

Exercise 6-8 — Zone of Positive Stress

1. With one or more persons you know well compare and contrast your zones of positive stress on a scale of 0-100 (see below). What signs of stress indicate your upper and lower limits? The limits of others with whom you compare yourself?
2. How has your zone of positive stress changed over time?
3. How well does your zone of positive stress match up with the demands of your environment?

Positive Stress Zones

Very High Stress	100_____
	90_____
	80_____
	70_____
	60_____
	50_____
	40_____
	30_____
	20_____
	10_____
Very Low Stress	0_____

MONITORING EIGHT COMMON STRESS DIFFICULTIES

Chapter 3 also included a description of eight common stress difficulties. There are problems with too much or too little arousal, which can be easily understood and applied to yourself within the framework of "zone of positive stress." Go back and review this section in Chapter 3 if nessessary to recall these stress difficulties. In order to know your stress pattern more completely, and as an additional basis for targeting your stress management efforts, you may want to complete the following exercise.

Exercise 6-9 — Monitoring Stress Difficulties

Please indicate by checking the appropriate blank how often you have experienced each of the following stress difficulties during the *past three months.*

	Occurred Almost Constantly	Occurred Several Times	Occurred Once or Twice	Did Not Occur
Too High Baseline Stress Level	_____	_____	_____	_____
Too Low Baseline Stress Level	_____	_____	_____	_____
Hair-Trigger Stress Reaction	_____	_____	_____	_____
Too High Peak Arousal	_____	_____	_____	_____
Too Slow Recovery	_____	_____	_____	_____
Recovery Not Low Enough	_____	_____	_____	_____
Stress Build-up	_____	_____	_____	_____
Recovery Too Low	_____	_____	_____	_____

Now go back and underline stress difficulties that you have encountered during the past week.

1. What have you learned?

2. Specifically what do you need to do to prevent this (these) from recurring so often in the future? When will you start?

3. What do you need to do *now* to remedy the item(s) you underlined for this week? Do it.

Exercise 6-10 — Others' Perceptions of Your Stress Difficulties

Now ask someone close to you to give you scores on the same eight stress difficulty items.

1. Were his or her ratings of you similar to or different from your own?

2. What can you learn from this?

3. Discuss.

ASSESSING YOUR ANXIOUS REACTIVITY

According to Girdano and Everly, anxious reactivity, measured by Exercise 6-11, encompasses three of the stress difficulties: hair-trigger reaction, high peak arousal, and slow recovery.[2] In the extreme, the anxious reactive person can become incapacitated because of the loop-back effect whereby awareness of arousal and fear of its consequences further elevates arousal. Two charts explaining the role of cognitive reactivity and visceral and muscular skeletal activity in the anxiety feedback loop are presented in Figures 6-1 and 6-2.

FIGURE 6-1

COGNITIVE ACTIVITY IN THE ANXIETY FEEDFACK LOOP[3]

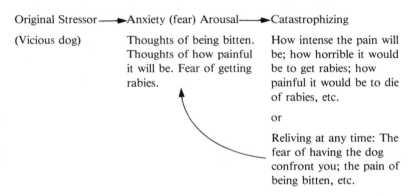

Original Stressor ──▶Anxiety (fear) Arousal──────▶Catastrophizing

(Vicious dog)   Thoughts of being bitten.   How intense the pain will
                  Thoughts of how painful   be; how horrible it would
                  it will be. Fear of getting be to get rabies; how
                  rabies.   painful it would be to die
                                                of rabies, etc.

                                                or

                                                Reliving at any time: The
                                                fear of having the dog
                                                confront you; the pain of
                                                being bitten, etc.

FIGURE 6-2

VISCERAL AND MUSCULO-SKELETAL ACTIVITY IN THE ANXIETY FEEDBACK LOOP[4]

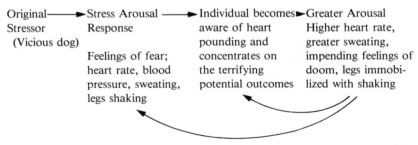

Original──────▶Stress Arousal ──────▶Individual becomes▶Greater Arousal
Stressor   Response   aware of heart   Higher heart rate,
 (Vicious dog)   pounding and   greater sweating,
               Feelings of fear;   concentrates on   impending feelings of
               heart rate, blood   the terrifying   doom, legs immobi-
               pressure, sweating,   potential outcomes lized with shaking
               legs shaking

185

Exercise 6-11 — Anxious Reactivity Index

You are invited to complete the following scale. Read the explanation following the scale to assess your score.

Anxious Reactivity Index[5]

Choose the alternative that best summarizes how you usually react during anxious moments and place your response in the space provided.

When I'm anxious I . . .

_____ 1. Tend to imagine all of the worst possible things happening to me as a result of whatever "crisis" made me anxious to begin with.
(a) Almost always true   (b) Often true
(c) Seldom true   (d) Almost never true

_____ 2. Do everything I can to resolve the problem immediately; if I don't it will drive me crazy worrying about it later.
(a) Almost always true   (b) Often true
(c) Seldom true   (d) Almost never true

_____ 3. Will relive in my mind the crisis over and over again even though the crisis may be over and resolved.
(a) Almost always true   (b) Often true
(c) Seldom true   (d) Almost never true

_____ 4. Will be able to picture the crisis clearly in my mind as long as a week after it's over.
(a) Almost always true   (b) Often true
(c) Seldom true   (d) Almost never true

_____ 5. Can feel my heart pounding in my chest.
(a) Almost always true   (b) Often true
(c) Seldom true   (d) Almost never true

_____ 6. Feel my stomach sinking and my mouth getting dry.
(a) Almost always true   (b) Often true
(c) Seldom true   (d) Almost never true

_____ 7. Notice that I sweat profusely.
(a) Almost always true   (b) Often true
(c) Seldom true   (d) Almost never true

_____ 8. Notice my hands and fingers trembling.
   (a) Almost always true   (b) Often true
   (c) Seldom true   (d) Amost never true

_____ 9. Have difficulty speaking.
   (a) Almost always true   (b) Often true
   (c) Seldom true   (d) Almost never true

_____ 10. Can feel my muscles tensing up.
   (a) Almost always true   (b) Often true
   (c) Seldom true   (d) Almost never true

Scoring: a = 4, b = 3, c = 2, d = 1   Score_____

Items 1 and 2 in the scale in Exercise 6-11 measure catastrophizing tendencies — perceiving the stressor as far worse than it really is. According to Girdano and Everly, the "catastrophizer" often views all psychosocial stress as "life or death" in urgency and severity, which of course aggravates stress from the original stressor. Items 3 and 4 measure the tendency to relive any and all crises over and over in the mind for days or weeks after the incident is over. The "reliver" suffers from distress everytime he or she relives the incident. It should be apparent how catastrophizers and relivers can both produce the stress response.

Items 5, 6, and 7 measure the sensitivity of internal visceral (intestines, stomach, heart, etc.) and musculo-skeletal systems to tension. Items 8, 9, and 10 measure the activity of striated muscles, those attached to tendons and which you can control voluntarily. These two muscle symtoms can feed on each other, adding to the anxiety of the already anxious person. For example, awareness of trembling in musculo-skeletal areas (trembling, muscle tension, for example) can cause the heart to beat faster, and the stomach to become upset. Similarly, growing awareness of the pounding heart can cause the throat to tighten and hands to shake.

The high-anxious reactive individual, then, is hypersensitive to stressors and becomes quickly overstressed, having difficulty restraining his emotions and thoughts, and having a difficult time returning his body to a normal, stable homeostasis because of anxiety feelings.

Exercise 6-12 — Assessing Anxious Reactivity Patterns.
1. Is your score a true reflection of your reactivity in real life?

2. In what situations during recent days or weeks has this anxiety loop-back process occurred for you?

3. What is the potential role of meditation or other forms of deep relaxation in reducing anxious reactivity tendencies? Aerobic exercise? Altering perception of stressors? On-the-spot tension reducers? Precisely how, physically and mentally might these stress management practices work to reduce tension?

4. Discuss with someone who knows you well.

ASSESSING YOUR FRUSTRATION

Frustration is"... the thwarting or inhibiting of natural desired behaviors or goals."[6] It is what you experience when blocked from what you want to do or get. The feeling is familiar — a sense of irritation, upset, indignation, perhaps wanting to lash out. Beneath these feelings is nervous and hormonal arousal as part of the stress response. Girdano and Everly point out that four features of contempory urban and suburban America are especially likely to trigger frustration: overcrowding, economic conditions, bureaucracy, and discrimination.[7]

These social circumstances are familiar to all of us, of course, and as we stated in Chapter 10, an important option for reacting to them is to become actively engaged in political or other causes for seeking solutions. Frustration leading to such engagement is "positive frustration."

At the same time, becoming so highly frustrated that our bodies and minds suffer ill effects does little good for anyone, oneself included or for the effort which one might be motivated to work for. According to Girdano and Everly, "such inhibition is capable of producing psychological stress realities which are expressed in the forms of anger, aggression, increased sympathetic nervous activity, and an increase incidence of mental trauma."[8]

Therefore, it makes good sense to understand what frustration is, to assess your own level, now and in the days ahead, and to develop means of keeping it within reasonable limits.

Exercise 6-13 — Frustration Index

You are invited to complete the following index which helps in measuring frustration levels.

188

Frustration Index[9]

Choose the most appropriate answer for each of the 10 statements below as it usually pertains to you. Place the letter of your response in the space to the left of the question.

_____ 1. When I can't do something "my way," I simply adjust to do it the easiest way.
   (a) Almost always true   (b) Often true
   (c) Seldom true   (d) Almost never true

_____ 2. I get "upset" when someone in front of me drives slowly.
   (a) Almost always true   (b) Often true
   (c) Seldom true   (d) Almost never true

_____ 3. It bothers me when my plans are dependent upon the actions of others.
   (a) Almost always true   (b) Often true
   (c) Seldom true   (d) Almost never true

_____ 4. Whenever possible, I tend to avoid large crowds.
   (a) Almost always true   (b) Often true
   (c) Seldom true   (d) Almost never true

_____ 5. I am uncomfortable having to stand in long lines.
   (a) Almost always true   (b) Often true
   (c) Seldom true   (d) Almost never true

_____6. Arguments upset me.
   (a) Almost always true   (b) Often true
   (c) Seldom true   (d) Almost never true

_____7. When my plans don't "flow smoothly," I become anxious.
   (a) Almost always true   (b) Often true
   (c) Seldom true   (d) Almost never true

_____ 8. I require a lot of room (space) to live and work in.
   (a) Almost always true   (b) Often true
   (c) Seldom true   (d) Amost never true

_____ 9. When I am busy at some task, I hate to be disturbed.
   (a) Almost always true   (b) Often true
   (c) Seldom true   (d) Almost never true

_____10. I believe that "all good things are worth waiting for."
          (a) Almost always true   (b) Often true
          (c) Seldom true   (d) Almost never true

Scoring: 1 and 10: $a = 1, b = 2, c = 3, d = 4$
                   2 - 9: $a = 4, b = 3, c = 2, d = 1$ Score:_____

Items 1 and 10 measure flexibility and patience, while Items 2-9 measure tendency toward frustration in situations where wants and desires are temporarily thwarted.

Exercise 6-14 — Questions About the Frustration Index

1. Is your score higher than you would like?

2. What are the major sources of frustration in your daily life? In your micro-environment? In the macro-environment?

3. What are the psychological and physical pathways through which frustration can adversely affect your health, state of mind, and behavior?

4. How might specific stress-control ideas in this book aid you in controlling unnecessarily high frustration?

ASSESSING YOUR QUALITY OF LIFE

Exercise 6-15 — Quality of Life Index

You are invited to complete the following scale.

1. Circle the number below which best describes how much *in control of your own life* you feel these days.

1	2	3	4	5	6	7	8	9	10
Not at all in control				Moderately in control				Completely in control	

2. Circle the number below which best describes your *emotional tension* these days.

1	2	3	4	5	6	7	8	9	10
No emotional tension at all				Moderate emotional tension				A great deal of emotional tension	

190

3. Circle the number below which best describes your feeling of *depression* these days.

1	2	3	4	5	6	7	8	9	10

No depression
at all   Moderate   A great deal
                              depression   of depression

4. Circle the number below which best describes how *satisfied* you are with *life as a whole* these days.

1	2	3	4	5	6	7	8	9	10

Not at all   Moderately   Completely
satisfied   satisfied   satisfied

5. Circle the number below which best describes how *satisfied* you are with *health* these days.

1	2	3	4	5	6	7	8	9	10

Not at all   Moderately   Completely
satisfied   satisfied   satisfied

6. Circle the number below which best describes how *satisfied* you are with your *job* these days.

1	2	3	4	5	6	7	8	9	10

Not at all   Moderately   Completely
satisfied   satisfied   satisfied

7. Circle the number below which best describes how *satisfied* you are with your *home life* these days.

1	2	3	4	5	6	7	8	9	10

Not at all   Moderately   Completely
satisfied   satisfied   satisfied

8. Circle the number below which best describes how *optimistic* you are about your *health* during the next five years.

1	2	3	4	5	6	7	8	9	10

Not at all   Moderately   Completely
optimistic   optimistic   optimistic

9. Circle the number below which best describes how *optimistic* you are about your *life as a whole* during the next five years.

1	2	3	4	5	6	7	8	9	10
Not at all optimistic				Moderately optimistic				Completely optimistic	

10. Circle the number below which best described how *happy* you are these days, all things considered.

1	2	3	4	5	6	7	8	9	10
Not at all happy				Moderately happy				Completely happy	

11. Circle the number below which best describes how much *fun and playfulness* you are having these days.

1	2	3	4	5	6	7	8	9	10
None at all				Moderate amount				A great deal	

Exercise 6-16 — Questions About The Quality of Life Index

1. How satisfied are you with the picture you see of yourself through these scores?

2. Which scores would you especially like to improve? Why?

3. What would it take, within yourself or within your life circumstances, or both, to improve your scores?

Exercise 6-17 — The Wellness Antidote

And now, so you will not take all this too seriously you are invited to complete the following scale.[10]

In May, 1975, 100 questions (which were later to become the Wellness Index) were tested on 25 staff persons at the Department of Health Services Research, U.S.P.H.S. Hospital in Baltimore. Within 24 hours after distribution of the questionnaire, a counter-attack was launched in the form of a spoof by the "guys" in the computer division. Subsequently labeled the Wellness Antidote, it will gauge your ability to break your seriousness about wellness. Scoring is an individual matter. One method for doing it is to rate your responses to each question:

0 points — didn't move a muscle
1 point — partial smile
2 points — wide smile
3 points — chuckle in throat
4 points — chuckle in belly
5 points — audible laughter
6 points — uproarious laughter
7 points — uncontrollable response, falling off chair.

I. PRODUCTIVITY, RELAXATION, SLEEP

_____1. I enjoy goofing off.
_____2. I seldom go to bed before passing out.
_____3. My bed is at least two feet off the floor.
_____4. I rarely bite or pick my nose.
_____5. My room is bolted down to prevent spinning.

Bonus Points for Strangers
_____6. Although not centered, I usually try to stay within the outer limits.

TOTAL _____

II. PERSONAL CARE AND HOME SAFETY

_____1. I smoke only during and immediately after sex.
_____2. I regularly check my sex.
_____3. I keep an up-to-date record of all germs in the house.
_____4. I wash my hands in the toilet before handling food.
_____5. I avoid nuclear explosion like the plague.

Bonus points for Women
_____6. I keep my pap covered in cold weather.

TOTAL _____

III. NUTRITIONAL AWARENESS

_____1. I drink beer instead of water because it's less polluted.
_____2. I salt only spoiled food.
_____3. I eat labels on packages rather than the contents.
_____4. I know the basic types of alcohol and try to keep an ample stock of each.
_____5. I avoid eating large quantities of wood pulp.

TOTAL _____

193

IV. ENVIRONMENTAL AWARENESS

_____1. I recycle my septic system by using it to wash my windows.

_____2. I set my thermostat on the window before going to bed.

_____3. My car burns less than 3 gallons of oil per 100 miles.

_____4. I throw burns into the dumpster.

_____5. I use public showers and eat at the "Y".

TOTAL _____

V. PHYSICAL ACTIVITY

_____1. I jump off buildings rather than use the stairs.

_____2. I kick doors down instead of opening them.

_____3. I participate in orgies every week.

_____4. I yodel at least 20 minutes 4 times a day.

_____5. I jog to the liquor store.

TOTAL _____

VI. EMOTIONAL MATURITY AND EXPRESSION OF FEELINGS

_____1. I am frequently sober enough to think.

_____2. I am able to punch people out without taking it personally.

_____3. I am frequently nice to idiots and don't hesitate to use that word.

_____4. I prefer to get money but still accept compliments.

_____5. I would seek help from friends if I had any.

TOTAL _____

VII. COMMUNITY INVOLVEMENT

_____1. I vote early and often at each election.

_____2. If I saw a broken kid in the street, I would put him out of his misery.

_____3. I know who my neighbors are and swear at most of them.

_____4. I love my neighbor's wife.

_____5. I am a member of one of the more subversive organizations.

TOTAL _____

VIII. CREATIVITY, SELF EXPRESSION

_____1. I enjoy expressing myself Period.
_____2. I like myself because I'm so irresistible.
_____3. I enjoy being touched by my hamster.
_____4. I am emotionally close to at least 5 hamsters.
_____5. I enjoy spending time doing just about anything
       with Farah Fawcett.

TOTAL _____

IX. AUTOMOBILE SAFETY

_____1. I know what a car looks like.
_____2. I do not mind spending $4.50 a quart for oil.
_____3. I drive on the road usually.
_____4. I check my dome light frequently.
_____5. I carry an emergency fifth at all times.

TOTAL _____

X. PARENTING

_____1. I allow my kids to play with the fan belt only while
       the car is idling.
_____2. I use what is left over from washing the windows
       to prepare baby food — it's really organic.
_____3. I frequently beat the little bastards.
_____4. I do not store loaded shotguns in the crib.
_____5. I do not allow any child over 50 lbs. to eat.

TOTAL _____

GRAND
TOTAL _____   RANGE OF SCORES AND EVALUATIONS

above 350 points	you'll probably live forever
above 300 points	add 10 years to life expectancy
200-299 points	add 4 years to life expectancy
100-199 points	have another drink
50-99 points	you need a vacation
25-49 points	you need a long rest
10-24 points	call the hospital
0-9 points	call the morgue.

REFERENCES

1. Regina S. Ryan and John W. Travis, *Wellness Workbook.* Berkeley, CA: Ten Speed Press, 1981, p. 14.

2. Daniel Girdano and George Everly, *Controlling Stress and Tension.* Englewood Cliffs, N.J.: Prentice-Hall, Inc., 1979, p. 114.

3. Ibid., p. 115.

4. Ibid., p. 116.

5. Ibid., p. 112.

6. Ibid., p. 63.

7. Ibid., pp. 63-67.

8. Ibid., p. 66.

9. Ibid., p. 62.

10. Ryan and Travis, Ibid., p. 166-167.

CHAPTER 7

MONITORING AND MANAGING STRESSORS

It is well established that the mere fact of knowing what hurts you has an inherent curative value.[1]

Hans Selye

A distinctive feature of the lifestyle approach to stress management is that attention is given not just to techniques for *adapting* to stressors, but to *identifying* and *managing* those stressors themselves, insofar as possible. Many times you can do nothing about the political, economic, community, occupational, or family circumstances that cause distress for you. But often you can.

Helplessness breeds passivity. Assertiveness based on awareness and courage leads to action — doing something about stressors. This chapter offers a variety of guidelines and techniques for sharpening awareness of stressors and for controlling them whenever possible.

AN OPENER

A useful starting point in better monitoring and managing stressors is to complete 7-1 below.

Exercise 7-1 — Distressing Stressors.

Use the following chart to identify distressing stressors for you during the past *three* months. List up to three distressing stressors within each cell. Use school and work only if applicable.

Distressing Stressors During Past Three Months

	Work	School	Family	Self	Other
Episodic Stressors	1 2 3	1 2 3	1 2 3	1 2 3	1 2 3
Chronic Stressors	1 2 3	1 2 3	1 2 3	1 2 3	1 2 3

Next *underline* those three stressors that have been most distressing of all to you during the past three months. Now, for each one of these answer the following questions.

1. What distress symptoms have resulted in mind and body in response to this stressor?
2. Is this easy, difficult, or impossible to change?
3. Is it changeable by me, others, both, or neither?
4. Which of the following alternatives is or are most practical and promising in dealing with the above stressors?
   — Change the stressor in some way.
   — Avoid or withdraw from the stressor.
   — Adapt to the stressor, but lower distress by:
     — Perceiving it differently.
     — Learning to physically and mentally relax when faced with the stressor.
     — Act differently toward it.
     — Strengthen lifestyle buffer to be better prepared for it.
5. Which specific actions will I take to better change or adapt to each of these stressors?

COPING WITH CLUSTERED LIFE CHANGES
Exercise 7-2 — Life Changes

Complete either Scale 1 or Scale 2, which measure the clustering of potentially distressful life events. Use Scale 1 if you are not a student and Scale 2 if you are a student.

Life Change Scale

Think of what has happened to you during the past twelve months. Write the point value on each line as many times as each of these events occurred during the year. Then add your total score.[2]

Life Event	Stress Rating	Your Score
Death of Spouse	100	_____
Divorce	73	_____
Marital separation	65	_____
Jail term	63	_____

Life Event	Stress Rating	Your Score
Death of close family member	63	_____
Personal injury or illness	53	_____
Marriage	50	_____
Fired from job	47	_____
Marital reconciliation	45	_____
Retirement	45	_____
Change in health of family member	44	_____
Pregnancy	40	_____
Sex difficulties	39	_____
Gain of new family member	39	_____
Business readjustment	39	_____
Change in financial state	38	_____
Death of close friend	37	_____
Change to different line of work	36	_____
Change in number of arguments with spouse	35	_____
Mortgage over $10,000	31	_____
Foreclosure of mortgage or loan	30	_____
Change in responsibilities at work	29	_____
Son or daughter leaving home	29	_____
Trouble with in-laws	29	_____
Outstanding personal achievement	28	_____
Wife begins or stops work	26	_____
Begin or end school	26	_____
Change in living conditions	25	_____
Revision of personal habits	24	_____
Trouble with boss	23	_____
Change in work hours or conditions	20	_____
Change in residence	20	_____
Change in schools	20	_____
Change in recreation	19	_____
Change in church activities	19	_____
Change in social activities	18	_____
Mortgage or loan less than $10,000	17	_____
Change in sleeping habits	16	_____
Change in number of family get-togethers	15	_____
Change in eating habits	15	_____
Vacation	13	_____
Christmas	12	_____
Minor violations of the law	11	_____
Your Total		_____

Life Change Scale for Youth[3]

The following table, developed by Martin B. Marx, ranks life changes in order of the amount of stress they cause teenagers. For each time one of the events listed below has happened in your life in the past year, add the stress value to your total. A score of less than 600 suggests a low life change and a small possibility of illness in the coming year; 600 to 1,000 points represents a medium of change; anything exceeding 1,000 is high. A high score does not mean you will necessarily get sick. But it does mean that in a large sample of people like you, a substantial percentage will get sick.

You can minimize your risk of illness, researchers believe, by taking extra precautions in times of high life change. The average score of entering freshmen at the University of Kentucky in 1972, for whom this scale was based, was 891. The highest score was 3,890.

Life-Change Scale of Youth

Events	Scale of Impact
Death of spouse	100
Divorce (of yourself or parents)	73
Pregnancy (or causing pregnancy)	68
Marital separation	65
Jail term	63
Death of close family member	63
Broken engagement	60
Engagement	55
Personal injury or illness	53
Marriage	50
Entering college	50
Varying independence or responsibility	50
Conflict or change in values	50
Drug use	49
Fired at work	47
Change in alcohol use	47
Reconciliation with mate	45
Trouble with school administration	45
Change in health of family member	44
Working while attending school	42
Changing course of study	40
Sex difficulties	39
Changing dating habits	39

Events	Scale of Impact
Gaining a new family member	39
Business readjustments	39
Change in financial state	38
Changing participation in courses, seminars	38
Death of a close friend	37
Change to different line of work	36
Change in number of arguments with mate	35
Trouble with in-laws	29
Outstanding personal achievement	28
Mate begins or stops work	26
Begin or end school	26
Change in living conditions	25
Revision of personal habits	24
Trouble with boss	23
Change in work hours or conditions	20
Change in residence	20
Change in schools	20
Change in recreation	19
Change in church activities	19
Change in social activities	18
Going into debt	17
Change in sleeping habits	16
Change in frequency of family gatherings	15
Change in eating habits	15
Vacation	13
Christmas	12
Minor violation of the law	11

Total score _____

Scale 1 above is a slightly modified version of the scale described in Chapter 4, which has been widely used to measure clustering of life events. You may recall that the higher your score, the higher your chances of mental and physical illness. Holmes and Rahe have reported the following probabilities of becoming seriously ill during the next two years:

0-149 — less than 33 percent chance of illness
150-199 — 33 percent chance of illness
200-299 — 50 percent chance of illness
300 and over — 80 percent chance of illness

Four important guidelines are useful to consider in dealing with clustering of multiple life events:

1. Insofar as possible avoid clustering of life changes.

2. Anticipate the likely additive effects on stress of a life change you are contemplating — before deciding.

3. Maintain an effective lifestyle buffer to be prepared for unavoidable clustering of life changes.

4. Cope constructively, rather than destructively, with any distress that does result from clustering of life changes.

5. When experiencing lots of change, control those parts of your life that are controllable.

Exercise 7-3 — Other Advice on Coping With Life Changes

Read the following advice from another writer on stress from too much change in too short a time. How could this advice apply to you? Write your thoughts in a journal or discuss with a friend.

It all sounds pretty grim. But there may be ways in which you can soften the blow. Change is not entirely random. You have a large amount of personal control over whether and when to marry, go to college, move or have a family. You may have little control over whether to get divorced, change jobs, take out a loan or retire. But you may have a pretty good idea of when these events might take place.

So the future is not a complete blank. You can predict it to a certain degree. And to this degree, you can order your life by managing the change that is a vital part of living. You can weigh the benefits of change against its costs, pace the timing of the inevitable changes and regulate the occurrence of voluntary change to try to keep your yearly life-change score out of the danger zone.

If you are considering your third job change in two years, you might stay for a while and consider a more long-lasting alternative. Or if divorce is imminent, you might avoid the temptation to plan to remarry right away and give yourself time to sort out the implications of all the changes that divorce brings with it. If you are approaching 65, a gradual rather than sudden transition from full-time work and responsibility could help reduce the feeling of uselessness that often accompanies retirement.[4]

DAILY OVERLOAD

Perhaps the greatest threat to health is chronic daily overload which results in never-ending elevation of the stress response. A common cause of overload is personal and time disorganization. To assess how organized you are, you are invited to complete the following scale.

Exercise 7-4 — How Organized Are You?[5]

Score one point for every question you answer "yes".

1. Are you almost always late to meetings and appointments?
2. Do you find yourself always making apologies for being disorganized?
3. Do you plan only a day at a time — never weeks or months in advance?
4. Do you find that you "don't have time" for those essential activities that help you take care of yourself — exercise, relaxation, preparing and eating good food, music and arts, quality time with family and friends?
5. At the end of a day do you often feel that you've been dealing with trivia and haven't done the more important things?
6. Do you feel you'd like to be more organized, but your life is such a mess you wouldn't know where to begin?
7. Is your refrigerator badly in need of cleaning?
8. Do you often forget or misplace your keys, glasses, handbag, briefcase, appointment book, etc.?
9. Do you find yourself constantly running out of essential supplies at home or at work?
10. Have you forgotten a scheduled appointment within the past month?

If you score:

0-1	2-4
Congratulations! You have things pretty well under control.	Somewhat disorganized.
5-7	8-10
Fairly disorganized. Following guidelines in this article should be helpful.	Highly disorganized. Life is probably pretty difficult. The guidelines in this article and in the book listed in *Resources* could change your life.

Another cause of chronic daily overload, as we saw in Chapter 3 is hurry sickness or Type A behavior. You are invited to complete the following Pace of Life Index, which measures hurry sickness.

Exercise 7-5 —   **PACE OF LIFE INDEX**

Indicate how often each of the following applies to you in daily life.

	3 Always or Usually	2 Sometimes	1 Seldom or Never
1. Do you find yourself rushing your speech?	_____	_____	_____
2. Do you hurry other people's speech by interrupting them with "umha, umhm" or by completing their sentences for them?	_____	_____	_____
3. Do you hate to wait in line?	_____	_____	_____
4. Do you seem to be short of time to get everything done?	_____	_____	_____
5. Do you detest wasting time?	_____	_____	_____
6. Do you eat fast?	_____	_____	_____
7. Do you drive over the speed limit?	_____	_____	_____
8. Do you try to do more than one thing at a time?	_____	_____	_____
9. Do you become impatient if others do something too slowly?	_____	_____	_____
10. Do you seem to have little time to relax and enjoy the time of day?	_____	_____	_____
11. Do you find yourself over-committed?	_____	_____	_____

12. Do you jiggle your knees or tap your fingers?   _____   _____   _____

13. Do you think about other things during conversations?   _____   _____   _____

14. Do you walk fast?   _____   _____   _____

15. Do you hate dawdling after a meal?   _____   _____   _____

16. Do you become irritable if kept waiting?   _____   _____   _____

17. Do you detest losing in sports and games?   _____   _____   _____

18. Do you find yourself with clinched fists or tight neck or jaw muscles?   _____   _____   _____

19. Does your concentration sometimes wander while you think about what's coming up later?   _____   _____   _____

20. Are you a competitive person?   _____   _____   _____

TOTAL SCORE   _____

Exercise 7-6 — Questions About the Pace of Life Index

Now obtain your Pace of Life Index score, using 3-2-1 as indicated at the top of the scale. Here are categories for assessing your score:

45-60   High Hurry Sickness

35-44   Medium Hurry Sickness

20-34   Low Hurry Sickness

1. Is your score higher than you wish?

2. During the next two days, focus on reducing hurry sickness by modifying two or three specific things on which you scored "always or usually."

3. Ask your mate or friend to rate you on this scale. Then ask for his or her suggestion for how you might slow down, if needed.

Exercise 7-7 — Mr. A and Mr. B — A Personal Comparison

Which of the following most clearly describes you and your daily life, Mr. A. or Mr. B?

ONE DAY IN THE LIFE OF MR. A AND MR. B[6]

Potential Stressors	Mr. A: (Stressed, ineffective responses)	Mr. B: (Relaxed, effective responses)
1. 7:00 a.m. Alarm clock did not go off. Overslept.	**Action** Rushed through shaving, dressing. Left without any breakfast.	**Action** Called colleague to say he would be 30 minutes late. Got ready for work and breakfast as usual.
	Thoughts I can't be late. This is going to foul up my whole day.	**Thoughts** This is not a big problem. I can manage to make up the 30 minutes later on.
	Results Left home in a hurried state.	**Results** Left home in a relaxed state.
2. 8:00 a.m. Traffic jam caused by slow driver in fast lane.	**Action** Honked horn, gripped steering wheel hard; tried to pass and later tried to speed.	**Action** Waited for traffic jam to end. Relaxed and listened to the radio while waiting; later drove at his normal rate.
	Thoughts Why can't that jerk move into the slow lane? This infuriates me.	**Thoughts** I'm not going to let this upset me since there is nothing I can do about it.

208

Results
Blood pressure and pulse rate rose. Arrived at work hurried and harried.

Results
Remained calm and relaxed. Arrived at work fresh and alert.

3. 10:00 a.m. Angry associate blew up over a staffing problem.

Action
Was officially polite but nonverbal behavior signaled impatience and anger.

Action
Relaxed while listening attentively and mentally rehearsed how to handle this encounter. Remained calm in demeanor.

Thoughts
This guy is a prima donna. I can't tolerate outbursts like these; I'll never get my work done.

Thoughts
Beneath all his anger he does have a point. I can take care of this problem now before it gets more serious.

Results
Associate stormed out unsatisfied. Mr. A. was too aggravated to take care of important business on his agenda.

Results
Associate's temper was calmed. He thanked Mr. B. for hearing him out. Mr. B. was glad that he was able to take care of the problem.

4. 12:00 noon Behind.

Action
Ate lunch in office while working. Could not find needed materials in files. Made telephone calls but parties were out.

Action
Went for a 20-minute walk in park. Ate lunch in park.

Thoughts
I'll never get out from under all this work. I'm going to plow through this if I have to work through dinner.

Thoughts
A break in routine refreshes me. I work better when I allow myself intervals to relax.

Results	**Results**
Made mistakes in work because of exasperation.	Returned refreshed. Proceeded with work rapidly and with fresh insight.

5. 11:00 p.m.
   Bedtime

Action	**Action**
Couldn't get to sleep. Had insomnia for two hours.	Fell asleep rapidly.

Thoughts	**Thoughts**
Why don't I accomplish more? I am a disappointment to myself and my family.	This has been a good day. I'm glad I was able to head off several potential problems.

Results	**Results**
Awoke exhausted and depressed.	Awoke refeshed and happy.

Exercise 7-8 — Altering Type A Behavior[7]

Type A behavior and resulting chronic daily overload are not genetically determined. They are learned. Therefore, they can be altered. Read the following list of suggestions and check those items you could benefit from doing more or better. After you have done this, underline the two steps you will begin today.

— If you are usually too busy, leave details to someone else whenever possible — the income tax return, fixing your car, office details.

— Move through your day slowly enough to experience beauty in your environment — on your way to school or work, for example.

— Learn to live with unfinished tasks — only a corpse is completely finished.

— Leave enough time between activities so that you minimize overlap.

— Schedule only as many tasks each day as you can reasonably finish without pressure.

— Leave time in your schedule for the unexpected.

— Leave early enough so that you need not rush to get where you are going, even if this means rising 20 minutes earlier in the morning.

— Say no to new opportunities or responsibilities if they would overload or rush your day.

— Take steps to "center," in order to know your priorities.

— Find a work environment that is not chronically high-pressured or harried. Avoid Type A organizations. Find another job if necessary.

— Learn to slow your pace of talking, walking, eating.

— Find time each day to relax, meditate, exercise.

— Avoid doing more than one thing at a time.

— Tell yourself at least once a day that failure seldom results from doing a job too slowly or too well. But failure often is caused by mistakes of judgment or from too much hurrying.

— Ask yourself at least once each week: apart from eternal distress and hurry, what is really important to me?

— Measure success by quality, rather than quantity.

— "Screen out" whenever possible, — even if this risks disapproval or missing something you may have thought important.

— Surround yourself with symbols of tranquility — soft music, plants, pleasant colors and lighting.

— Use your noon hour for deep relaxation, exercise, or something else which will slow you down, lift your spirits, and restore energy.

— Find time and space to be alone each day other than at your desk or in your car.

— Associate with Type Bs whenever possible.

— Practice quiet listening. Never interrupt with yes, yes, uhuh, uhuh, and similar signals of impatience.

— Catch your free-floating hostility in progress. Stop it. Take deliberate actions of graciousness and patience.

— Ask whether something in fact must be done this hour or this day. Would catastrophe ensue if you could not squeeze it in?

— Whenever you catch yourself racing through a yellow light, penalize yourself by immediately turning right and going around the block.

— Use waiting in line as an opportunity to observe people around you and to practice deep breathing techniques while you are waiting.

— Whenever you find yourself jiggling your knees or tapping your fingers, immediately practice an on-the-spot tension reducer.

— Each day use realistic to-do lists, written in large handwriting to free your mind from preoccupation with all you have to do.

— Stop blaming others for falling short of your day-to-day accomplishment goals. Accept responsibility for trying to do too much in too short a time or for being poorly organized.

Exercise 7-9 — A Model for Time Management[8]

Time management involves matching the best combination of time demands with your supply of available time. The following steps provide a means of achieving that goal.

Time Demands

1. List all of the tasks that need to be completed within the given time interval. For example, on Monday consider what things need to done during the coming week.

2. Estimate how much time will be needed to complete each task.

3. Go back and increase each of the time estimates in step 2 by 10-15%. This will provide some cushion for error or for unexpected problems.

Time Supply

4. Look at your calendar for the week. Identify the blocks of time available each day for completing the necessary tasks.

5. Match the tasks with the available time blocks in such a way as to make use of available time most constructively.

6. Many times you will find that there is simply not enough time available to complete all of the tasks. Therefore, you must *prioritize* the tasks. List the tasks in order of their importance so that the most important tasks will be completed. If extra time becomes available, you may go on to other, less important tasks.

Exercise 7-10 — Controlling Your Time

Webber, a time-management specialist, points out that our time can be divided into two categories: discretionary (under your own control) and non-discretionary (controlled by others).[9] One important step in controlling the stressors in our work and non-work lives is to put as much time under your own control as possible. Once this is done, Webber suggests, you can protect your discretionary time by the following means:

- Insulation: Screening and sorting incoming information and tasks one time each day for processing outgoing information
- Isolation: Finding a place to work without interruption
- Delegation: Especially those activities over which you need not exercise direct control and which others are competent to perform
- Simplification: Grouping similar tasks into time-blocks whenever possible
- Concentration: Working from prioritized lists and doing one thing at a time.

Which of the above guidelines can you incorporate into your daily life for more effective control of time?

Which of the following suggestions from the same time management expert can you usefully adopt?[10]

- List goals and set priorities
- Make a daily list of tasks to complete and prioritize these tasks
- Work on high-priority tasks first
- Constantly ask: Am I using available time wisely?
- Handle each piece of paper only once
- Do not procrastinate.

BOREDOM

Exercise 7-11 — Assessing High Risk Factors for Boredom

When you have had periods of extended boredom, which of the following high-risk factors for boredom were present?

	Very True	Somewhat True	Not Very True	Not At All True
Not Enough Challenge				
Too much isolation				
Too much routine				
Meaninglessness				

Exercise 7-12 — Distress-Causing Job Conditions and Experiences

PLEASE WRITE A NUMBER BESIDE EACH OF THE FOLLOWING ITEMS ACCORDING TO HOW TRUE IT IS OF YOUR PRESENT JOB.

> 3 = Very true of my job
> 2 = Somewhat true of my job
> 1 = Not very true of my job
> 0 = Not at all true of my job

____Not sure what is expected of me

____Isolated from others during work

____Work is meaningless to me

____Pay is too low

____Bad fit between my personality and demands of the job

____Unchallenging

____Too little time to do all that's expected of me

____Too frequent changes in work assignments or conditions

____Lack of influence over my job conditions

____Difficult to please everyone

____Poor equipment or supplies

____Seldom told whether or not I am doing a good job

____Bad air

____Bad lighting

____Too much noise

____Too many people around me, too little privacy

____Too many interruptions

____Too little freedom to do the work my own way

____My abilities are not fully used

____Too much routine

____Personality conflicts among my co-workers

____Personality conflicts between me, others I work with

____Workload sometimes too heavy, other times too light

____Little opportunity for advancement

MICRO-STRESSORS

Exercise 7-13 — Assessing Hassles of Daily Life

For many people, the major sources of distress are quite minor when taken one at a time but quite major when clustered together into myriad daily hassles. Part of learning to regulate these stressors and your reac-

214

tions to them is to recognize them clearly. For this reason, keep a diary for three full days, writing in it several times daily, if possible. List all the micro-stressors which resulted in even a minor disturbance of your internal physical or emotional harmony. Indicate beside each one whether it was:

1. Barely irritating at all, physically or emotionally.
2. Somewhat irritating physically or emotionally.
3. Quite irritating physically or emotionally.
4. Very irritating physically or emotionally.

This exercise is intended to help you recognize more clearly what elements in your daily life are stressful for you. Share what you have discovered with at least one other person.

Exercise 7-14 — Daily Hassle Index for College Students

Students are invited to complete the following Daily Hassle Index for college students.

Below is a list of daily hassles that commonly irritate college students. Please indicate how often each one is an irritation to you.

_____Almost never an irritation to me
_____Sometimes an irritation to me
_____Frequently an irritation to me

_____Parking problems around campus
_____Careless bike riders
_____Library too noisy
_____Roommate too noisy
_____Preparing meals
_____Too little time
_____Too little money
_____Deciding what to wear
_____Laundry
_____Materials unavailable in library
_____Getting up in the morning
_____My weight
_____Not enough time to exercise
_____Noisy neighbors

_____Too little intimacy
_____Other students are unfriendly
_____Getting to class on time
_____Car problems
_____Quality of meals
_____Future plans
_____Relationship at work
_____Tensions in love relationship
_____Conflict with family
_____Crowds
_____Other drivers
_____Missing my family
_____No mail
_____Being lonely
_____Being unorganized

_____Conflicts with roommate

_____Instructor not available

_____Boring instructor

_____Constant pressures of
studying

_____Instructor difficult to under-
stand

_____Not enough close friends

_____Not enough time to talk with
friends

_____Too few dates

_____Room temperatures

_____How I look

_____Others' opinions of me

_____Roommate's messiness

_____Problems with own or room-
mate's pet

_____Too little sleep

_____Shopping

_____Taking tests

_____Writing term papers

_____Household chores

_____Fixing hair in morning

_____Physical safety after dark

The Daily Hassle Index for College Students was developed by asking several dozen students to list their common daily hassles. From the resulting list the 50 most common items were selected. The Index is scored as follows:

0 ✓ Almost never

5 ✓✓ Sometimes

10 ✓✓✓ Frequently

In a recent study of 106 undergraduate students, the medium score was 115. The higher the Daily Hassle Index score, the higher were scores on the Distress Symptom Scale, as well as on scales of depression, emotional tension, and internal control.

Exercise 7-15 — Assessing Your Daily Hassle Index Score

1. What is your Daily Hassle Index score?
2. Is it higher than you would like?
3. In what degrees is your score a result of objective life circumstances? Your attitudes and perceptions?

Exercise 7-16 — Stressors During A Hot Summer[11]

A. Air conditioning that flakes out when the temperature is 121°.

B. Bicycling through town is dehydrating, dangerous, debilitating and damn foolish at 108°.

216

C. Crime has me vexed as I would like to use Upper Bidwell Park as much as the next guy.

D. Dogs who wander in gangs and dig up the plants, poop on the lawn and chase my cat.

E. E.F. Hutton gave me a bum steer, and I lost my swimming fins in the summer crash of '82.

F. Finding someone fishing in my favorite hidden hole and junking up the place with litter and entrails

G. Getting crank calls at 3:00 every night for a week and then have the sucker miss a night.

H. High prices and low pay, worry about a war, social services cut, inflation run wild and grades.

I. Ice cream doesn't make it from the store to the house, ice doesn't either, neither do I.

J. Justice is blind when you are in gas lines, grocery stores, queues, and cordons at the Department of Motor Vehicles.

K. Kisses that are too moist, slithery, perspiry, damp and clammy.

L. Lost everything for camping somewhere in the garage, Suntan Oil, Coleman gear, boyfriend.

M. Maintaining the home front as paint peels, shingles fly, swimming pool cracks, fence falls.

N. Numbers for the P.G. & E. for summer ups, winter ups and generally a big unexplained increase.

O. Overload of tasks, demands, obligations, harvesting, walking the dog, cleaning the fish bowl.

P. Protection of real and acquired property requires too many hours, gadgets, dogs and alarms.

Q. Quick rise in temperatures from 85° at 7:00 AM to 124° by 3:00 PM.

R. Rise in price of essentials: beer, wine, Pepsi, ice, gas, inner tube rentals.

S. Sun stroke hits the Shop-n-Save parking lot by 10 A.M.

T. Taxes on pet food, clothing, motels, toilet paper, liquor, cleaning supplies, and parking meters.

U. Underalls splitting when you are doing your daily housework.

V. Visiting friends who come uninvited, park for a week, expect to be entertained, and drain the bank book.

W. Weight Watchers vs. wearing swim suits to the July Fourth Bar-B-Que.

X. X marks the spot where every ant, roach, bee, mosquito, fly, and garden pest is — my house

Y. Yard work that makes demands when you want to go vacationing....and.... ZZZZZZZ.....zzzzzz

Exercise 7-17 — Minimizing Noise

Below are a number of guidelines from the U.S. Environmental Protection Agency for creating a quieter home environment.[12] Which can apply?

Some Helpful Hints for a Quieter Home

— Use carpeting to absorb noise especially in areas where there is a lot of foot traffic.

— Hang heavy drapes over windows closest to outside noise sources.

— Put rubber or plastic treads on uncarpeted stairs. (They are safer too.)

— Use upholstered rather than hard-surfaced furniture to deaden noise.

— Install sound-absorbing ceiling tile in the kitchen. Wooden cabinets will vibrate less than metal ones.

— Use a foam pad under blenders and mixers.

— Use insulation and vibration mounts when installing dishwashers.

— Compare, if possible, the noise outputs of different makes of an appliance before making your selection.

— Install washing machines in the same room with heating and cooling equipment, preferably in an enclosed space away from bedrooms.

— If you use a power mower, operate it at reasonable hours. The slower the engine setting, the quieter it will operate.

— When listening to a stereo keep the volume down.

— Place window air conditioners where their hum can help mask objectionable noises. However, try to avoid locating them facing your neighbor's bedrooms.

— Use caution in buying children's toys that can make intensive or explosive sounds. Some can cause permanent ear injury.

GENERAL GUIDELINE FOR MANAGING STRESSORS

Habit is a double-edged sword. On one hand, it makes life easier by adding predictability and routine. One the other hand, habit can stunt growth, prevent exploration, lead to blind inertia.

Habit exerts tremendous force in all of our lives. So much, in fact, that it can be called a basic drive. The force behind habit is the *repetition compulsion*. Like everyone else, you possess a strong drive to be and to do what is familiar. Habit is comfortable and secure. Risk and change create tension. Habit requires little effort. Changing can require that you exert yourself as never before.

Becoming aware of the force of habit in your own life can be very important in helping you to manage stress because, like most people, you may need to work hard to overcome destructive habits. As pointed out earlier, some stressors — death of a loved one, fire, injury — cannot be changed. These you must learn to accept, with as little harmful effect as possible. But most stressors in your daily life can be controlled — some easily, others with great effort.

Learning to tailor to your own needs the number, variety, and intensity of stressors to which you expose yourself is most important. This requires attention both to pace of life and to major life changes. There are a number of specific ways you can improve your ability to manage your stressors. All of these are based on what you have already learned in previous chapters.

1. *Become more aware of the nature of stressors in your daily life.* Understanding and anticipating stressors can strengthen you in advance, help to reduce their harmful impact, and assist you in controlling them. For example, knowing in advance that starting a new job probably will upset your sleep patterns, energy level, personal relationships, and appetite can help you to handle this potentially difficult transition.

2. *Take personal responsibility for your pace in life and for major life changes.* You are partly a product of your social environment, and your roles and responsibilities do shape your behavior to a large extent. But you need not — in fact, you must not — be entirely passive. You can act upon your world as well. Ultimately *you* are responsible for how fast or how slow you live or how many changes you bring upon yourself in a year's time. Blaming society, your

teacher, your boss, your parents, or your spouse is passing the buck. They may play a part in creating the stressors you must face. But over the long haul, you must control your own stressors.

3. *Know your comfort zone.* People vary in the range of stimulation that is comfortable, healthy and productive of growth. You need to discover how much stimulation is right for you. Too much activity for too long can lead to distress from overload. Too little can lead to boredom and stunted growth. Becoming more sensitive to internal cues which tell you your limits in both directions is an important step toward the wide management of your pace of life.

4. *Find a good fit between your own needs — your comfort zone — and the demand of your environment.* If you need to live relatively slowly, don't become a corporation executive. If you thrive on a relatively rapid pace, find friends, an intimate partner, and a job that will allow and support such a lifestyle. A bad fit can lead to continuing tension both within you and between you and others. A good fit can minimize stress-related problems.

5. *Know how rapidly and how much your comfort zone can change.* Your comfort zone is not set *for* all time. You can change stimulation activity levels according to circumstances and personal choice. Flexibility is essential. Become sensitive to how rapidly and how much you can change your comfort zone.

6. *Anticipate the probable stressful effects of major life changes.* Many people consider only financial benefits or prestige in changing jobs. Others consider only emotional factors in beginning or ending a romantic involvement. Few of us think about the likely effects of a major life change on stress levels. Is the timing right? Are the likely stress effects too great to justify the change — at least for now? Are too many major changes occuring simultaneously? Are the long-run gains from a major change likely to offset the temporary stress effects? For example, how large an adjustment is needed in a prospective geographic move? How long is it likely to take? Are the potential benefits great enough to justify this amount of stress?

7. *Avoid clustering too many major life changes.* If you have experienced a death in the family, a change of residence, the end of an intense romance, and a major illness within the past few months, this may not be a good time to change jobs. Correct spacing of major life

changes is vital to intelligent management of stress. To the extent that you can control your major life changes, you should keep them in line with your comfort zone.

8. *Manage daily life — micro-engineer your time — so you have optional lead time, afterburn time, and time for unfinished business.* Again, what is "optimal" depends on the person. You may be able to move quickly from one intense activity to another or to carry, with little adverse effects, a host of unexpressed feelings and incomplete tasks. Your "correct" lead-time, afterburn time, and number of pieces of unfinished business may differ drastically from those of a friend whose time needs are different. Control your time, insofar as possible, to fit your own needs and style.

9. *Establish clear priorities and values so you can select opportunities and challenges wisely in a world of overchoice.* The Quakers refer to this as being "centered." Others call it "being clear" or "having your head on straight." Whatever words you prefer know what is important and unimportant, desirable and undesirable for you. If you don't, you run the risk of being overwhelmed by options and of having decisions made for you by others. Clear values can provide guidelines for specific decisions.

10. *Select activities and challenges that are meaningful to you and avoid meaningless ones whenever possible.* Dr. Selye maintains that we possess two types of adaptive energy: superficial and deep.[13] Superficial adaptive energy is not depletable. In fact, it can be increased through good health and fitness. Deep adaptive energy is like an inherited fortune, held in reserve for times of intense stress. Selye suggests that our deep adaptive energies may be limited and finite, like oil reserves in the earth. In times of distress, we use up small amounts of this reserve. "Chemical scars" remain. As the reserve is depleted, we wear down. This is aging. Total depletion brings death.

Wise management of pace of life means using deep adaptive energies sparingly and for the right purposes. As Selye states, "we can squander our adaptability recklessly, 'burning the candle at both ends', or we can learn to make this valuable resource last long, by using it wisely and sparingly, only for things that are worthwhile and cause least distress".[14] Proper pacing is vital in daily life, just as in running a marathon. So is choosing activities and goals that are meaningful — worth using up some of our deep adaptive energy.

Many people hate their work; others hate their social life. Alienation, boredom, and symptoms of distress too often follow. Sometimes, of course, you must do things that have little meaning or make little sense to you. But when you can exercise choice, spend your time on challenges and activities that are meaningful to you. Develop sensitivity to your talents, deep interests, and personal preferences. Become good at things you enjoy. Enjoy those things you do best. Being "centered" helps. Some people refer to this as following your own destiny.

11. *Take enough risks so you are challenged but not so many you are overwhelmed.* Abraham Maslow, the humanistic psychologist, wrote that we all face a tug and pull between the drive for safety and the drive for growth through risks[15]. Taking risks in work, in school, in your relationships, or in sports is essential for growth. Always staying safe — out of fear of failure, rejection, or the unknown causes stagnation, as shown in Figure 11 below.

Taking too much risk can be foolish, leading to distress or disaster. Intelligent, properly aimed risk-taking is essential for fulfilling your potentials. Knowing when to take risks and when not to, when to be content and when to push into new frontiers, knowing your best *pace* of growth — these are vital ingredients of stress management and making stress work for you.

FIGURE 7-1

RISK AND SAFETY

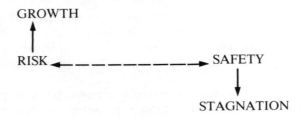

No matter how well you take care of yourself through exercise, good diet, or adequate sleep, your stresses will turn into distress if you push too hard for too long, if you are continually under-stimulated, or if your activities have little meaning to you. In this chapter, you have read about methods for managing stressors so you face enough challenge for growth

222

yet avoid overload. Other methods were discussed in the chapter on hurry sickness and heart disease.

Managing stressors depends on your special human resources of awareness and choice. Failing to use these resources is to sell yourself short. Using awareness and choice to control your pace of life and major life changes is to promote your own health and growth.

REFERENCES

1. Hans Selye, *The Stress of Life.* New York, New York: McGraw-Hill, 1976, p. 406.

2. T.H. Holmes and R.H. Rahe, "The Social Readjustment Rating Scale." *Journal of Psychosomatic Research,* Vol 11 (1967), p. 213.

3. M.B. Marx, T.F. Garrity, and F.R. Bowers, "The Influence of Recent Life Experience on the Health of College Freshman," *Journal of Psychosomatic Research,* Vol 19 (1975), pp. 87-98.

4. T.H. Holmes and T.S. Holmes, "How Stress Can Make Us Ill," *Stress.* Chicago: Blue Cross Association, 1974, p. 75 (Copyright by Blue Cross Association).

5. *Medical Self-Care,* Number 16 (Spring, 1982), p. 26.

6. John W. Farquhar, *The American Way of Life Need Not Be Hazardous To Your Health.* Stanford, California: Stanford Alumni Association, 1978, pp. 64-65.

7. For more detailed suggestions on altering Type A behavior, see Meyer Friedman and Ray Rosenman, *Type A Behavior and Your Heart.* Greenwich, Conn.: Fawcett Publications, Inc. 1974. Also see Leon Belshin and Dean T. Mason, *Love Your Heart.* Davis, CA.: International Dialogue Press, 1982.

8. Daniel Girdano and George Everly, *Controlling Stress and Tension.* Englewood Cliffs, N.J.: Prentice-Hall, Inc., 1979. p. 151.

9. R.A. Webber, *Time and Mangement.* New York: Van Nostrand Reinhold, 1972, p. 89.

10. *Ibid.*, p. 121

11. Written by Donna Ensele, student in my Harnessing Stress class at California State University, Chico.

12. U.S. Environmental Protection Agency, cited in Regina S. Ryan and John W. Travis, *Wellness Workbook*. Berkeley, California: Ten Speed Press, 1981., p. 79.

13. Hans Selye. *Stress Without Distress.* Philadelphia: J.B. Lippincott, 1974, p. 40.

14. *Ibid.*, p. 40

15. Abraham Maslow, *Toward A Psychology of Being.* New York: Van Nostrand, 1962, p. 46.

CHAPTER 8

MONITORING AND MANAGING YOUR LIFESTYLE BUFFER

The previous chapter focused on steps for sharpening awareness of stressors and on selected measures for managing those stressors whenever possible. This chapter emphasizes the positive steps you can take to build resistance against potentially distressing stressors. We will suggest means of strengthening your lifestyle buffer, that is, attitudes and actions that can add mental and physical protection against distress.

Stressors affect people in different ways. In response to the same situation, such as starting a new job, one person will experience only mild positive stress, while another will become nervous, withdrawn, or even ill. Some people "flip-out" or become distraught in response to circumstances many of us handle easily. Others experience little distress throughout their lives, even when faced with great adversity.

Consider, for example, this case:

...One of the 'healthiest' telephone operators was a woman who had been an effective and well-liked worker throughout the entire period of her employment. As evidenced by medical examinations and interviews, by the testimony of friends and employees, by the testimony of unbroken records covering the entire period, she had been healthy all of this time. Her history indicated that she was the daughter of an alcoholic longshoreman and a teenaged immigrant girl. She had been born into a household of great poverty, constant conflict, and much turmoil. Four of her nine siblings had died in infancy of infection and apparent malnutrition. When she was three years of age, her father had deserted his family. When she was five years of age, she had been placed in an orphanage by community action because her mother had been neglecting her and had been adjudged unfit to raise her. She had had a barren childhood in orphanages. When she was thirteen, she had been put out to work as a servant. At the age of sixteen, she had left the place at which she was working and had lived, as she put it, 'all around the town' with another teenage girl. During this time, she had had a number of casual sexual attachments and many jobs. When she had obtained her present job as a telephone operator, she was twenty-seven, she had married a chronically ill,

227

neurotic plumber's helper, whom she had had to support thereafter. They had no children. He died in her arms of a massive gastric hemorrhage when she was forty-four years old. Thereafter, she lived alone as a widow. At the age of fifty-four, when we examined her and interviewed her, we found her to be a well-liked and highly respected employee. She had had only two episodes of sickness disability in thirty-one years. The only significant illnesses that we could uncover on extensive questioning and examination had been a few colds. However, she said she did have a few days of 'nervousness' after her husband's death. [1]

No one knows for certain why this remarkable woman and others like her remain healthy in the face of enormous difficulties. However, this case does illustrate the fact that some people possess personal qualities that can soften the impact of stressors on mental and physical health. Perhaps a genetic endowment of physical hardiness contributes. So too might some touch of inherited psychological strength. Loving, responsibility-generating childrearing practices certainly can help, though apparently not in the life of the above woman.

Willpower or courage to persevere through adversity also are vital. Such self-determination springs from the person's unique center or inner self. Just as can physical strength, this psychological strength can be nurtured, even in later years. It can add immeasurably to a sense of well-being and hardiness, even in cruel and threatening circumstances.

This chapter focuses on positive steps you can take to strengthen your own lifestyle buffer through:
— Running and other types of aerobic exercise
— Deep relaxation
— Nutrition
— Social support
— Personal anchorages

Exercise 8-1 — Wellness Behavior Test [2]

You are invited to complete the following Wellness Behavior Test, which yields a beginning picture of how well you take care of yourself, thereby contributing to a strong or weak lifestyle buffer. Scoring instructions are provided at the end of the test.

Response

1. Do you take time to get completely away from work and other pressures to unwind?
   - 4_____ Frequently
   - 3_____ Fairly often
   - 2_____ Sometimes
   - 1_____ Seldom
   - 0_____ I "just can't"

2. Do you sleep well? Fall asleep easily? Sleep through the night?
   - 4_____ Very well
   - 3_____ Fairly well
   - 2_____ Not so well
   - 1_____ Have trouble
   - 0_____ "Certified insomniac"

3. Do you take, or feel you need aspirin, tranquilizers, sleeping pills, stomach medicines, or laxatives?
   - 4_____ Seldom or never
   - 3_____ Occasionally
   - 2_____ Fairly often
   - 1_____ Quite often
   - 0_____ I'm hooked

4. Do you practice a form of deep relaxation (e.g., meditation, progressive relaxation, autogenic training, etc.) daily?
   - 4_____ Nearly every day
   - 3_____ Often
   - 2_____ Occasionally
   - 1_____ Seldom
   - 0_____ What's deep relaxation?

5. Can you run a mile (at any speed) without becoming exhausted?
   - 4_____ Easily
   - 3_____ Fairly well
   - 2_____ Can barely make it
   - 1_____ Can't do it at all
   - 0_____ Can't walk a mile

6. Can you play a fast game of tennis or other strenuous sport without becoming exhausted?
   - 4_____ Easily
   - 3_____ Fairly well
   - 2_____ Get very tired
   - 1_____ Get exhausted
   - 0_____ Wouldn't try it

7. Do you jog or engage in some other very active exercise several times a week?
   - 4_____ Usually
   - 3_____ Fairly often
   - 2_____ Occasionally
   - 1_____ Seldom
   - 0_____ Allergic to exercise

8. Are you fairly strong and physically able?

4_____	Very
3_____	Moderately
2_____	Adequate for my purposes
1_____	Quite weak
0_____	I can stand up in a strong wind

9. Are you overweight? (Just check to see how much surface fat is visable on your body.)

4_____	Not at all
3_____	Mildly overweight
2_____	Moderate amount of flab
1_____	Quite a paunch
0_____	Butterball

10. Do you smoke?

4_____	Never
3_____	2 or 3 a day
2_____	Half-pack a day
1_____	Pack or more a day
0_____	Chain smoker

11. Do you drink liquor (including wine or beer)?

4_____	Rarely or never
3_____	Socially and seldom
2_____	One a day
1_____	Several a day
0_____	I'm an alkie

12. Do you drink coffee, tea, cola drinks, or other sources of caffeine and sugar?

4_____	Rarely or never
3_____	1 or 2 a day
2_____	Several a day
1_____	Regularly, including with meals
0_____	Can't do without it

Total

This Scale is scored similar to a grade point average:

A = 4.0
B = 3.0
C = 2.0
D = 1.0
F = 0.0

RUNNING AND OTHER AEROBIC EXERCISE

Two health-related trends have marked the twentieth century:

1. Acceleration in pace of life. This takes two forms: more personal changes in shorter periods of time and a faster daily tempo, topics discussed in earlier chapters.

2. Sedentary living. At the turn of the century, most of our grandparents were physically active. They depended more on their own bodies than on machines to move from place to place, to work, to maintain their households, to play. In 1860, one-third of the American economy was directly human-powered. Today that figure is less than one percent.

How do these two historical trends effect stress and health? Increasing personal adjustments are required, year by year, and day by day. Tension mounts, physically and mentally. Without sufficient release through physical activity, this tension turns into bound energy, pulling and tearing inside our bodies.

Stress-induced illnesses result. Included, for example, are migraine headaches, ulcers, back pain, high blood pressure, atherosclerosis. These ailments can have other causes as well, of course. Emotional distress abounds, evidenced by irritability, joylessness, depression, chronic anxiety, insomnia. Overweight reaches epidemic proportions. Destructive coping behavior is rampant; alcohol and drug abuse, smoking, violence, escapism, attraction to cults, overeating.

A vital step in harnessing stress and preventing illness is to restore exercise into daily life. You may not be able to harness the pace of change around you. But you can control your readiness to cope with it, partly by becoming physically active again — like your grandparents and your own young children.

For many, work affords little chance for physical exercise. Housework requires lots of movement but little real exercise of any benefit for stress control or health. The answer is to set aside 30 to 60 minutes each day to exercise.

The human body was designed to be exercised. That is why research studies show the following: that longshoremen with lifting and carrying jobs live longer than fellow workers with desk jobs;[3] that among 17,000 graduates of Harvard over a 34-year period, those who vigorously exer-

231

cised several times each week had fewer heart attacks and a longer life span than those who did not exercise;[4] that middle-aged men who began to regularly walk, run, or swim lowered their cholesterol, blood pressure, weight, anxiety, and depression.[5]

Social and technological changes have deluded us into the false belief that inactivity is a normal way to live. But the fact is that exercising — if not during work, then during play — restores your body to its true optimum condition. Those who take time to exercise live as the body was intended to live. Exercise reduces bound energy, that is, stress.

Judy Marshall, a woman in her mid-thirties, wrote to me in a letter:

> *I had such a lovely run yesterday. I left home at 5:30 a.m. trying to race the sunrise to the top of my ridge two and one-half miles away (up). I run on a winding dirt road until the last two hundred feet or so. Then it is straight to the top. Just as I rounded the last bend and could see the top, the sun broke over the hills and across the valley. The sky was a brilliant red-orange and pink with rays of sunlight streaking up through high rain clouds. Standing in the middle of the road on the horizon were a doe and buck (his horns were in full velvet) staring at me. The deer silhouetted against the sky was incredible. At that point, even though I was running uphill, I lost all conscious feeling of my running. The sight before me and movement of my body simultaneously become one glorious experience. I ran another three miles on top of the ridges with the cool early morning air and the sun bathing me. It then suddenly began to softly rain large summer rain drops. Wow! I was home by 6:30. I had already experienced so much and my day was just beginning! Stress? What stress?[6]*

Running can be immensely rewarding and surprisingly easy. People often associate running with pain and competition. Many athletes stop exercising after high school or college because of their memories of painful training or pressure from coaches to win. And fans who watch them never begin for the same reasons.

Recently millions of Americans have discovered an entirely new way to run — for health, friendship, and the beauty of body-in-motion. Some compete in low-key races, but competition is less important than the process of running. This type of running can be started at any age, regardless of ability. It can become a regular part of everyday life. And it can be continued into old age.

Running for the purposes of enjoyment and good health has several features. First, it is done as regularly as eating or sleeping. You do not feel guilty about taking time to eat, or read the newspaper. Nor do runners feel guilty about taking 20 to 60 minutes each day or two to run. Rain or shine, good mood or bad, they run.

Second, running involves a minimum of strain or pain. Runners usually run at a pace at which they can carry on a reasonable conversation. They are willing to push into the "pain zone" once in a while, but not every day. For they know they can achieve substantial benefits by running fairly easily — and can enjoy it at that pace.

Third, runners can run alone or with others. They do not require the presence of others to get their regular run, but they often do "run socially." Sometimes, in fact, deep friendships develop "on the run."

Fourth, running is a long-term proposition. Continuing to exercise in this way over many years is more important than achieving short-range goals. Running, therefore, is approached with patience. Comments from runners interviewed by Glasser for his book on positive addictions include these:

> When I am settled into my run I concentrate on running as much as possible but the mind wanders to thoughts of most anything. The state of mind is one of almost total complacency and privacy. Although you are in sight of people, cars, buses, school kids, dogs, etc., I feel a very privateness when I run. People may yell at me or a kid may bug me for a few hundred yards, but due to the nature of running (it is hard and physically demanding) you are pretty much left to yourself and no one can invade your runners' world because they physically are not able. If another runner enters or intrudes it is fine because he is running for the same reasons and for a lot of the same feelings.

> Running is extremely personal to each runner. Its importance shapes the lives of many people who enjoy running long distances. I can really never see myself quitting unless an accident should occur. It has been an integral part of my life for a number of years, and I am quite happy with myself and my life and I wouldn't trade places with anyone.

> I can describe two states of mind when I have settled into my run. Sometimes both will occur when I am settled into a run.

Strangely enough these minds seem to be a function of the weather.
Nice crisp days yeah, hot humid days, too. Novelty of the course,
physical features of the course include whether the course is
beautiful, easy to run, etc. The first mind state that I would describe
is that of a rational cognitive nature and coincides with runs that are
generally unsatisfactory in some way. The weather is hot, the dogs
are harassing me, the course is becoming boring because I have been
on it many times. The second mind state is (and here I believe he
describes the PA state quite clearly) not cognitive or rational, instead
it is ego-transcending. I simply perceive as I run. I react instinctively
to obstacles which suddenly appear. I float. I run like a deer. I feel
good. I feel high. I don't think at all. My awareness is only the pre-
sent. Even that cannot be called awareness. Brain chatter is gone.
This mind set normally coincides with running along a cross-country
course in autumn on a crisp day but definitely appears other times of
the year as well.[7]

Running is among the most popular forms of aerobic exercise today.
However, it is not the only form. Let us turn now to a series of practical
questions about aerobic exercise and stress management.

What is Aerobic Exercise?

Aerobic literally means "activity with air." Other main forms of exercise are anaerobic exercise ("without air") such as all-out sprinting or
swimming underwater while holding breath; strengthening exercises, such
as weight training and isometrics; and stretching, such as yoga and pre-
running stretches. Still other forms of physical activity combine these
various ways within the context of recreation or competitive games, such
as golf, softball, volleyball, or ping-pong. Aerobic exercise is any form of
activity in which heart rate is elevated substantially above resting level in
response to sustained movement. Examples of aerobic exercise are:

> Running (and "jogging" which is simply slower running)
> Brisk walking
> Swimming
> Bicycling
> Stationary bicycling
> Brisk raquetball
> Cross-country skiing
> Mini-trampolining
> Aerobic dancing.

How Much Aerobic Exercise Is Needed?

For minimum cardio-vascular fitness, the following criteria need to be met, according to exercise physiologists:

Frequency — at least three times per week.

Intensity — heart rate between 70 and 85 percent of maximum for entire exercise session. To estimate these percentages, subtract your age from 220, then multiply that figure times .70 and .85. This is called the aerobic training zone.

Time — At least 20 minutes per session.

My experience with stress management clients leads me to recommend the following for purposes of *effective stress control* and *high level wellness* — beyond minimal cardiovascular fitness.

Frequency — five to seven days per week.
Intensity — heart rate between 70 and 85 percent of maximum.
Time — at least 30-40 minutes per session.

What Physiological Changes Will My Body Experience If My Exercise Program Meets These Criteria?

Three main changes will occur, all of which improve your overall energy level through more efficient use of oxygen. This is called the "aerobic training effect." The aerobic training effect can be summarized as follows:

1. Improvement in *oxygen intake*
   — Strengthening of diaphragm muscle
   — Greater lung flexibility and capacity
   — New and larger capillaries in lungs

2. Improvement in *oxygen circulation*
   — More output per heart beat
   — Slower heart rate at given exertion level
   — More blood volume
   — More red corpuscles
   — Less blood stickiness
   — Expansion in size of blood vessel and capillaries
   — Opening of new capillary networks

3. Improvement in *oxygen use*
   — More efficient extraction of oxygen from blood
   — More efficient burning of oxygen
   — More efficient discharge of carbon dioxide

How Can Aerobic Exercise Help to Control Stress?

Physical stress-related benefits are likely to include:[8]

— Fine-tuned awareness of body signals, not only during the workout but throughout the day.
— Release of muscle tension
— Burning off stress-produced adrenalin, which leaves the bloodstream and is consumed in the muscles
— Post-exercise quieting of the sympathetic nervous system (the part of the system that produced tension)
— Post-exercise reduction of adrenalin output
— Production of endorphin, the body's own morphine-like pain-killer and source of sense of well-being
— More energy for daily living — and for coping with stressful situations
— Lower baseline (hour after hour) tension level
— Lower peak stress during intense, demanding situations
— Faster recovery time from acute stress
— Reduction of other coronary risk factors: cholesterol, low-density lipoprotein cholesterol, triglycerides, blood sugar, body fat, blood pressure, smoking.

Psychological benefits related to tension control are likely to include the following:[9]

— Release of pent-up emotional tension
— Creative problem-solving during the exercise session
— Enhanced self-esteem
— Greater sense of competence and internal control over events
— Greater mental clarity after exercise
— Feeling of well-being and calm
— Less anxiety
— Less depression
— Mood stabilization
— Fun, play, joy

In his best selling book, *Aerobics,* Dr. Kenneth Cooper uses the following exchanges with a patient to underscore the central importance of cardiovascular fitness for health and vitality:

Doc, I don't need much endurance. I work at a desk all day, and I watch television at night. I don't exert myself any more than I have to, and I have no requirements for exerting myself. Who needs large reserves? Who needs endurance?

You do, Everyone does. Surely you know the usual symptoms caused by inactivity as well as I do. Yawning at your desk, that drowsy feeling all day, falling asleep after a heavy meal, fatigue from even mild exertions like climbing stairs, running for a bus, mowing the lawn or shoveling snow. You can become a social cripple, 'too tired' to play with the kids, 'too tired' to go out to dinner with your wife, 'too tired' to do anything except sit at your desk or watch television, and maybe you're even getting tired of doing that. And the final clincher, 'I guess I'm getting old.' You're getting old all right, and a lot sooner than you should.''[10]

Aerobic exercise is a highly potent approach to harnessing stress and increasing daily energy. It is never too late to start.

What is the Best Way to Start?

There are several ways to get going.

— Follow one of the walking and running plans given below.
— Follow a plan suggested in one of many fine exercise books now on the market.[11]
— Take a beginning exercise class in your community.
— Start with a more experienced friend.

Here are several other suggestions:

- If you are over 30, and especially if you are out of shape, overweight, smoke, have high blood pressure, or have a family history of heart disease, you should consider a treadmill stress electrocardiogram before starting a vigorous exercise program. Even if stress EKG shows evidence of coronary artery disease or other cardiac problems you still can exercise, but at a lower level of intensity and under medical guidance.
- Stretch for at least five minutes before and after exercising. Especially important are the muscles in the back of the legs and hips, which tend to be more injury-prone and can tighten as you begin your aerobic program.
- Start moderately, progress gradually, be patient. Getting fit need not be painful.

- Make a four-month commitment and stick with it.
- Keep a record, including exercise, and after a five-minute rest.
- Learn to take your pulse for 15 seconds, then multiply times four.
- Avoid the heat, especially if running. Running in rain, or even snow, is fine with proper clothing.
- If running, use good shoes. Avoid cheap sneakers.
- Enjoy your exercise time, guilt-free. Do you feel guilty when you eat? Brush your teeth? Shower? Sleep? Aerobic exercise is just as vital for good health.
- Be consistent. Make exercise a part of your life. Don't give it all up because you miss a day or even several days.
- Find a group or partner for support, companionship, and encouragement if you dislike running alone and especially if you get discouraged.
- Run at whatever time of day suits you best, morning, noon, late afternoon, or evening. Physiologically, and emotionally, benefits accrue whenever you exercise. Find the most convenient and pleasant time of day for you.
- Watch for significant overtraining signs — chronic fatigue, depression, unusual loss of weight, accelerated heart rate for several days.
- Occasional low-key races or fun runs can be challenging, and can provide an opportunity for runners to meet others who have also just begun. Runners who have achieved a higher level of fitness after a few months may find occasionally low-key races quite enjoyable.
- Be patient, increasing distance and pace very gradually. Some experts recommend increasing distance at no more than 10 percent per week.

Here are several simple beginning walk-run plans. Find the one that fits you through a few days of experimentation. In picking your own level, remember to keep your heart rate in the aerobic training zone — 70-85 percent of estimated maximum. Be flexible with your program, staying longer at one week at a given level, for example, if necessary, or accelerating faster than listed here.

For beginning plans in swimming, bicycling, and other aerobic activities, see Kenneth Cooper's fine book, *The Aerobics Way.* [12]

30 MINUTE WALK-RUN PLANS*

	Plan 1 MINUTES		Plan II MINUTES		Plan III MINUTES		Plan IV MINUTES	
Week	Walk	Run	Walk	Run	Walk	Run	Walk	Run
1	30	0	15	1	5	2	3	3
2	14	1	12	2	4	2	2	3
3	12	1	10	2	4	3	2	4
4	10	1	8	2	2	3	1	4
5	9	1	6	2	2	4	1	5
6	8	1	3	2	2	5	1	6
7	6	1	3	2	2	6	½	6
8	4	1	2	2	2	8	½	7
9	3	1	1	2	1	8	½	8
10	2	1	1	3	1	10	½	10
11	1	1	1	4	1	12	½	12
12	1	2	1	5	1	15	½	15
13	1	2	1	6	1	15	0	30
14	1	3	1	8	1	15	0	30
15	1	4	1	10	1	15	0	30
16	1	5	1	12	0	30	0	30

*Each workout session should include the walk-run cycle until 30 minutes is reached.

Are Physical Activities Other Than Those Listed
Below as Aerobic Also Valuable?

Yes, research shows that quality and length of life also benefit from such activities as walking several blocks to work, climbing stairs rather than taking elevators, doing yoga and other stretching exercises, and working vigorously on the job. Other physical activities, such as gardening, fishing, hunting, softball, and golf also have diversionary and recreational value. All these activities certainly can be beneficial in controlling tension and rejuvenating the spirits. But aerobic exercise is the most beneficial of all for maintaining high-level wellness and managing stress. As noted earlier, this is simply returning the body to its normal state of existence.

Exercise 8-2 — Personal Exercise Planning

1. Do you now meet minimal criteria of aerobic exercises described above (frequently, intensity, and time)?
   If not, what are the barriers now interfering (e.g., time, habit, cost, baby-sitter, etc.)?

2. If you were to start, which aerobic activity would you choose?

3. Where would you do it?

4. When?

5. With whom?

6. What equipment and supplies would you need?

7. What barriers do you expect to interfere with starting? Continuing?

8. What specific steps will you take to overcome these barriers?

9. How long a commitment are you making, rain or shine, no matter what?

Exercise 8-3 — Exercise Log

You are invited to reproduce and use the following record-keeping log, both for aerobic exercise and for deep relaxation, which we will discuss in the next section.

EXERCISE AND DEEP RELAXATION LOG

WEEK OF _____

	Sunday	Monday	Tuesday	Wednesday	Thursday	Friday	Saturday
I. Aerobic Exercise							
Type							
Time of Day							
Duration							
Distance							
Heart Rate Before							
Heart Rate During							
Heart Rate After 2 min. rest.							

Comments:

	Sunday	Monday	Tuesday	Wednesday	Thursday	Friday	Saturday
II. Deep Relaxation							
First Session							
Time of Day							
Duration							
Second Session							
Time of Day							
Duration							

Comments:

DEEP RELAXATION

In Chapter 2 we noted that just as the body possesses the natural ability to arouse, to prepare for action, it has a built-in ability to relax. Through the parasympathetic nervous system and quieting of the endocrine system, the ability is a natural tendency, on its own, to restore homeostasis through quieting of the fight-or-flight response. Unfortunately, our fast-pace lifestyle often keeps the stress response activated so permanently that the body and mind stay aroused at an excessively high level for days, weeks, or even years, without release or recovery. The result is wear and tear, breakdown, and stress illnesses such as these reviewed in Chapter 3.

Research during the past decade on biofeedback and meditation has shown conclusively that the mind is able to deliberately produce the relaxation response, not just back down to the level of beginning homeostasis, but below that to a psychological and physical state of *deep* quiet or deep relaxation.[13] Research also has shown that when this condition of deep relaxation is produced once or twice every day for 15 or 20 minutes, substantial benefits follow for stress control and health enhancement.[14] In this chapter we will describe in detail what deep relaxation is, how it can be created, and practical issues in beginning to practice deep relaxation.

Hypometabolic and Hypermetabolic
Approaches to Stress Control

Aerobic exercise and deep relaxation are opposite approaches to controlling stress and tension. Running, swimming, and other aerobic activities temporarily elevate metabolism — indeed the entire physical system — in order to meet the demands for more energy output voluntary placed on it by the person exercising.

Deep relaxation, on the other hand, temporarily quiets metabolism and all the physical processes associated with it. With both activities, the mind and body both return to a level below the starting point in terms of subjectively felt tension and even objectively measurable body activity. With aerobic exercise, it takes longer for the body to reach that post-exercise level of deeper quiet, perhaps even several hours after an intense workout as the body cools down.

As shown in Figure 8-1, a common pattern is for baseline stress level to begin low in the morning, then to rise as the day progresses, finally falling off with two martinis, T.V., or sleep in the evening. Another even more destructive pattern is for baseline stress level to begin at an elevated point as soon as the person awakens, then to stay up all day, never returning even at night.

As shown by the solid line, aerobic exercise and deep relaxation are complimentary approaches to keeping baseline stress level down so it seldom leaves the person's zone of positive stress. Note that in both cases, the post-session level of stress is lower than beforehand. It makes eminent good sense, then, to practice both nearly every day, preferably with several hours separating the two.

Remember, they both are preparation for activity and stress, as well as recovery from tension already accumulated. Therefore, they are best done every day whether you subjectively feel you need them or not. Their effect is cumulative over weeks, months, and years in keeping tension under control.

Methods of Producing Deep Relaxation

Meditation. This is a simple, very old technique using a repeated focus to quiet rational thought, which in turn quiets the hypothalamus, the sympathetic nervous system, and the endocrine system.[15] The mental focus may be a mantra as in Transcendental Meditation ("om," "sharoom," "ee," for example), a color, a prayer, your breathing, or a word such as "one." Your mind will wander away from the focus part of the time. This is natural. Simply become aware that it is wandering, then gently bring it back to the focus. Rational thinking about an idea is not meditation. Instead it is contemplation and probably will not succeed in producing deep relaxation, at least as deeply. The Benson method of meditation is described later in Exercise 8-4.

FIGURE 8-1
Two Approaches to Tension Control

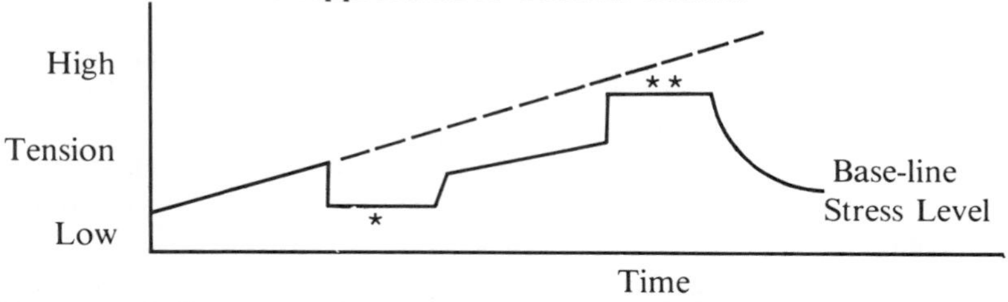

* Hypometabolic approach
  to relaxation:
  Deep Relaxation

**Hypermetabolic approach
  to relaxation:
  Aerobic Exercise

Autogenic Training. This is a method of producing the relaxation response originally created by a German physician over 30 years ago and now gaining widespread attention in the United States. [16]. This method involves sitting or lying for 20 to 30 minutes, although it can be done more briefly, and using concentration and mental images to produce a feeling of warmth, heaviness, and calm in each separate part of the body.

Biofeedback. A highly useful aid for learning deep relaxation, especially when used in conjunction with other methods, is biofeedback.[17] There is nothing mysterious about biofeedback. Each time you look in the mirror, take your pulse or temperature, feel your skin temperature, or take your blood pressure, you are using biofeedback.

During recent years, more sophisticated methods have been developed to measure internal physiological processes and states formerly not directly detectable. For example, the EMG (Electromyogram) measures muscle activity, the EEG (Electro-encephalogram) measures brain waves, the GSR (Galvanic Skin Response) measures electrical conductance on the skin's surface, the finger thermometer measures skin temperature. Through simple electronic monitoring, each of these measures is translated into sound or dial movement. The higher the tension, the higher the pitch or tone, and the greater the movement to right or left of the needle on the dial.

The point of biofeedback training is to discover subjectively how relaxation feels and then to induce the feedback indicator downward through conscious focus of the mind. This usually is done with a therapist, stress consultant, or technician in a comfortable chair in an office or clinic setting. The individual then learns to reproduce the same state of deep relaxation at home or work. Biofeedback has been found to be especially useful for treating specific distress symptoms, such as neck pain and headaches.

Hypnosis and Self-Hypnosis. Hypnosis is a very old and effective method of producing deep relaxation. Hypnosis is a condition of very deep mental and physical quiet induced by the hypnotic suggestion of a trained person who uses key words and images to elicit the desired internal change. He or she then gives post-hypnosis suggestions which, acting through the subconscious, can be very powerful in reducing fears, phobias, smoking, overeating, anxiety, and other problems. When deep relaxation is suggested, the physiological changes associated with the relaxation response can be induced.

Hypnotists also can be helpful in teaching self-hypnosis, which is using self-suggestion to take the mind and body into a deep quiet.[18] Self-hypnosis also can be learned through instructional tapes. It is very close to meditation and autogenic relaxation in that the mind is internally directed and deliberately quieted in order to bring the body's arousal to a very low level.

Progressive Relaxation. Developed by Edmund Jacobson, progressive relaxation is a method of letting go of physical and mental tension, by alternating tensing and relaxing of each muscle of the body through an established sequence.[19] For example, one might tense and relax first the right hand, then the left hand, the right arm, the left arm, the right leg, the left leg, etc. This technique seems to be especially useful for people who have difficulty settling down through passive relaxation, but who do better with this active approach.

Progressive relaxation is best done in a prone position, the full sequence taking about 30 minutes with alternating tensing and relaxing each muscle for 10-15 seconds. Muscles become more relaxed after tensing than before. At the end of the exercise, the person has experienced extremes of relaxation and tension, which can heighten a sensitivity to these states throughout the day as well as resulting in deep quiet immediately after the session. This technique can be adapted to be used for one to three minutes while focusing on a specific limited part of the body, such as hands and arms.

Yoga. Certain forms of yoga can produce the same effects using a combination of stretching and mind focus. According to Benson, this too can induce the relaxation response.[20]

Visualization. Visualization, also called mental imagery or guided day-dreaming, is another technique which reduces rational mental activity and induces deep quiet.[21] This is a method of imagining yourself in some very pleasant place, usually a natural setting, where you or someone guiding you through the experience takes you into a deep, pleasant quiet. Another name for visualization as we shall see in a later chapter is "movies of the mind."

Physiology of Deep Relaxation

Research shows that during deep relaxation, physical and mental responses are the opposite of the fight-or-flight response:

Slower breathing
Lower oxygen use rate
Slower heart rate
Less blood per heart beat
Relaxed muscles and skin
Decreased blood lactate
Slowing down of brain waves
Greater harmony among brain waves
Quieting of key hormonal glands.[22]

This gives the body time to restore itself, to recuperate from the stresses of daily life. After deep relaxation, your energy level increases. You feel rested, and you are able to recover more quickly from unexpected threats or alarms.

Figure 8-2 shows brain wave differences between the waking state (beta waves) and deep relaxation (alpha or theta waves). Metabolism during deep relaxation is slower, even after a minute or two, than during the deepest sleep after five or six hours as shown in Figure 8-3.

Benefits of Regular Practice of Deep Relaxation for Stress Control

Since 1970, hundreds of careful studies have been conducted on various forms of deep relaxation, especially Transcendental Meditation and biofeedback, showing a number of specific benefits including:

Increased measured intelligence
Increased recall, both long-term and short-term
Better "mental health" (decreased anxiety, depression, aggression, and irritability and increased self-esteem and emotional stability)
Greater perceived self-actualization or realization of potential
Better academic performance in high school and college
Improved job performance
Improved job satisfaction
Improved athletic performance
Better mind-body coordination
Increased perceptual awareness
Normalization of blood pressure
Relief from insomnia
Normalization of weight
Reduced drug abuse.[23]

FIGURE 8-2

Brain Waves During Normal State of Awareness

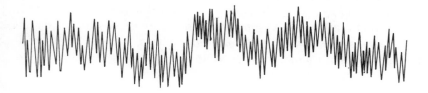

Brain Waves During Deep Relaxation

FIGURE 8-3

Metabolism During Sleep and Relaxation Response[24]

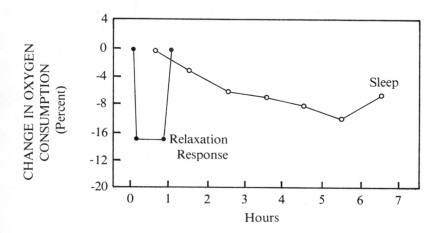

Glasser, who maintains that meditation is a positive addiction similar to running, reports the following comments about the subjective benefits from transcendental meditation.

Subjectively, almost everyone remarks that he or she feel 'less tense, less worried.' Most mention that they had previously experienced some kind of tension, some degree of strain. Students even speak of the 'anxiety I felt about school and my future' but 'now,' said one man, 'I feel a certain easiness, everything is smoother,' 'The main benefit of meditation for me,' said another, 'is the almost total reduction of serious worry. That means worry in the sense of non-productive, nervous disruption. I can still be deeply concerned about important matters.

One man stated that 'for the first time since I can remember, I can relax, without drugs or drink.' A girl wrote, 'Before I began the Transcendental Meditation program, I used drugs, methedrine and narcotics. The effects of the drugs were that I was incredibly tense. Physically, my shoulders were up so high that one could barely see my neck.' She said that, immediately after receiving instruction in the TM technique, 'my shoulders had dropped, all the tension in my face was gone so that my whole facial structure had changed, and most important to me, I was completely at ease. My tension didn't come back.[25]

Advocates of TM maintain that the positive effects of meditation result not only from physiological processes, but also from coming into greater harmony with one's inner nature. Later in this chapter, this is referred to as "centering" or tuning into one's "inner light." Whatever the term, there is growing evidence that meditation and other forms of deep relaxation foster realization of higher potentials — and help to reduce stress.

Exercise 8-4 — The Benson Method of Meditation

Dr. Herbert Benson of the Harvard Medical School has shown that the following method of meditation can produce the same physiological changes associated with Transcendental Meditation.[26]

— "Sit quietly in a comfortable position
— Close your eyes
— Deeply relax all your muscles, beginning at your feet and progressing up to your face. Keep them relaxed.
— Breathe through your nose. Become aware of your breathing. As you breathe out, say the word, 'ONE': IN... OUT, 'ONE': etc. Breathe easily and naturally. Continue for 10 to 20 minutes. You may open your eyes to check the time, but do not use an alarm.

248

When you finish sit quietly for several minutes, at first with your eyes closed and later with your eyes opened. Do not stand up for a few minutes.

— Do not worry about whether you are successful in achieving a deep level of relaxation. Maintain a passive attitude and permit relaxation to occur at its own pace. When distracting thoughts occur, try to ignore them by not dwelling upon them and return to repeating 'ONE'. Practice the technique once or twice daily, but not within two hours after any meal, since the digestive processes seem to interfere with the elicitation of the Relaxation Response."

Exercise 8-5 — Schafer Deep Relaxation Tape

As an aid to learning deep relaxation you might consider my simple 18-minute instructional tape which I urge all participants in our 12-week stress control program to use for several weeks. It combines visualization, autogenic relaxation, and meditation into a simple, very effective deep relaxation method. To purchase the tape by mail, write to me at Enloe Hospital, Chico, CA 95926.

Exercise 8-6 — Seeking Information on Deep Relaxation Training

For further information about various types of instruction in deep relaxation available in your area, call the Psychology Department of a nearby college or university for references. They may not know all that is available, but you can start with the information they provide.

Exercise 8-7 — A Private Place

You are invited to try the following visualization exercise repeated here from the *Wellness Workbook*.

A PRIVATE PLACE: An exercise in Creative Imagination.[27]

"This exercise serves a number of useful purposes. Doing it will take you into a state of relaxation. The images you form will stay with you for a long time, and provide you with an imaginary place to retreat to for refreshment and healing. Then too, it will exercise your imagination, and excite you as you realize how resourceful you can be. Finally, it may suggest some possibilities for changing your real environment.

Find a quiet, relaxing place, and give yourself thirty uninterrupted minutes to do this excercise. It is helpful to have a friend read it to you so you can close your eyes and give your imagination free rein. You could also tape record it and play it back to yourself. Now, in your mind, journey to your bedroom. See it as vividly as possible. Look it over, wall by wall, remembering what is there. Notice that a new door has appeared on one wall. The door has a door knob. Approach it and put your hand on the knob, notice its texture and temperature. When you open the door, you are going to find yourself in a new room, an addition to your house, a room that you have never seen before. The room will be empty, except that it will have several windows. Go inside now and survey your space.

First, decide upon the light in the room. Where are windows placed? Determine what views you would like to have out of each. (One woman looked out upon the ocean from one, a redwood forest from another, and a snow covered mountain from a third.)

Now cover the floors if you wish. Next attend to the walls — color, paintings, murals, shelves? Now furnish it for yourself — include a special chair or pillow or couch on which you can rest and dream. Want a work space? — an art studio, a dance floor, a writing desk? Make it happen immediately. If you like music, listen for it. Or add a piano, organ, flute, and music stand. Many people who have done this report that they added elements of the outdoors into their environment — an indoor waterfall, a floor-to-ceiling bird cage, a tree in the middle of the room.

Be as courageous and as outrageous as you can be. Remember there are no limits. Now sit back and enjoy your place. Tell yourself that you can go to it to solve your problems, to relax in the midst of a hassled day, to prepare yourself for sleep. The uses are as many and as varied as your needs. Have fun with it.

Now you may wish to draw or paint what you have created in your mind. Share it with a friend. Build an addition. It's up to you."

Exercise 8-8 — Planning To Begin Deep Relaxation

1. What type of deep relaxation exercise are you most attracted to?
2. When will you start?
3. What steps will you take to learn a deep relaxation technique?
4. When and where will you practice deep relaxation each day?
5. What difficulties do you expect to encounter?

6. How will you overcome each of these difficulties?

7. For example, what will you do six months from now when your schedule becomes so busy that you think you just don't have time to practice deep relaxation every day?

NUTRITION

Research is sparse linking food with stress. Yet a number of statements can be made, some backed by sophisticated research, others by common-sense knowledge about how certain foods can create the stress response, add to it, or make the individual more vulnerable to prolonged stress arousal.[28]

1. Insufficient calories weaken the human organism, making it more susceptible to stress illnesses.

2. Insufficient vitamins and minerals can have the same weakening effect as too few calories. For example, deficiencies of vitamins in the B complex can lead to anxiety reactions, depression, insomnia, cardiovascular problems, stomach irritability, and muscle weakness. Included are thiamine, riboflavin, niacin, pantothenic acid, pyrodoxine hydrochloride, and chlorine, and imositol.

3. It is possible that prolonged high stress can use up unusual amounts of certain vitamins. For example, B_1 (thiamine), B_2 (riboflavin), and niacin are consumed at high rates during chronic stress, because of their roles in carbohydrate metabolism and gluco-biogenesis (forming of glucose for more energy), Pantothenic Acid, C, and choline go into the construction of adrenal hormones, which are secreted in high amounts during chronic stress.

4. Excessive consumption of certain vitamins, such as A, D, E, and K, for example, can be toxic because they can be stored in the body, rather than excreted like other vitamins taken in excess.

5. Refined sugar taken in excess is a quick source of energy, but can have several negative side effects. First, it can lead to tooth decay — itself stressful. Second, it can lead to insulin blood sugar swings (reactive hypoglycemia), stimulating manic depressive swings on a smaller scale. Third, many sugary products such as candy, cookies, soft drinks for example, are virtually devoid of vitamins and minerals. Therefore, the body must "borrow" vitamins, especially B vitamins from other food

sources to complete the metabolism process. This can lead to a B-complex deficiency in the body. When a high-sugar, unbalanced diet is combined with a long elevated stress period, a vitamin B deficiency can develop, aggravating the stress symptoms already present through heightened anxiety, irritability, and general nervousness.

6. Caffeine, taken in coffee, tea, cocoa, colas, and chocolate, is a "sympathomimetic" agent which itself produces the stress response. More than two or three cups per day can induce elevated blood pressure, increased heart rate, increased oxygen demand on the heart, heart arrhythmias, insomnia, and anxiety.

7. Foods high in cholesterol, saturated fats, and sodium (salt) add to the risk of high blood pressure and plaque build-up in the coronary arteries, thereby intensifying the harmful effect of hypertension on heart disease from other stress factors. Excessive fluid retention from too much sodium can also lead to discomfort and distress directly.

8. Smoking and probably inhaling secondary smoke uses up greater than usual amounts of vitamins C, adding to the deficiencies already created by high stress which smokers often experience — both from other stressors and from smoking itself. (More will be discussed about smoking in Chapter 12.)

9. Too many calories, especially combined with inactivity, leads to obesity, which is directly stressful on the body and often psychologically distressful as well because of the drag on energy it creates, low self-esteem it generates, and the negative feedback which often results. Overweight decreases the individual's coping abilities because of the decreased energy available for dealing with daily problems.

10. There is some evidence that food additives and colorings contribute to the stress response, perhaps contributing to "hyperactivity" in certain children. This is not a closed matter, and considerable research is still being conducted.

Based on these considerations, a number of specific recommendations can be suggested. Let us begin by calling your attention to the guidelines offered by the McGovern Committee on Nutrition and Human Needs. These recommendations, which are sound, balanced, and moderate, are stated in terms of U.S. dietary goals and related recommended changes in food selection and preparation.[29]

Dietary Goals:

— Increase the consumption of complex carbohydrates and naturally occurring sugars from about 38% of energy intake to about 48% of energy intake;

— Reduce overall fat consumption from approximately 40 to 35% of energy intake;

— Reduce saturated fat consumption to account for about 10% of total energy intake; balance that with polyunsaturated and mono-unsaturated fats, which should each account for about 10% of energy intake;

— Reduce cholesterol consumption to about 300 mg a day;

— Reduce the consumption of refined and processed sugars by about 45% to account for about 10% of total energy intake;

— Reduce salt consumption by about 50 to 85% to approximately 5 gm a day;

— Consume only as much energy (calories) as is expended to avoid overweight; if overweight, decrease energy intake and increase energy expenditure.

Changes Required to Meet Goals:

— Increase consumption of fruits and vegetables and whole grains;

— Decrease consumptionn of animal fat, and choose lean meats (with the least amount of marbling), poultry and fish which will reduce saturated fat intake;

— Decrease consumption of foods high in fat and partially substitute poly-unsaturated fat (such as safflower, corn, sunflower seed oils) for saturated fat;

— Substitute non-fat or low-fat milk for whole milk;

— Decrease consumption of eggs and other high-cholesterol sources (such as butter and shortening); some consideration should be given to easing the cholesterol goal for pre-menopausal women, young children and the elderly in order to obtain the nutritional benefits of eggs in the diet.

— Decrease consumption of sugar and foods high in sugar content;

— Decrease consumption of salt and foods high in salt content.

Stress-Related Nutritional Recommendations

In addition, a number of more specific recommendations related to nutrition and stress can be offered.

1. Avoid more caffeine than you would consume in one or two cups of coffee per day.

2. Eat balanced meals every day to be assured of ample intake of essential calories, vitamins, and minerals.

3. Eat as many natural, unprocessed foods as possible to assure you are getting adequate vitamins and minerals and are minimizing intake of potentially harmful chemicals.

4. Avoid eating in response to stress, especially foods high in refined sugar.

5. If your fast-paced life results in unbalanced or irregular eating, consider a multiple vitamin each day to plug any gaps which may exist. Otherwise food supplements probably are not necessary.

6 If you smoke or regularly inhale others' smoke, consider taking vitamin E and C supplements.

7. Enjoy your eating. If you engage in exercise regularly, you can eat more and still stay thin — plus you can occasionally eat no-no foods, such as hot fudge sundaes with no harmful effects at all.

8. Dieting in absence of exercise usually will prove futile.

9. Avoid fad diets.

10. Minimize intake of salt, saturated fats and cholesterol.

Exercise 8-9 — Food Scripting

Recall some childhood experience which involved food and eating. What messages did you receive about food and eating from family and friends? Examples might be, "If you love me, you will eat everything I put on the table." "Good times always have food connected with them." "Follow my example and eat in response to stress." What problems, if any, did they cause you? What steps can you take to update these messages?

Exercise 8-10 — Food Diary

Keep a food diary for the next three days. What can you learn about good and bad foods you eat? About how eating and drinking relate to stressful events in your life? What can you do differently to improve your diet for better buffering against distress? For more effective reactions to distress?

Exercise 8-11 — Eating Inventory

You are invited to complete the following "Wellness and Eating" self-inventory.[30]

Always or Usually	Often	Sometimes, Maybe	Occasionally, Rarely	No, never or hardly ever		
___	___	___	___	___	1.	I pay attention to the quality and quantity of foods I eat.
___	___	___	___	___	2.	I am aware of the difference between refined carbohydrates (white flour, sugar, etc.) and complex (natural carbohydrates.
___	___	___	___	___	3.	I minimize my intake of refined carbohydrates and hidden sugars.
___	___	___	___	___	4.	I avoid fast foods and greasy, over-cooked, restaurant meals.
___	___	___	___	___	5.	I am aware of feeling differently when I eat different foods.
___	___	___	___	___	6.	I am satisfied with my diet.
___	___	___	___	___	7.	I minimize my intake of fats.
___	___	___	___	___	8.	I have fewer than five alcoholic beverages per week.
___	___	___	___	___	9.	I don't take medications, including prescription drugs.
___	___	___	___	___	10.	I drink fewer than five soft drinks per week.
___	___	___	___	___	11.	I add little or no salt to my food.
___	___	___	___	___	12.	I read the labels for the ingredients of the foods I buy.
___	___	___	___	___	13.	I am aware of the benefits of fasting and fast regularly.
___	___	___	___	___	14.	I eat at least two raw fruits or vegetables each day.
___	___	___	___	___	15.	I drink fewer than three cups of coffee or tea per day (except of herbal teas).

___ ___ ___ ___ ___ 16. I have a good appetite and maintain a weight within 15% of my ideal weight.

___ ___ ___ ___ ___ 17. I enjoy eating and take time for leisurely, relaxing meals.

___ ___ ___ ___ ___ 18. I have a well-stocked, well-equipped kitchen and I enjoy cooking.

___ ___ ___ ___ ___ 19. I know and feel the difference between 'stomach hunger" and "mouth hunger."

___ ___ ___ ___ ___ 20. I chew my food thoroughly.

___ ___ ___ ___ ___ 21. I add unprocessed bran to my diet to provide roughage if my diet is largely processed foods.

___ ___ ___ ___ ___ 22. I steam or stir-fry my vegetables (instead of boiling them).

___ ___ ___ ___ ___ 23. I eat whole (unrefined) grains and stoneground 100% whole wheat bread.

___ ___ ___ ___ ___ 24. I minimize my intake of red meats.

___ ___ ___ ___ ___ 25. I have a bowel movement each day.

___ ___ ___ ___ ___ 26. I am aware that my diet contributes to the health of my skin, hair, and teeth.

___ ___ ___ ___ ___ 27. I don't use food for reward, escape, or self-punishment.

___ ___ ___ ___ ___ 28. If most of the food I eat is commercially grown, I take mineral and vitamin supplements.

___ ___ ___ ___ ___ Total

29. If weight is not a problem for you, skip the next five statements, otherwise quickly complete the sentence with the first thoughts which come to mind.

30. When I binge, I feel_____

_____

31. Aspects of my regular diet that I would like to change are_____

_____

_____

32. Food habits which contribute to my weight problems are_____

_____

_____

_____

33. The kinds of experiences I have had with dieting are_____

_____

_____

_____

34. When I want to lose/gain (as applicable) weight I _____

_____

_____

_____

Exercise 8-12 — Food and Coping

Please complete the following if you are overweight.

1. My present feelings toward food are:

_____

_____

_____

_____

_____

_____

_____

2. My present feelings toward my body are:

_____

_____

_____

_____

_____

_____

_____

3. I use food in the following ways to cope with stress:

_____

_____

_____

_____

_____

_____

_____

4. I will do the following to use food more constructively in dealing with stress:

_____

_____

_____

_____

_____

_____

_____

SOCIAL SUPPORT

A researcher name Henry (1969) has been able to produce persistent hypertension in mice by placing the animals in boxes all fixed to a common feeding place, thus developing a state of territorial conflict. Hypertension only occurred, however, when the mice were "strangers." Populating the system with litter mates did not produce these effects.[31]

Berkman and Syme (1979) ...analyzed data gathered between 1965 and 1974 on 2,229 men and 2,496 women, aged 30 to 69 in 1965 and randomly sampled from the population of Alameda, California. They assessed whether the presence or absence of four kinds of social ties in 1965 — marriage, contacts with friends, church memberships, and informal and formal group associations — affected the likelihood of the person dying over the next nine years. People low or lacking in each type of social tie were 30 percent to 300 percent more likely to die than those who had each type of relationship. Generally, these trends held for both sexes and at all age levels, although marriage had the strongest protective effect for men, while contact with friends was most protective for women.... The more intimate ties of marriage and friendships were stronger predictors than were ties of church and group membership.[32]

These two studies, one on mice and the other on humans, clearly illustrate the direct effect of social support on stress, health — and death. Many other studies lead to the same conclusion.[33]

Not only does social support directly influence the chances of whether you will remain ill or well and the probability of a shorter or longer life, your connectedness with other people also can influence whether stressors have greater or lesser impact. In short, social support can have a buffering effect as well as a direct effect.

Before proceeding further, let us be clear what social support is. You already probably have an intuitive sense — it means belonging, sharing, giving and receiving love, and caring. It is all these things and more. A well-known expert defines social support as:

....an interpersonal transaction involving one or more of the following:
1. Emotional concern (liking, love, empathy)
2. Instrumental aid (goods or services)
3. Information (about the environment)
4. Appraisal (information relative to self-evaluation).[34]

He goes on to note that "...both experts and lay persons tend to believe support is most important..."[35] Social support can vary in degree in two ways:

— Number of ties
— Intensity or closeness of ties.

The Alameda County study cited above measured only the number of ties. However, another well-known scholar showed the importance of *quality* of support for health.

Recently 10,000 married men who were 40 years of age or older were followed for five years in Israel. The researchers, Jack H. Medallie and Yuri Goldbourt, wanted to find out how many new cases of angina pectoria developed. They assessed each man's medical risk factors for heart disease and then asked, among other items, this question: Does your wife show you her love?

The answer turned out to have enormous predictive power. Among high-risk men — men who showed elevated blood cholesterol, electrocardiographic abnormalities, and high risk of anxiety — fewer of those who had loving supportive wives developed angina pectoris than did those whose wives were colder (52 per 1,000 versus 93 per 1,000).[36]

This dramatic finding on the apparent protective or buffering role of close social support is consistent with other studies which show that health also is affected by the amount of self-disclosure — the sharing of personal feelings back and forth — in a relationship. So having enough relationships and affiliations and the presence of at least a few very close relationships no doubt can help buffer you against harmful effects of stressful events.

Exercise 8-13 — Assessing Social Support Related to Your Job

Here are nine questions about social support related to your job.[37] If you are working or have recently held a job, you are invited to complete each question.

(Put one check on each line)

	Very much	Somewhat	A little	Not at all
How much does each of these people go out of their way to do things to make your *work life* easier for you?				
Your immediate superior	_____	_____	_____	_____
Other people at work	_____	_____	_____	_____
People outside work	_____	_____	_____	_____
How much can each of these people be relied upon when things get tough at work?				
Your immediate superior	_____	_____	_____	_____
Other people at work	_____	_____	_____	_____
People outside work	_____	_____	_____	_____
How much are the following people willing to listen to your personal problems?				
Your immediate superior	_____	_____	_____	_____
Other people at work	_____	_____	_____	_____
People outside work	_____	_____	_____	_____
How easy is it to talk with each of the following people?				
Your immediate superior	_____	_____	_____	_____
Other people at work	_____	_____	_____	_____
People outside work	_____	_____	_____	_____

What can you learn from your answers? Research shows that the greater the social support from each source (especially supervisors and co-workers), the better the health and the lower the stress.[38] Moreover, at a given level of perceived stress, each type of support was found to have a buffering or protective effect on health.

1. What do your above responses tell you about how much support you feel you receive from each potential source?
2. How do you think this affects you?
3. What might you do to initiate greater closeness? For example, if you were to give more support, might you receive more in return?

Another approach to social support groups is provided by Greenberg.[39]

Support groups exist in so many kinds and forms and affiliations that it is sometimes confusing to identify what the basic ingredients are. Some of the necessary factors seem to be the following:

1. The same people attend.
2. The group meets regularly, once a week or more.
3. The group has met for an extended period of time — until closeness develops.
4. There is an opportunity for informality, spontaneity, and incidental contacts.

Greenberg identifies a number of types of groups which meet these criteria. The following exercise gives you the opportunity to see how important each type is to you at present.

Exercise 8-14 — Assessing Your Social Support Groups[40]

Do Not Belong	Belong, Not an Important Social Support for Me	Belong, an Important Source of Support for Me

List each group under the heading that fits for you:

— An informal group of co-workers.
— A formal co-worker group, for example, a weekly luncheon group, a monthly management organization, an executive club, and the like.
— A sports or hobby group, for example, a singing group, a square dance club, a racquetball club, and the like.
— One's own large, kinship family (there are still some around)
— An activity group, for example, a weekly discussion, book reading, play reading, and the like.
— Service group (Kiwanis, Rotary, etc., and especially small informal satellite shoot-offs from these large groups).
— Extended families (artificial, intentional families developed in churches, community organizations, etc.).

- Racial, ethnic, and nationality groups (associations, clubs, etc.)
- Vocational groups (organized and formal).
- Church and other community groups.
- Strictly social groups, for example, singles' clubs, men's groups, women's consciousness raising groups, and the like.

Greenberg also maintains that the most important way true social support takes place in groups like those above is not through the central activity of the group, but through informal, incidental contacts, such as the following:

- Driving to and from meetings with someone
- Having dinner together before or after the meeting
- Having a group potluck meal
- Meeting in someone's house
- Talking during coffee breaks, in the social get-together after the "formal" meeting
- Chats, separate social get-togethers, and the like
- Solving problems and making decisions together
- Pairing up outside the group with another group member
- Going on a trip together, to a convention, or to a retreat setting[41]

Which of these types of contacts do you engage in? Might you in the future?

PERSONAL ANCHORAGES

One man I know has run through a series of love affairs, a divorce and remarriage — all within a very short span of time. He thrives on change, enjoys travel, new foods, new ideas, new movies, plays and books. He has a high intellect and a low "boring point," is impatient with tradition and restlessly eager for novelty. Ostensibly, he is a walking exemplar of change.

When we look more closely, however, we find that he has stayed on the same job for ten years. He drives a battered, seven-year-old automobile. His clothes are several years out of style. His closest friends are long-time professional associates and even a few old college buddies.

Another case involves a man who has changed jobs at a mind-staggering rate, has moved his family thirteen times in eighteen years, travels extensively, rents cars, uses throw-away products, prides himself on leading the neighborhood in trying out new gadgets, and generally lives in a restless whirl of transience, newness and diversity. Once more, however, a second look reveals significant stability zones in his life: a good, tightly woven relationship with his wife of nineteen years; continuing ties with his parents; old college friends interspersed with the new acquaintances.[42]

These two cases illustrate the vital importance in a world of swirling change to maintain personal anchorages. A personal anchorage is any one of the following which is meaningful and relatively stable through time regardless of other changes:

— Objects
— Linkage to a place
— Activities
— Beliefs, moral codes, and values
— Persons
— Groups

Personal anchorages help hold you steady, even when the surrounding environmental or other aspects of your life crumble, shift, or reorganize. To reduce distress, it can be highly useful to consciously create meaningful personal anchorages. Here is Toffler's suggestion in *Future Shock* about objects in our daily lives.

> *We can, for example, cut down on change and stimulation by consciously maintaining longer relationships with the various elements of our physical environments. Thus, we can refuse to purchase throw-away products. We can hang onto an old jacket for another season; we can stoutly refuse to follow the latest fashion trend; we can resist when the salesmen tells us it is time to trade in our automobile. In this way, we reduce the need to make and break ties with the physical objects around us.*[43]

We already have focused on persons and groups as anchorages in the previous section. Approaching social support from this vantage point may emphasize even more the importance of developing and maintaining strong interpersonal and group ties.

For most people, beliefs, values, and moral codes are vital anchorages or guideposts that remain steady even when the waters are troubled. For me, that includes in the ultimate value of promoting my own high-level wellness (good health, life satisfaction, productivity, and self-development) and high-level wellness of others whose lives I touch. My moral code says that anything which interferes with or decreases high-level wellness of myself or others is immoral. My own beliefs also include a strong recognition of an "inner light" to which I seek to remain attuned. For Quakers, the Sunday Friends meeting is for the purpose of "centering" — keeping one's mind attuned to that seed of God within. As Dag Hammerskjold said, "the more faithfully you listen to the voice within you, the better you will hear what is sounding outside."[44] For some, living in tune with inner direction is called the "will of God," for others it is simply living in harmony with the self in the world. For me, believing in and listening to my own inner light unquestionably leads to this harmony. The result is less rather than more distress — and greater high-level wellness.

Exercise 8-15 — Examples of Personal Anchorages

List at least five examples of each of the following types of personal anchorages — whether or not they exist in your own life:

- Objects:

- Linkage to a place:

- Activity:

- Belief, value, or moral code:

- Person:

- Group:

Exercise 8-16 — Personal Anchorages in Your Life

Now identify several items of each type which exist in your life now — and which you want to add in the near future.

	Exist Now	Will Add in the Near Future
• Objects:		
• Linkage to a place:		
• Activity:		
• Belief, value or moral code:		
• Person:		
• Group:		

What specific actions will you take to add each new personal anchorage? When?

BUILDING RESISTANCE TO DISTRESS THROUGH THE LIFESTYLE BUFFER

This chapter has focused on practical steps you can take to build resistance against distress. You cannot avoid troublesome or challenging stressors, and you would not want to. In fact, fulfillment of human potential depends upon being challenged again and again throughout one's life. The point is to be able to see and meet those challenges with vigor, enthusiasm, and good health. Maintain an effective lifestyle buffer is the means of doing so. In this chapter, we have focused on several practical steps you can take to strengthen your own buffer:

— Regular aerobic exercise
— Daily deep relaxation
— Good nutrition
— Social support
— Personal anchorages.

An effective lifestyle buffer adds to resistance against distress through two pathways:

— Improving the body's ability to cope with challenge, change, and crisis.
— Improving mental outlook.

To a substantial degree, an improved mental outlook will follow naturally and predictably from an improved lifestyle buffer. Yet how you perceive and interpret stressors deserves special attention, to which Chapter 9 is devoted.

REFERENCES

1. Lawrence E. Hinkle, Jr. "The Effects of Exposure to Culture Change, Social Change, and Changes in Interpersonal Relationships on Health," in B. Dohrenwend and B. Dohrenwend, Editors, *Stressful Life Events: The Nature and Effects*. New York: John Wiley and Sons, Inc., 1974, p 21.

2. Karl Albrecht, *Stress and The Manager*. Englewood Cliffs, N.J.: Prentice-Hall, Inc., 1979. p 228-230.

3. Ralph S. Paffenbarger and W.E. Hale, "Work Activity and Coronary Heart Mortality," *New England Journal of Medicine,* 292: 545-550, 1975.

4. Ralph S. Paffenbarger, Alvin L. Wing, and Robert T. Hyde, "Physical Activity as an Index of Heart Attack Risk in College Alumni," *American Journal of Epidemiology,* 108: 161-175, 1978.

5. Peter S. Wood, "Does Running Help Prevent Heart Attacks?"*Runner's World,* December 1979, pp 84-93.

6. Walt Schafer, *Stress, Distress and Growth.* Davis, California: International Dialogue Press, 1978, p 183.

7. William Glasser, *Positive Addiction.* New York: Harper and Row, 1976, pp 108, 109, 113.

8 For summaries of research on these topics, see, for example, Peter S. Wood, *Run To Health.* New York: 1980; "The Marathon: Physiological, Medical Epidemiological and Psychological Studies."*Annals of the New York Academy of Sciences.* 301, 516-724, 1977. (Edited by P. Milvy); Per-Olaf Astrand and Kaare Rodahl, *Textbook of Work Physiology: Physiological Bases of Exercise.* New York: McGraw-Hill, Inc., 1977; David Costill, *A Scientific Approach to Distance Running.* Los Altos, CA.: Track and Field News, 1979, Covert Bailey, *Fit or Fat?* Burlington, Mass., 1978. Kenneth Cooper, *The Aerobics Way.* New York: M. Evans, 1977.

9. For summaries of research on the psychological effects of running, see, for example, *Psychology of Running,* Michael H. Sachs and Michael L. Sacks, editors, Champaigne, Ill.: Human Kinetics Publishers, Inc. 1981; T. Kostrubala, *Joy of Running.* New York: J.B. Lippincott, 1976; P. Milvy, *Ibid.;* James Fixx, *The Complete Book of Running.* New York: Random House, 1977.

10. Cooper, *op cit.*, p 11.

11. See, for example, Fixx, *op cit.*; Joe Henderson, *Jog, Run, Race.* Mountain View, CA.: World Publications, 1977; Tom Collingwood and Robert Carkhuff, *Get Fit for Living.* Amherst, Mass.: Human Performance Development Press, 1976. Rory Donaldson, *Guidelines for Successful Jogging.* Washington, D.C.: National Running and

Fitness Association, 1977: Wood, *op cit*.; Joan Ullyot, *Women's Running*. Mountain View, CA.: World Publications, 1976.

12. Cooper, *op cit.*

13. Herbert Benson, *The Relaxation Response*. New York: William Morrow and Company, Inc. 1975.

14. Ibid: R.K. Wallace, "Physiological Effects of Transcendental Meditation". *Science,* 1970, 167, 1751. P.C. Ferguson and J.C. Gowan, "Psychological Findings on Transcendental Meditation", *Scientific Research on the Transcendental Meditation Program,* Switzerland, MERU Press Publication, 1975 (1, Number 3180).

15. *Benson, op cit.;* Wallace, *Ibid*.; R.K. Wallace and H. Benson, "The Physiology of Meditation. *Scientific American,* 1972, *226,* 84-90.

16. J. Schultz and W. Luthe, *Autogenic Training: A Psychophysiologic Approach in Psychotherapy*. New York: Grune and Stratton, 1959; W. Luthe, editor, *Autogenic Therapy* (Vols. I-III). New York: Grune and Stratton, 1969.

17. Barbara B. Brown, *Stress and the Art of Biofeedback*. New York: Bantam Books, 1977; T. Barber, et *al*, editors, *Biofeedback and Self-Control*. Chicago: Aldine, 1971. Kenneth R. Pelletier, *Mind as Healer, Mind as Slayer*. New York: Delcourte, 1977, Chapter 8.

18. Leslie M. Lecron, *Self-Hypnotism: The Technique and its Use in Daily Living*. Englewood Cliffs, N.J.: Prentice-Hall, Ind., 1964; Martha Davis, Elizabeth Eshelman and Matthew McKay, *The Relaxation and Stress Reduction Workbook,* Second Edition, Oakland, CA.: Ken Harbinger Publications, 1982, Chapter 7

19. Davis, Eshelman and McKay, *Ibid,* Chapter 3; Edmund Jacobson, *Progressive Relaxation,* 2nd Ed. Chicago: Chicago Press, 1938; Kenneth R. Pelletier, *Holistic Medicine: From Stress to Optimum Health*. New York: Delcourte, 1979.

20. Benson, *op cit.,* p 70.

21. Pelletier, *Mind as Healer, Mind as Slayer, op cit.,* Chapter 7; Adelaide Brye, *Visualization*. Harper and Rowe: New York, 1978,

L. John Mason, *Guide to Stress Reduction.* Culver City, CA.: Peace Press, 1980; Davis, Eshelman and McKay, *op cit.,* Chapter 6.

22. Benson, *op cit:* Wallace and Benson, *op cit.*

23. *For summaries of this research, see, for example, Benson, ibid.,* Ferguson and Gowan, *op cit;* David R. Frew, *Management of Stress: Using TM at Work.* Chicago, Nelson-Hall, 1977; John F. Beary and Herbert Benson, "A Simple Psychophysiologic Technique which Elicits the Hypometabolic Changes of the Relaxation Response," *Psychosomatic Medicine.* Vol. 36, No. 2 (March-April, 1974) pp 115-120.

24. Benson, *op cit.,* p 65.

25. Glasser, *op cit.,* p. 32; also see Harold Bloomfield, *et al., TM: Discoving Inner Energy and Overcoming Stress.* New York: Del

26. Benson, *op cit.;* Herbert Benson, *et al.,* "Decreased Blood Pressure in Pharmacologically Treated Hypertensive Patients who Regularly Elicited the Relaxation Response," *The Lancet,* Feb. 23, 1974; Herbert Benson, Martha Greenwood and Helen Klemchuk, "The Relaxation Response: Psychological Aspects and Clinical Applications," *International Journal of Psychiatry in Medicine,* Vol. 6 (1/2), 1975, pp 87-98.

27. Regina S. Ryan and John W. Travis, *Wellness Workbook.* Berkeley, CA.: Ten Speed Press, 1981, p 143.

28. For more on the stress-nutrition connection, see, for example, the following: Daniel Girdano and George Everly, *Controlling Stress and Tension.* Englewood Cliffs, J.J: Prentice-Hall, Inc.., 1979, Chapter 7; Pelletier, *Holistic Medicine, op cit.,* Chapter VI; Davis, Eshelman and McKay, *op cit,* Chapter 15; Mason, *op cit.,* pp. 144-158. Donald B. Ardell, *High Level Wellness,* New York: Bantam Books, 1977, pp. 124-144.

29. Issued by the Senate Select Committee on Nutritional and Human Needs, February 1977, Revised January 1978.

30. Ryan and Travis, *op cit.,* pp. 32-33.

31. J. Cassel, "The Contribution of the Social Environment Host Resistance," *American Journal of Epidemiology 102* (2): 107-123.

32. Quote by James S. House, *Work Stress and Social Support.* Reading, Mass.: Addison-Wesley, 1981, p. 52; L.F. Berkman and S.L. Syme, "Social Networks Host Resistance and Mortality: A Nine-year Follow-up Study of Alameda County Residents," *American Journal of Epidemiology 109* (2): 186-204.

33. House, *ibid;* G. Caplan, *Support Systems and Community Mental Health.* New York: Behavioral Publications, 1974; G. Caplan and M. Killilea, *Support Systems and Mutual Help.* New York: Grune and Stratton, 1976; S. Cobb, "Social Support as a Moderator of Life Stress, *"Psychosomatic Medicine,"* 38 (5): 300-314; S. Gore, "The Effect of Social Support in Moderating the Health Consequences of Unemployment," *Journal of Health and Social Behavior. 19:* 157-165.

34. House, *ibid,* p. 39.

35. Ibid, p. 39

36. Maya Pines, "Psychological Hardiness: The Role of Challenge in Health" *Psychology Today,* December, 1980, p. 43.

37. This is a slightly modified version of a questionnaire developed by House and Wells. See House, *op cit.,* p. 71.

38. House. *op cit.*

39. Herbert M. Greenberg, *Coping With Job Stress.* Englewood Cliffs, N.J.: Prentice-Hall, 1980, pp 142-143.

40. *Ibid,* p. 143.

41. *Ibid,* p. 144.

42. Alvin Toffler, *Future Shock.* New York: Bantam Books, 1971, p. 378.

43. *Ibid,* p. 52.

44. Ryan and Travis, *op cit,* p. 217.

CHAPTER 9

MONITORING AND MANAGING YOUR PERCEPTION OF STRESSORS

When a man loses his job, he can see it either as a catastrophe — an irreplaceable loss which shows he is unworthy and predicts his downfall — or as an experience that falls within the range of risks he accepted when he took the job. In some cases, he may even view it as an opportunity to find a new career that is better suited to his abilities. Similarly, when an elderly couple is forced to sell their home because it has become too expensive and too difficult to keep, they can view the change either as a tragedy or as a chance to find housing that is safer and perhaps closer to children.[1]

Situations are never inherently distressful. Situations become distressful only when seen as threatening. Throughout this book, we have referred to the fact that perception intervenes between stressors and the stress response.

A major research project at the University of Chicago recently identified three key qualities of stress-resistant people:

— Challenge: viewing change as a challenge rather than a threat
— Commitment: engaging life, rather than hanging back
— Control: perceiving one's ability to have an impact on events.[2]

Given the same exposure to stressors (high life-change scores, for example) persons scoring high on these factors tend to become ill less often than persons scoring low. Stress-resistant people perceive and interpret stressors in ways that minimize their harmful impact.

Here is another illustration of the powerful impact of perception of the situation on emotional and behavioral response.

You are standing in the middle of a crowded elevator waiting for it to take its long ride to the eleventh floor. The elevator stops at the floor and the people behind you begin to move towards the exit. The door hesitates for a moment and the person behind you nudges, bumps, and then literally jabs you from behind. What is your immediate emotion? Chances are good that you are feeling mildly irritated, angry, or very volatile. Think of what you might have said to yourself immediately before experiencing the emotion. "What the hell is going on? Can't that person see that the elevator door is not open yet. How stupid and inconsiderate! He or she should not be doing that." One or more of these statements probably instantaneously popped into your consciousness and provoked the feeling of mild or intense anger.

You turn around to say something to this rude person and are surprised by what you see. The individual is wearing dark glasses and is carrying a cane. It was the cane that provided the jabs that ultimately aroused your emotions. You may even feel guilty for getting angry. Think of the thoughts that you may have experienced as you realized that the individual was blind. "This person is blind. No wonder he or she hit me from behind. How stupid of me to get angry." The change in your emotions from anger to compassion resulted from a change in your appraisal of the event. The content of your silent self-dialogue helped determine the nature of the emotion that you experienced.[3]

Two points are central to this chapter:

— Your perception of stressors rather than stressors themselves create distress.
— You can control your perception of stressors.

This chapter focuses on the role of faulty perception in causing distress and on steps for altering those faulty perceptions.

HELPLESSNESS, THREATENING EVENTS AND DISTRESS

My reading, personal experience, and work with hundreds of highly stressed people have led me to the following conclusions about the part perception plays in distress.

1. **Stressors are distressors only when they are perceived as threatening.**
   Stressors may be perceived as a threat to any one of several parts of your existence.
   — To life and safety: "I could get shot by this guy robbing me."
   — To basic needs: "Getting laid off my job will eliminate income for me and my family."

274

- To self-worth: "Her bad grades mean I am a failure as a parent."

- To image or reputation: "My co-workers in this meeting will think I am incompetent if I don't give an intelligent answer to this question."

- To acceptance or approval: "If I don't do things just right tonight, he will never ask me out again."

- To satisfaction and enjoyment: "I will be miserable for two weeks if I blow this project."

- To pain limit: "This is more than I can bear."

2. **Sometimes it is rational and realistic to perceive stressors as threatening and therefore to be temporarily distressed.**
   For example:

   - Fear and physical tension at hearing an earth-slide up the hill from your house.

   - Grief and pain at word of death of a loved one.

   - Concern, disappointment, and temporary insomnia at word of an unwanted job transfer.

   - Anger and readiness for action at an attack by a neighbor's dog on your child.

3. **Stressors often are unnecessarily and unrealistically perceived as threatening, thereby causing unnecessary distress.**
   This is especially true of perceived threats to self-worth, image, acceptance, and satisfaction. As we shall see, alternative perceptions are possible.

4. **Stressors are unnecessarily perceived as threatening when you:**
   • Perceive yourself as helpless to control your reactions to stressful situations.

   - "I can't do anything about my test anxiety."
   - "I can't control my temper when she makes me angry."
   - "My depression is out of my control."
   - "I can't help feeling like a wall flower."
   - "I can't cope."
   - "I'm totally overwhelmed."
   - "I will have a nervous breakdown if this happens."

   • Perceive yourself as helpless to influence events or people in the surrounding environment.

— "There is nothing I can to about that neighbor kid's blaring stereo."
— "Vandalism is out of control in this neighborhood."
— "My boss is oppressive and insensitive, but I am just a little guy here and can't do anything about it."
— "There is no way the poor quality of teaching in this school can be changed."
• Perceive the environment as unrealistically dangerous.
— "I know those teachers are out to get me, pure and simple."
— "Those bright graduate students will make me look bad for sure."
— "All whites (or blacks) are a threat to me."

5. **Unnecessarily perceiving a specific stressor as threatening results from broader irrational beliefs.**
    A number of common irrational beliefs behind the specific faulty appraisals of participants in my stress control program are these:

— "I must maintain an image of strength and invulnerability."
— "I must be sure to act so others will like me."
— "I must always please others."
— "If I don't say yes to this, I will never have the opportunity again."
— "Anything new is dangerous."
— "I must appear feminine at all times — to both men and women."
— "I must appear masculine at all times — to both men and women."
— "If I relax, disaster will strike."
— "If I relax, I will fall behind."
— "Spending time on exercise, relaxation, or fun is wasteful."
— "If I am really me, I will get hurt."
— "Taking one hour a day for me would be selfish."
— "If I don't do it, nobody else can or will."
— "I must always say yes when asked to help."
— "My actions are the main cause of others' emotions."
— "Most people are out to get me."

Albert Ellis pinpointed ten irrational ideas which people often hold.[4] Some of these overlap with the list just given.

1. You must — yes, must — have sincere love and approval almost all the time from all the people you find significant.

2. You must prove yourself thoroughly competent, adequate and achieving, or you must at least have real competence or talent at something important.

3. You have to view life as awful, terrible, horrible, or catastrophic when things do not go the way you would like them to go.

4. People who harm or commit misdeeds rate as generally bad, wicked, or villainous individuals and you should severly blame, damn, and punish them for their sins.

5. If something seems dangerous or fearsome, you must become terribly occupied with and upset about it.

6. People and things should turn out better than they do and you have to view it as awful and horrible if you do not quickly find good solutions to life's hassles.

7. Emotional misery comes from external pressures and you have little ability to control your feelings or rid yourself of depression and hostility.

8. You will find it easier to avoid facing many of life's difficulties and self-responsibilities than to undertake more rewarding forms of self-discipline.

9. Your past remains all-important and because something once strongly influenced your life, it has to keep determining your feelings and behavior today.

10. You can achieve happiness by inertia and inaction or by passively and uncommittedly "enjoying yourself."

Aaron Beck maintains that much irrational or disorganized thinking results from the following four cognitive defects:

— Dichotomous reasoning: to think in terms of extremes of opposites. Internalized statements that indicate a tendency to think in absolutes are: "Everybody is against me." "Nobody seems to like me."

— Overgeneralization: To generate a series of thoughts and beliefs on the basis of a small amount of data. An individual who overgeneralizes allows one incident of failure and criticism to influence thoughts and attitudes about other, similar incidences. "I'll never confide in my boss again. He'll always criticize me and see me as a failure."

— Magnification: to view events as much more threatening and dangerous than they are in reality. Hypochondriacs, for example, tend to assume that each ache and pain in their body represents the beginning of a dreaded disease.

— Arbitrary inference: to base beliefs and conclusions on evidence that is totally unrelated to the context of the present situation. This tendency reflects a failure in discrimination. For example, the boss's bad mood is taken very personally. "I don't know why he or she's mad at me, I didn't do anything to warrant that reaction."[5]

6. **Faulty perception resulting in unnecessary distress can be prevented or altered in two ways:**
   — Altering irrational beliefs which lead to faulty threatening perception of specific stressors
   — Controlling perceptions as they occur in the immediate distressing situation.

Exercise 9-1 — Faulty Perceptions During Past Month

Looking back over the past month, identify circumstances in which you:

1. Felt unnecessarily helpless to control your emotional or behavioral reactions to a stressor.

2. Felt unnecessarily helpless to influence people or events around you.

3. Unnecessarily perceived the surrounding environment as dangerous.

In retrospect, how might you have thought and acted more positively in order to create less distress for yourself?

Exercise 9-2 — Monitoring Threatening Perceptions

During the next three days, identify each instance when you feel emotionally or physically distressed. You may want to use a diary for this.

1. To what part of your experience do you perceive the stressor to be a threat in each instance? (Safety, basic needs, self-worth, image, approval, satisfaction?)

278

2. Is your perception realistic or faulty?

3. What alternative perceptions might you have used in each case?

Exercise 9-3 — Monitoring Your Irrational Beliefs

Which of the irrational beliefs under point five above are consistent with your own thinking? How do you think they influence your perceptions, stress level, and behavioral reactions in specific situations?

Exercise 9-4 — Irrational Beliefs by Parents of Special Children

Below are a number of faulty beliefs sometimes held by parents of special children who are physically handicapped, retarded, or emotionally disturbed. Do you harbor any of these or similar beliefs? Do you know anyone who does?

1. When I take my child out and he/she acts bizarre, it reflects badly on me as a person.

2. I should always protect others (such as grocery clerk, milkman, person on the street) from the inappropriate behavior of my child.

3. I can always determine my child's behavior if I try hard enough.

4. I always must be all things to my child.

5. I cannot take time for myself until I have fulfilled all my child's needs and wants.

6. Having a handicapped child reflects negatively on my own character.

7. I have a handicapped child. Therefore, I must have done something to deserve this fate.

8. I cannot control my emotional reactions to my child's actions — or to anything else.

9. People will automatically look down on me because of my child.

10. Having a handicapped child is a special blessing which I proudly display.

11. If I truly love my child, I will never consider placing him/her outside the home. If I ever take this step, I would fail as a parent.

12. My other children always must remember our child *is* handicapped and treat him/her accordingly.

13. If I never raise the topic of sex, my child will never think about it.

14. If I truly love my child, I should be able naturally to communicate with him/her. And if my child truly loves me, he/she should be able automatically to communicate easily with me.

15. If my child truly loves me, he/she always will do what I say.

16. Professionals always know what is best for my child and should never be questioned.

17. If professionals (especially physicians) determine my child's abilities and limits, I should never question this judgment by expecting more (or less).

ALTERING IRRATIONAL BELIEFS

The key to altering irrational, faulty thinking is internal dialogue or self-talk. Specifically, internal messages must be given to questions and counter irrational beliefs. This can be done through the following simple steps which Ellis calls disputations.[6]

1. What symptoms of distress do I want to reduce or eliminate?

2. What stressor is associated with my distress?

3. What specific perception intervenes between the stressor and my distress symptoms?

4. What is the irrational belief causing me unnecessary distress which I want to change? Here is an illustration in the life of John Smith, a young university professor.

John Smith frequently "freezes" and stumbles when talking in a Department faculty meeting. He perceives the situation as threatening because he believes the impression he leaves on colleagues will influence their votes for or against his tenure next year. His fear of looking bad creates the very blundering he so much wants to avoid. The irrational belief he wants to change is: "If I don't say the proper intelligent things in the proper intelligent manner, they will think I am not a worthy professor and will vote against me next year."

What evidence is there that this belief is true?

John: "None really. Tenure votes are influenced much more by publication records and teaching evaluations than on impressions left in faculty meetings."

What evidence is there that this belief is false?

John: "I have never known or heard of anyone who failed to be granted tenure because of what he or she said or did not say in a faculty meeting. Besides, no one has ever given any sign that they think less of me because of what I say or don't say in these meetings."

What alternative rational beliefs can I substitute for this irrational one?

John: "It makes no real difference whether any colleagues approve or agree with what I say in faculty meetings. If I just relax, be myself, and do the important parts of my job well, I will probably get tenure, even if I don't, I will survive."

This process of disputation can be applied verbally with someone such as spouse, close friends, or counselor who can assist you to re-think your irrational beliefs and try to change them.

Exercise 9-5 — Steps for Disputing Your Own Irrational Beliefs

Apply the disputation steps described above to two of your own irrational beliefs, either by yourself, or preferably with someone else, using the following format.

1. Distress symptoms?

2. Stressor?

3. My perception of the stressor?

4. Irrational beliefs influencing my perception?

5. Evidence this belief is true?

What was your perception of the situation? Your stress response? Your behavior? Your feelings afterwards? Discuss your experience with someone who knows you well.

Exercise 9-6 — The A B C Technique

Use the following format to analyze how you might think in situations that are repeatedly distressful for you. (This is Ellis's ABC technique.)[7]

    A. Activating agent (stressor)

    B. Old thoughts about A   B. New thoughts about A

C. Old consequences — mental,   C. New consequences
physical, and behavioral

In this chapter, we have focused on steps for monitoring and managing your perceptions of specific stressors. As noted in the previous chapter, a good lifestyle buffer will directly and naturally contribute to a more positive mental outlook. Yet specific attention to your attitudes, interpretations, and beliefs sometimes is needed. This chapter acquaints you with tools for assessing and, if needed, altering your perceptions.

REFERENCES

1. Maya Pines, "Psychological Hardiness: The Role of Challenge in Health." *Psychology Today,* December, 1980, p. 39.

2. *Ibid,;* Suzanne C. Kobasa, Robert R.J. Hiliker, and Salvatore R. Maddi, *Journal of Occupational Health,* 21 (1979) pp. 595-8. Suzanne C. Kobasa, "Stressful Life Events, Personality and Health: An Inquiry into Hardiness," *Journal of Personality and Social Psychology* 37 (1979), pp. 1-11.

3. John J. Parrino, *From Panic to Power: The Positive Uses of Stress.* New York: John Wiley and Sons, 1979, p. 120.

4. Albert Ellis and Robert Harper, *A New Guide to Rational Living.* Englewood Cliffs, N.J., Prentice-Hall, 1979.

5. A. Beck, "Cognitive Therapy: Nature and Relation to Behavior Therapy", *Behavior Therapy,* 1970, *1,* 184-200. Quoted here from Parrino, *op cit.,* p. 124.

6. Albert Ellis, *How to Live with a Neurotic.* New York: Crown, 1975, pp. 137-140.

7. Albert Ellis and Robert A. Harper, *A Guide to Rational Living.* N. Hollywood: Melvin Powers, Wilshire Book Company, 1975.

CHAPTER 10

MONITORING AND MANAGING YOUR STRESS REPONSE

The first time Joe gave a class presentation during his first semester in college, he trembled beforehand, sweated, stumbled several times over simple words and phrases, and developed a temporary mental block in the middle of his speech. Afterwords, he felt extremely depressed, resolving never to get up before a group again.

Six weeks later, after working with a stress counselor, it was his turn to give another speech. This time he practiced his deep relaxation technique two hours beforehand, practiced his speech before the mirror one hour beforehand, and accepted the modest tension build-up during the hour before the talk as natural. Immediately before his turn arrived, he did a deep breathing exercise, relaxed his muscles, took his time, and presented a flawless speech with composure. Afterwards, he gave himself several internal pats on the back for doing so well — and in mastering his fear of speaking.

CONTROLLING EMOTIONS INDIRECTLY

Joe's challenge was to control his physical stress response and emotions closely associated with that response in such a way that his speech would be effective the second time around. In short, he needed to learn to control thoughts and feelings so his behavior could be up to potential.

In this situation and others like it, emotions, thoughts, and behavior are interwoven in an intricate, complex web. The parts can be separated only for purposes of discussion and analysis. In reality, they occur together.

Yet, which do we focus on in the immediate stress situation like Joe's class presentation? A key assumption in this book is that while emotions, thinking, body, and behavior are interwoven and inseparable, the key targets are:

— Controlling perception of the stressor
— Controlling the physical stress response
— Controlling the coping response in relation to the stressor

This leaves out emotions. This does not mean that emotions are unimportant or to be denied. To the contrary, I believe them to be a valuable, central part of human experience, during stress and all other parts of life. But emotions occur and change largely in response to what we think, do, and experience in our bodies. While we will give attention to feelings in this chapter, we assume they can best be controlled or altered by controlling what we think and do and by how we regulate our bodies.

This view is consistent with Lazarus who emphasizes the role of mental and behavioral coping in determining emotions. "You will note that this analysis reverses the usual wisdom that coping always follows emotion (or is caused by it) and suggests that coping can precede and even influence its form and intensity."[1]

Parrino expresses a similar view within his holistic "human response system" framework.

In the human response system model, emotions do not precipitate problems, rather problems or maladaptive responses lead to emotional upset and disturbance. Human responses such as disordered thinking habits can precipitate anger in frustrating situations. A nervous system that is easily aroused by threatening life events can produce a state of chronic anxiety and tension. Behavioral habits such as procrastination can induce deep states of depression. In summary, habits of living are seen as the instigators of emotional reactions.[2]

Of course, through a loop-back effect, emotions in turn affect physical arousal, thinking, and behavior. But in terms of a stress control strategy, it is best in stressful situations to approach emotions indirectly through one of these other channels, rather than directly. In fact, this probably is the only way. In Chapter 12, we will present methods of handling distress emotions in this fashion. Chapter 10 focuses on means of controlling stress in the immediate situation when confronting or interacting with a stressor.

BREATHING TECHNIQUES

Below are a number of simple breathing techniques for controlling or reducing the physical stress response in the immediate stressful situation. Each counters the arousal associated with either a mini- or maxi-fight-or-flight response with a brief release of the relaxation response. Contraction and relaxation are intrinsic parts of the breathing cycle as you inhale and exhale. These exercises simply build upon this fact.

Each of the following is presented as an exercise which you are invited to experience as you read, as well as in later stressful situations.

Exercise 10-1 — One Deep Diaphragmatic Breath

With straight back, draw a long, deep breath by first pushing out your stomach, then your chest. You will experience a rolling effect up the front of your abdomen. Hold your breath for 4-8 counts, then exhale long and completely. As you do, allow your entire body to fall and become limp and slack. Leave your breath out for a few seconds before inhaling again. You will experience an immediate calming effect on mind and body, taking your stress level down a few degrees.

This can be done with eyes open or closed, with others or alone. Few others will ever detect you doing this exercise.

As you begin to use this simple technique, repeat it once every hour for two or three days. After that, you will find yourself doing it regularly throughout the day, especially in tense situations.

Exercise 10-2 — Three-Breath Release

Here is another technique which you can practice on-the-spot, during or before meetings, tests, performances, confrontations.[3] It is very simple and very effective. Try it at least once each day or week.

1. If possible, let your eyes fall closed. (This is not essential.)

2. Draw a comfortable deep breath, preferable into the deeper end of your lungs (this is diaphragmatic breathing). As you let go, allow your whole body to loosen and go slack at once. Feel your entire musculature relax and soften. As you let go, recall how your body feels at the end of a good, deep relaxation session, and let your body sink toward that feeling of slackness and heaviness — all in one long, comfortable exhale. (Don't worry if you are standing or sitting, you will not fall over. If you are standing and want to let your eyes close, you can keep your balance by placing your hand on something solid next to you.)

3. Draw a comfortable deep second breath. As you inhale, randomly choose a particular muscle (or pair) in the head, neck, or shoulder area. Usually you will find yourself focusing on a muscle that you suspect to be tense — the brow, the jaws, the shoulder-lifting muscles. As you exhale, focus all your awareness in that muscle, and imagine you feel it dissolving, draining of

tension even more completely than it might have during exhale number one.

4. Draw a comfortable deep third breath. As you release it, focus inside your forearms and hands, and imagine them feeling heavier, warmer and calmer, as if you just completed a full deep relaxation session.

5. Open your eyes and continue about your business. No judgments, no analysis. Just let it go at that. You do not have to "perform" this technique — just do it, with your awareness clear and inward for the moment, but without effort. With practice, its value will become more and more obvious.

Exercise 10-3 — Breathing Countdown

This technique, actually a form of brief meditation, is a very effective on-the-spot tension reducer.

1. Close eyes in sitting or lying position.
2. Take one deep breath, hunching shoulders and holding breath for six seconds.
3. Breath out slowly and completely.
4. Resume normal breathing.
5. On first out-breath, silently say "10". On the next out-breath silently say "9". On the next out-breath, silently say "8", etc., down to "1".
6. When you reach "1", you can repeat "1" over and over, count back to "10" or let your mind wander.
7. Continue for 3-10 minutes.
8. Slowly open eyes, resume normal activities.

Exercise 10-4 — Focus Attention on Breathing

This simple technique can help your mind and body in tense situations. It is very simple. Without trying to change anything, simply allow your mind to be fully aware for several moments of your breathing. Dwell on the rise and fall of your chest, the cooler air coming in, the warmer air passing out. Be aware of whether your breaths are shallow or deep, quick or slow, comfortable or uncomfortable. Dwell on the passage of air in and out of your right nostril for a few breaths, then your left, simply allow this attentiveness to settle you, to quiet distracting or racing thoughts. It is important to accept what you observe, simply be with it. Do not concern yourself with trying to change it.

288

Exercise 10-5 — Breathing Slowly for Calming Effect

Another technique, very effective for many people before a difficult speech, performance, interview, physical performance, or athletic performance, is to deliberately breathe calmly and slowly, thinking of this slow breathing as soothing and calming your entire body. Leaving your breath out longer than normal can be especially helpful.

Exercise 10-6 — Breathing Away Tension

1. Sit or lie in a comfortable position with hands open and legs uncrossed.
2. Be aware of the weight of your entire body on the floor, bed, couch, or chair. Your muscles need not help support your body at all.
3. Softly close your eyes.
4. Focus attention on your nostrils and "see" the air entering each side. Follow its path down into your lungs, "watch" it swirling around, and "observe" it moving back up and out.
5. As it leaves, tell yourself it is carrying away tension, pain, and disease if present.
6. Continue for 1-5 minutes.

Remember, the better your physical fitness, the better your ability to extract and process large amounts of oxygen during exercises such as these and throughout the day.

MUSCLE RELAXATION TECHNIQUES

The techniques described below are brief, on-the-spot tension reducers. You will recall that longer, deeper preventative muscle relaxation exercises were presented in Chapter 7 as part of the lifestyle buffer. These are intended to be used throughout the day, especially during or between challenging situations. The following exercises are quoted by permission from Jane Madder's fine book, *Stress and Relaxation*.[4]

STANDING

Stretch: Have a good stretch before you begin to relax. Notice how a cat gives a whole-body stretch and yawn before it settles down.

Stretch up and out as far as you can. If you feel like it, yawn.

Stretch up with one arm, let it drop and relax, then stretch both arms together.

Warming-up exercises: Athletes always do some exercises to warm up before strenuous activity to avoid the risk of injury when muscles are tense. Warm muscles relax more easily.

Slapping: Slap the muscles all over your body. There is an added advantage in this as it tones up the muscles, so pay special attention to the thighs and abdomen.

Big Circle: Large trunk movements provide the most effective way of warming up. Warning! Don't let anyone persuade you to touch your toes with your legs straight unless you are very supple and fit. It has little value and can hurt your back. So bend your knees as you reach down in the big circle.

Reach to the side and with your finger draw the largest circle in the air you possibly can, making big trunk movements in stretching, bending and turning. If you are short of space you can do this with your elbow making the circle instead of your hand.

Floppy jog: Let your arms go floppy and do a relaxed jog on the spot. Your feet hardly leave the ground. This, and many other exercises are more fun done to music.

ARMS

Floppy sway: Stand with your feet astride to give you a good base. Let your arms dangle straight down. Sway a little so that your arms move as a result. Then let them gradually come to a standstill. Get a partner to test how relaxed you are. He should lift one arm just above the elbow joint and it should feel heavy. When he lets go the arm drops immediately and you neither help nor hinder.

You can learn a lot about differences in relaxing if you test a number of people this way.

Swimmers' shake: (Swimmers often do this to loosen up before races.) Shake one arm with a rotary movement from your wrist up to your shoulder so that the arm muscles wobble. This is only successful if your arm hangs straight down, so don't lift it sideways. You can add to this a relaxed shake of your whole body.

The swish: Raise your arms in front at shoulder height. Let them flop loosely so that they swish past your thighs. Do this with relaxed arms for as long as you like, registering the feel of loose arms, and then end the sequence with a complete circle of your arms backwards. This helps to keep your shoulder joints mobile.

The chairoplane: This isn't easy at first but once you have got it going it does give a good feeling of relaxation.

Lead up to the exercise this way. Stand with your feet apart with your arms loosely by your sides. Twist your trunk so that your hips and shoulders face one way. Your arms are still by your sides. Turn to the other side. Then make this a rhythmical movement, turning from side to side and as you do this your arms float up of their own accord. Speed this up a little and your arms will float up and even wrap around you if they are relaxed. If you feel giddy, either close your eyes or, better still, keep your head facing forward as you turn. This exercise feels good when you have got it right; it just happens.

SITTING

Shoulders: Many people show tension on their shoulders and it is of two kinds: some hunch them and others draw them down stiffly. Sometimes these muscles remain contracted all day and as a result they become aching and tender to touch. Women who always carry shopping bags in one hand may find this an additional strain.

Hunch and pull: Tighten your shoulders just a little. This is only the amount of tension you use when you are fussed and anxious. Recognize this and let the tension go so that your shoulders drop. Then relax them even further.

A partner can feel the effects of slight tension this way: hands rest on top of the shoulders and when you tighten up even slightly he can feel the muscles tense. It is easy to understand why they ache when they are always held like this.

Then pull your shoulders down, keeping your neck long. Recognize this form of stiffness and then relax the muscles.

Circling shoulders: Circle your shoulders to relieve muscle tension and improve circulation. You can do this almost unobserved whenever your shoulders ache.

Massage by a partner is a great help in relieving muscle tension in shoulders.

During the day, notice when you hold these muscles tight: it may be when you are driving, doing housework, telephoning, or even when you are resting. Remember that you look more at ease and move with more grace when your shoulders are relaxed.

Flight: Raise your arms obliquely sideways and upwards. Keep your back straight and your neck long. Let your arms drop heavily and in a relaxed way so that they cross in front of you. Continue doing this in a rhythmical way and notice the feel and look of relaxed arms.

Stand with your feet astride with your arms raised obliquely sideways and upwards. Wait for a moment to feel poised and at ease, with your neck long and your shoulders relaxed. Let your arms drop downwards in a relaxed heavy way so that they cross in front of you (keep your body quite upright). Then raise your arms sideways and upwards again with a feeling of lift in your whole body so that your hands touch lightly overhead. Then let your arms fall sideways again to cross in front. Repeat this several times keeping this rhythm: "Drop and lift, and touch... drop, lift, and touch." You may prefer to lift the arms just obliquely upwards instead of the whole way in which case it will be: 'Drop and lift, drop and lift.' Whichever way you do it you will capture the delightful feeling of relaxed loose arms and the poised feeling of flight.

Legs: Many women hold their legs tightly together even when they are alone and resting, and these large muscles need to relax sometimes. Businessmen in high-powered jobs often hold their legs tightly in committee meetings and bend an ankle strongly upwards when they are annoyed. When you are sitting at rest, let your thighs fall apart a little and keep ankles relaxed.

Face: There is a very close relationship between the state of the muscles of the face and a state of mind. Much of our communication with other people is non-verbal, and a tense, anxious face signals to everyone messages of anxiety, and this is very catching. A forehead in a state of continual contraction also contributes to tension headaches.

First check up to make sure that your teeth are not held tightly together. The only time they need to meet is when you are eating, so let the jaw rest in the relaxed position.

Do the following exercise once only. There will be no need to do it again but it helps if you can observe the effects of emotions on forehead muscles, and realize the kind of message it gives to others.

Do this facing the mirror, or, if you can bear it, facing someone else:

Frown: This represents the fight reaction.

Raise your eyebrows: This represents surprise or flight.

Do both of these together. This represents conflict, when you can neither fight nor run away and it conveys a message of anguish and anxiety.

Now relax the muscles so that your forehead feels wider and higher than it did before. Give your forehead some massage to smooth out the worry muscles or better still get someone else to do it for you.

Palming: After a spell of concentrated mental work, 'palming' gives relief for eyes and neck.

Lean forward and rest your forehead on your cupped hands, hands crossed over your eyes, with your eyes closed. Combine this with relaxation and controlled breathing.

Neck: Make sure that your head is held in the middle and not to one side, or jutting forward. You can see this in the mirror, or get a partner to help you. He should stand behind you holding your head with his hands, and move it very gently with no opposition from you and then place it in the correct position. It may feel wrong to you but keep it there.

Turn your head to look first one way and then the other, keeping your shoulders square all the time.

Bend your head from side to side keeping your shoulders level.

Drop your head forward then lift it so that your head is held high. Keep your shoulders down and reach up with the back part of your head as if you were being pulled up by a tuft of hair at the back.

Some people, especially older ones, may get giddy if the head is bent far backwards so I do not include this. A small head roll, however, is useful to release tension in the neck.

293

Massage for the back of the neck is very helpful in releasing neck tension.

Neck Press: Sit with your neck well supported by a high-backed chair, or put a kitchen-type chair against the wall (use a cushion for your head if you like).

Press your neck against the support so that as much of it touches as possible. Then release the tension and let the muscles relax.

A neck-support pillow is useful for those whose neck is particularly curved forward or if there is neck pain.

Lips and cheeks: Pursed lips and tight cheeks may signal a wrong message to those around and make you look disapproving and severe. Photographic models often massage their lips to make them look relaxed.

Hands: Notice how often people show their tension in their hands. They are probably the easiest part of the body to learn to relax and when they are it induces general relaxation.

Shake your hands loosely as if you were flicking water from your fingers.

Clinch and Stretch: Clinch your fists, then stretch out your fingers as far as they will go.

Cradle: Rest with one hand cradled in the other. It is impossible to grip your hands tightly when they are cradled in this way, so use this position when you relax sitting down. The message received by your brain is that you're quiet and at rest so there is no need to be on guard. Use it also when you are feeling tense, for example, at the dentist, at take-off in a plane, watching television, waiting in the surgery. I know a busy physician who deliberately relaxes his hands while he is waiting for his next patient; he also notices signs of tension in his patients' hands. If you are doing intricate manual work, or typing, break off when you are tired and do a few hand exercises. Relaxed hands and arms are necessary for musicians and you will notice that eminent performers have beautiful relaxation in their movements.

Exercise 10-7 — Brisk Five-Minute Walk

The next time you have already accumulated physical tension or are about to enter a potentially distressful situation, take a brisk five-minute walk. This can release muscle tension, allow greater oxygenation in your brain and body, allow for mental diversion or positive affirmations. It can be amazingly effective.

MENTAL TECHNIQUES

Exercise 10-8 — I Am Relaxed — A Simple Form of Meditation and Relaxation[5]

This technique combines breathing with mental focus to create immediate relaxation.

1. Sit comfortably and quietly.
2. Tell yourself that you are going to use the next 5, 10 or 20 minutes to re-balance, to heal, to relax yourself.
3. Surrender the weight of your body, allowing the chair, or floor, to support you.
4. Close your eyes, gently cutting out visual stimulation and distraction.
5. As you inhale, repeat to yourself: "I AM...."
6. As you exhale say "....RELAXED."
7. Continue to breathe normally — not trying to change it in any way. Just watch it happening and continue to repeat: "I AM" with inhalation; "RELAXED" with exhalation.
8. As your mind begins to wander, gently bring it back to the awareness of your breath and your statement "I AM RELAX-ED." Be compassionate and loving with your "leaping frog" mind which wants to be anywhere but here.
9. Continue doing this for as long a time as you have established.
10. To conclude, discontinue the phrase and slowly stretch your hands and feet, your arms and legs, your whole body.
11. Open your eyes a sliver at a time — like the sun coming up in the morning.
12. Continue on your way.

Exercise 10-9 — Mental Rehearsal

Five or ten minutes before entering a difficult situation, use any of the relaxation techniques described elsewhere in this chapter to take your mind and body to a more relaxed state. Then visualize yourself moving through the situation with confidence and competence. Repeat several times before entering the actual situation. (This is discussed in more detail below in relation to desensitization in preparation for performance.)

Exercise 10-10 — Thought Stopping

This is a simple technique for stopping unpleasant, disabling, or other negative thoughts which threaten to interfere with full concentration or peace of mind.[6] Simply "hear" the word "stop" shouted inside your mind. This can help bring your thinking process to a halt, even briefly. Then immediately substitute a more positive, productive, useful line of thought. This technique can prove especially useful in situations which create personal fear or tightness.

Exercise 10-11 — Mental Diversion

This technique, an extension of thought stopping, merely involves substituting more positive thoughts for thoughts which are unnecessarily preoccupying or anxiety-provoking.[7] Here is one man's experience.

> *I discovered some time ago that, if I allowed myself to, I would spend the hour or two before conducting a large management seminar in worrying about whether I would do a good job. I'd go over my notes, check and recheck my materials, and keep asking myself whether I'd overlooked anything. After discovering the technique of mental diversion, I changed that pattern. Thereafter, I would prepare thoroughly for the seminar (or a meeting with executives, or an important presentation, or any other challenging task), get everything in order well in advance, and put it aside, I would then deliberately indulge in other mental activities that would bring me positive feelings, with the complete assurance that everything was taken care of. Driving to the location where I am to conduct a seminar, I frequently sing songs in the car — one of my favorite activities. This keeps my mind too busy to worry about the task ahead. I usually arrive at the location wishing I had more time to sing a half dozen other songs that have come to mind.*[8]

Exercise 10-12 — Positive Affirmations

As a sure confidence-builder, repeat affirmative statements over and over just before or even during a difficult situation. These can help alter your perception of threatening situations, relax your body, and drain away emotional anxiety. For example:

296

— I am prepared
— I am in control of this situation
— I have no reason to be afraid
— I like myself
— I will do this very well

Exercise 10-13 — Desensitization

Sometimes a serious aversion develops toward a specific activity such as giving a speech, meeting a new person of the opposite sex, airline travel, test-taking, a job interview, or speaking freely in a meeting. Desensitization is a systematic technique developed several years ago by Wolpe by which the person overcomes the fear or phobia by associating low physiological arousal with the anxiety-producing situation through deep relaxation and visualization. Sometimes an intermediate step of practicing the activity alone or with a friend also is used. Here is one way to use desensitization. If possible try it the first time under guidance of someone trained in this technique.

1. Choose an activating life event, one that precipitates disordered thinking, fear, anxiety.

2. Elicit the relaxation response by one of the muscular relaxation techniques described in this chapter. It is desirable to relax during imagery, but you can proceed with the following steps even if you are not completely relaxed.

3. Imagine the anxiety provoking situation as vividly as possible. Continue to imagine the situation until you feel that you are deeply involved in it. It helps to imagine it vividly enough to get mildly emotionally aroused by what you are imagining.

4. Alternate between imagining the scene and relaxing until you get more and more comfortable with the imagined event.

5. Plan a time to confront yourself with the situation and do it. If you aren't as comfortable in the situation as you would like to be, repeat the steps outlined above and try it once again.[9]

PREPARING FOR PEAK PERFORMANCE

Perhaps the most challenging of all efforts to control the stress response is preparing for performances such as in athletics, music, theater, or speaking. Sufficient adrenalin must be mobilized to be sharp, alert, and peaked, but not so much mental or physical arousal that it interfers with performance. Entering the situation near the upper range of one's zone of positive stress is probably most desirable.

Peak readiness depends on two main factors. First is technical preparedness through intense and repeated practice. Second is proper use of mental imagery or visualization before the event.

Several well-known athletes use visualization quite deliberately and systematically though they may never call it that.[10]

— Jean-Claude Killy, the multiple Olympic Gold Medalist, reported that preparation for one of his races was completely mental for several weeks beforehand. He skied the slope again and again in his mind. That is all he could do since he was recovering from an injury at the time. It turned out to be one of his best-ever performances.

— Jack Nicklaus maintains that 50 percent of a good golf shot is proper mental imagery beforehand. He runs a color mental movie through his mind before each shot. In his book *Golf My Way,* he states "First I 'see' the ball where I want it to finish, nice and white and sitting up high on the bright green grass. Then the scene quickly changes, and I 'see' the ball going there, its path, trajectory, and shape, even its behavior on landing. Then there is a sort of fade out, and the next scene shows me making the kind of motion that will turn the previous images into reality."[11]

— Jack Fosbury, former high jump world record holder, Olympic Gold Medalist, and inventor of the Fosbury Flop method of jumping, used the same technique of mental movies before each jump. "I would do a sequence of events. I would think of the last jumps, in practice or competition, and I would try to think what I was doing wrong, where I would come close to the bar. Then I would visualize what it felt like to do it right. I would remember back to my last good jump and try to emulate that. I would go over that in my mind a couple of times until I was sure, until I have the feeling in my head exactly what I was going to do for a good jump. Then I moved to another thought — all positive thinking — I was going to make the jump. When I had convinced myself, I would go. I made my body sensitive to my mind."[12]

Visualization can be highly effective in preparing for any event, athletic or otherwise, especially if it is part of a broader process of preparation. In a recent workshop for competitive roller skating club (figure, dance, and speed), I introduced the following plan for preparing for competition. It met with remarkable success in the case of several competitors and is adaptable to almost any type of challenging performance situation.

Exercise 10-14 — Harnessing The Mind Toward Peak Performance

1. Know why you are training and competing; be sure it's for the right reasons.
2. Don't be an extreme perfectionist. Set realistic, personal goals.
3. Don't gunnysack your feelings. "Unfinished business" can interfere with concentration and block energy.
4. Be totally prepared through thorough practice.
5. Avoid these traps: fear of failure and fear of success.
6. Learn to use visualization — "positive mental movies."
7. During the day of competition, be unhurried, uncluttered, soothed, focused.
8. Perform well for you, not for your impression on friends, teammates, coaches, parents.
9. Stop negative thoughts and feelings. Substitute positive feelings and images through "positive mental movies" and key confidence-building words.
10. Be aware of body and emotional signals of your own best "activation level."
11. Let yourself do it, rather than make yourself do it. Concentrate, don't bear down. Be totally absorbed.
12. Don't be distracted, discouraged, or stopped by an error in performance.
13. Use the following steps in preparing for competition:
    A. The night before competition, do deep relaxation, with a positive mental movie of your performance.
    B. Two to five hours before the event, repeat step one.
    C. On the site, use deep breathing and key relaxing words to control physical tension. Then create a brief, positive, relaxed mental movie of your performance.
    D. Now let your mind become totally absorbed in your performance. Create "A cocoon of concentration" — not bearing down but becoming "one" with your movement and your partner, if present.

E. Let your body take off and do its job.

14. After finishing, stroke yourself for what you *did* do well.

15. Remember the keys: practice, positive mental movies, and concentration.

Chapter 10 has included descriptions of a number of practical steps you can take to control your physical and mental arousal — that is, your stress response in challenging situations. These techniques have focused on breathing, muscle relaxation, and mental control. Experiment with several during coming weeks. Decide which ones work for you, then make it a habit to use them daily, especially in actual or potentially distressing situations.

In the next chapter, we will focus on how you interact with stressors.

REFERENCES

1. Richard Lazarus, "A Cognitive Oriented Psychologist Looks At Biofeedback," *American Psychologist,* 1975, *30,* 553-561.

2. John J. Parrino, *From Panic to Power: The Positive Use of Stress.* New York: John Wiley and Sons, 1979, p. 40.

3. Harold Gelb, *Killing Pain Without Prescription.* New York: Harper and Rowe, 1980.

4. Jane Madders, *Stress and Relaxation.* New York: Arco Publishing Company, Inc. 1979, pp. 48-60.

5. Regina S. Ryan and John W. Travis, *Wellness Workbook.* Berkeley, CA.: Ten Speed Press., 1981. p. 53. Quoted by permission of publisher.

6. Martha Davis, Elizabeth Eshelman and Matthew McKay, *The Relaxation and Stress Reduction Workbook.* Second Edition, Oakland, CA.: Harbinger Publications, 1982, Chapter 9.

7. *Ibid.;* Karl Albrecht, *Stress and the Manager.* Englewood Cliffs, N.J.: Prentice-Hall, Inc., 1979, pp. 204-5.

8. Albrecht, *Ibid,* p. 204.

9. Parrino, *op cit.,* p. 136.

10. Dan Sperling, "The Myth of the Natural Athlete," *Success Magazine,* November 1981, p. 31: Jerry Lynch, "Positive Thinking Techniques for Improving Performance," *The Runner,* July, 1982, p. 22.

11. Jack Nicklaus, *Golf My Way.* New York: Simon-Schuster, 1976.

12. Daily Program, 1980 Olympic Trials, Eugene, Oregon.

CHAPTER 11

MONITORING AND MANAGING YOUR COPING RESPONSES

Whether moderate and helpful stress becomes distress is determined in part by how you perceive the stressors, how you regulate your emotional and physical responses to them — and how you cope with those stressors, either internally or in behavior, the subject of this chapter. The coping response is influenced by and in turn influences your emotional and physical stress responses. For example:

— Feeling temporarily distressed at the perception of being overwhelmed by too many stressors leads to temporary withdrawal from the situation or to working hard to catch up.

— Similarly, thinking through the reasons for being overwhelmed and what to do about it can lead to a systematic, step-by-step approach to digging your way out of the overload.

— The emotion of depression contributes to physical fatigue, which slows down behavior.

— Attacking the tasks at hand vigorously can renew your spirit and rejuvenate your physical energy level.

Regulating how you think and feel and how your body responds is necessary but not sufficient for controlling your day-to-day stress level. You might meditate and run regularly, understand and handle your environment well, and think clearly. But if your behavior toward this stimuli in your environment is ineffective or maladaptive, your stress may well turn into harmful distress.

It would be unrealistic to attempt to prescribe a detailed plan for you to cope effectively with all the situations that may confront you. There is far too much complexity and individuality. In the end you must exercise judgment and take personal responsibility for your own coping style and coping responses. What we can do is suggest guidelines, directions, and a range of specific options to draw from, focusing both on do's and don'ts.

You will recall from the chart in Chapter 5 that loop-back arrows returned from both mental stress response and coping behavior stressors. Since coping necessarily involves what you think and feel toward stimuli, as well as what you do, we will include subjective as well as behavioral coping from time to time in this chapter.

CONSTRUCTIVE AND DESTRUCTIVE COPING RESPONSES

Your interactions with stressors can be divided into two broad categories.

— Constructive Coping Responses:
> Actions and attitudes toward stressors that promote your own health, enjoyment, productivity, and development while doing the same for others — or at least not adding to distress for others.

— Destructive Coping Responses:
> Actions and thoughts toward stressors that increase distress for self or others.

The standard by which to determine whether a specific set or thought is constructive or destructive (moral or immoral) is: What are the consequences for self and others? Does it promote personal well-being? The well-being of others? If so, it can be called constructive. Does it promote personal well-being at the expense of others? Does it add to the distress of both self and others? Then the act is destructive, and by my standards, immoral.

These distinctions are conceptually clear and distinct. In reality, of course, they are not always so clear, in part because consequences normally are mixed, rather than black or white. It also depends on who is interpreting the effect of an act or attitude — self, partners, or an outside observer. Nevertheless, the distinction does lead us toward useful distinctions for coping with situations and people in our environment.

MONITORING AND REDUCING DESTRUCTIVE COPING RESPONSES

A number of common behaviors and attitudes carry a high probability of being maladaptive or destructive for self and others. They can be divided into under-reactions, over-reactions, and inappropriate reactions. These lists are by no means exhaustive. Add your own.

Under-reactions

1. Apathy: Not caring about someone or something when the situation and your own best interest calls for engagement, involvement, a response.

2. Withdrawal: This may be mental, physical, or both. Not "being there," turning away with negative consequences for self and others is destructive. Withdrawal may be constructive, of course, under some circumstances.

3 . Escapism: A form of withdrawal, a result of apathy or denial. Using T.V., the car, reading, or sleep, for example, to avoid facing a stressor.

4 . Passivity: Being present, but responding with less than is responsible for your own or others' interest. Letting events or other people control you instead of taking responsibility and becoming involved.

5 . Procrastination: Putting off until another hour, day, year, forever. Makes stressors multiply fast.

6 . Not listening: Tuning out or distorting what others say.

7. Denial: Passively or actively denying that a stimuli calls for your response. Often a way of blindly blocking out political distress.

8. Acting depressed: Giving off messages that you are disinterested, devoid of energy, detached.

9. Avoiding risks: May be constructive or destructive, according to situation. Destructive if the situation or your own best interest calls for some type of risk-taking.

10. Playing martyr: Because of life script, helplessness, or simply habit. This is very common among the chronically ill, depressed, and abused persons.

Exercise 11-1 — Self-Monitoring of Under-Reactions

1. During the past week, which of the above under-reactions have you used? With what consequences for yourself? Others?

2. Watch your coping responses for the next two days, writing a diary if helpful. Which of the above do you use? With what effects or consequences for self? Others?

3. Consciously catch yourself in the future using one of these under-reactions.

4. What alternatives would be appropriate and effective?

Over-reactions

1. Aggression: Mentally or physically abusing others out of malevolence while seeking something you want for yourself. May take the form of procrastination, put-downs, or other subtle forms.

2. Anger explosions: Letting off steam and anger in such a way that it mentally or physically hurts others or lessens

your own success or well-being in the long-run.

3. Overworking: Typical for Type A's. Fine line between over-working and digging in intelligently to progress toward completing a task. Overworking is when consequences are adverse for your own health or others' well-being (especially wife, children, co-workers, who struggle to keep up).

4. Over-controlling: Also characteristic of many Type A's. Hyper-reactive in order to maintain rigid, complete mastery over others or events in general.

5. Dominating others: A form of over-controlling, but with specific reference to others at home or work. Often a defense to keep others at a distance or to avoid challenges to competence or emotional security.

6. Taking on others' burdens: May be appropriate and constructive, but when habitual beyond reason, will lead to being perpetually overwhelmed and martyred. Makes others dependent.

7. Making a mountain out of a molehill: This can occur with a task or communication from another person. Can lead to unnecessary distress for you as receiver of message and for the innocent sender who is bombarded with your emotional or task responses.

8. Defensiveness: Lash-out reactions which defend or otherwise seek to protect your own okayness, rightness, or righteousness. Usually stems from insecurity about own worth.

9. Foolish risk-taking: Risking life, limb, or fortune in response to opportunity or whim. Often characteristic of high sensation seekers. Wise risk-taking is vital to expansion and fun. Foolish risk-taking should be avoided.

10. Anger passion: Seeping anger which comes out, not directly or honestly, but indirectly and dishonestly through darts, put-downs, and sabotage. Terribly destructive for self and others. Equally harmful as explosions.

Exercise 11-2 — Self-Monitoring of Over-Reactions

1. During the past week, which of these over-reactions have you used? With what consequences for yourself? Others?

2. Watch your coping responses for the next two days, writing in a

diary if helpful. Which of the above do you use? With what effects or consequences for self? Others?

3. Consciously catch yourself in the future using one of these over-reactions.

4. What alternatives would be appropriate and effective?

Inappropriate Reactions

1. Unnecessary deviant behavior: Violating others' expectations, conventional norms, or laws so you or someone else is hurt in the long-run. Includes vandalism, murder, rape, drunkenness, capricious interruption of a meeting or class.

2. Rebellion: May be constructive or destructive depending on the situation, people, and rules involved. Often done quite inappropriately, for no good reason other than anger or hedonism, and with serious destructive consequences for self and others. Of course, rebellion is sometimes beneficial, depending on one's point of view.

3. Irresponsibility: Failing to perform a duty or activity which is rightfully yours. Sources of enormous potential grief for self and others, such as parents, spouse, neighbors, children, boss.

4. Rescuing: Opposite of irresponsibility in certain respects. Rescuing is appropriate when a person is drowning. It is inappropriate when he can very well swim and wants to, but your insistence on locking him into a lifesaving hold and pulling him to shore leads to dependency and non-responsibility, to dominance and self-righteousness. Also unnecessarily drains time and energy.

5. Missing the mark: Responding to or doing what was not asked or not responding or not doing what was asked. May result from rebelliousness, not listening, incorrect information, or even spite. Cause of much grief for self and others.

6. Rationalizing, supporting, defending, judging, parroting: See section on active listening below.

7. Excessive or untimely self-disclosure: Later we will contend that self-disclosure is generally to be desired. We do it too

little. But at appropriate times and in appropriate ways. If inappropriate, it can be distressing for both sender and receiver.

8. Using alcohol or drugs: This is often destructive, as we will discuss in Chapter 12.

Exercise 11-3 Self-Monitoring of Inappropriate Reactions

1. During the past week, which of these inappropriate responses have you used? With what consequences for yourself? Others?

2. Watch your coping responses for the next two days, writing in a diary if helpful. Which of the above do you use? With what consequences for self? Others?

3. Consciously watch yourself in the future using one of these inappropriate reactions.

4. What alternatives would be appropriate and effective? These, then, are a number of maladaptive or destructive coping responses which may cause or worsen distress, if not immediately, then in the long-run, and if not for self, then for others. Through banal or tragic life scripting, many people are hooked on such destructive behavior. Any script can be modified and even rewritten, however, through awareness, courage, effort, patience, and social support. Now we examine a number of types of constructive coping alternatives.

CONSTRUCTIVE COPING RESPONSES

Active Listening

When you listen to me without interruption or anything that feels like a judgment, you allow me the time and space to get more in touch with the many facets of me.

Thank you for never playing with my words, getting a laugh or recognition at my expense.

When you allow me to revise or restructure what I have said, I feel that you are truly committed to understanding me and what I'm about.

Thank you for not feeling that you necessarily have to do something about what I share.

When you listen, I feel that you are listening not only to my words but the feelings behind them.

Bless you for being you and thereby assisting me in my journey.

— Bennett Kilpack, M.F.C.C.[1]

Listening effectively is a basic ingredient in any effort to cope constructively with others.[2] Any exchange between two or more people has three basic elements:

— Sender
— Message
— Receiver

Active listening is a simple skill that is too seldom practiced. When used correctly, it can do wonders to assure that these three elements are in harmony. Clear and crisp exchanges of information and positive feelings between sender and receiver then are possible. Task accomplishment also benefits.

Let us assume the following message at 4:00 p.m. one day:

11-year-old boy to mother: "I'm sick of school."

At this point, mother can respond in any number of ways.[3] For example:

Mother to boy:

— "You are tired from staying up too late watching T.V. last night." (Psychologizing)

— "Are you saying you don't believe learning is good for you?" (Questioning)

— "No you're not." (Denying)

— "Oh, you are always complaining." (Discounting)

— "I can tell. I know school is a drag." (Sympathizing)

— "You know I have to send you to school every day. The law says so." (Defending)

311

— "You have no business feeling that way. You are only a sixth grader and will have to stay in school at least six more years." (Judging)

— "You must get to bed earlier, get your homework done on time and take a better attitude towards school. Then you will like it. No more of this." (Ordering)

— "Sounds like you're sick of school." (Parroting)

— "Let me tell you about one time I was sick of school when I was nine years old, blah, blah, blah." (Flipping to own story)

These are common, but defective responses. The boy is likely to feel no better. In fact, he probably will go away feeling unheard, put-down, intimidated, judged, belittled, attacked, and/or misunderstood.

Alternative responses, each an example of active listening, might be:

Mother to boy:

— "You seem pretty discouraged about school today."

— "You sound pretty tired today."

— "You sound really pooped."

— "You appear really down on school."

Any of these responses is likely to set in motion a fruitful exchange for the following reasons:

— The initial sender, the son, feels he is being truly heard.

— He will feel he is worthwhile because he is heard.

— The receiver, mother, checks out the accuracy of what she thinks she has heard.

— She invites him to say more, lowering his stress level by letting off steam and further reinforcing his sense of worth.

— She withholds her feelings, at least until she is clear what he is saying.

— He is given the chance to search for solutions himself, thereby promoting his own responsibility for his actions.

— Warmth and understanding are promoted between mother and son.

The basic format for active listening is simple:

You sound _____ about _____.[4]

The words cannot be mechanical or stilted, of course, but must flow naturally within the context of the person's own vocabulary and communication style.

The active listener is non-critical and non-controlling, at least in the early stages of the exchange. Sometimes it is appropriate, of course, to respond with an order, command or judgment, — but usually only after the sender has been fully heard. In most common daily interchanges at work and home active listening is entirely appropriate and beneficial. Chances are reduced that sender or receiver will unnecessarily build up tension or resentment.

In short, active listening includes:

— Showing attentiveness
— Clarifying content of sender's spoken message.
— Verifying non-verbal messages.
— Inviting more information and expression of feelings.
— Providing a genuine personal response.
— Promoting joint problem-solving or problem-solving by the sender alone.

Active listening is useful because it promotes:

— Accuracy of communication.
— Warmth and acceptance between sender and receiver.
— Self-worth of the sender.
— Elaboration of content.
— Full expression of feelings.
— Equality.
— Openness.
— Faith in sender's ability to solve problems.[5]

313

Active listening is a coping response which can aid immeasurably in reducing tension and in preventing unwanted distress in the first place.

Exercise 11-4 — Active Listening: Writing or Discussion Exercise

Provide an active listening alternative to each of the following responses:

Sender: "I don't have time for this nonsense."
Listener: "You sure as —ell do. Do it." (Ordering)
Active Listener: _____

Sender: "Why doesn't anyone ever take me seriously around here?"
Listener: "Poor John, no one ever listens to you." (Discounting)
Active Listener: _____

Sender: "I'll show those bums."
Listener: "You have no business talking like that." (Judging)
Active Listener: _____

Sender: "Nothing ever works around here."
Listener: "Oh, come on, you are just tired and hot tonight." (Psychologizing)
Active Listener: _____

Sender: "The administration of this place has no understanding of our problems."
Listener: "What business do you have talking like that?" (Judging)
Active Listener: _____

Sender: "I'm going to jump off the bridge, for sure."
Listener: "Poor John — feeling sorry for yourself again." (Discounting)
Active Listener: _____

Sender: "This workload is overwhelming."
Listener: "I know you've been putting in long hours." (Supporting)
Active Listener: _____

Sender: "I'm so angry, I could scream."
Listener: "What do you mean, I did the best I could." (Defending)
Active Listener: _____

Sender: "I'm convinced I'm going to keep everything to myself from now on. You can't trust anyone around here."
Listener: "You sound like you can't trust anyone around here." (Parroting)
Active Listener: _____

Exercise 11-5 — Role-Playing Active Listening

With a cooperative partner, role-play several exchanges using active listening. Extend the number of communications beyond one or two until you get the full feeling of active listening throughout the conversation.

Exercise 11-6 — Active Listening in Real Life

Deliberately try active listening in at least two situations today. Observe the consequences for you and your communication partner. What words best describe what happened? What was the result?

Appropriate Self-Disclosure

Bill R. has trouble making friends. His acquaintances all like him, but no one knows what he is really like.

Dorothy W. also has no close friends. Unlike Bill, however, she is not reluctant to let others know what she is feeling or what her problems are. In fact, she reveals personal things to almost everyone. People regard her as somewhat strange.

Terry is contemplating a divorce from her husband Ken. She now realizes that she has never really known him. For five years, she has lived with him, cooked and cleaned for him, and slept with him. In all that time, they have talked only about day-to-day concerns: what was for dinner, their week-end plans, and so forth. What is he really like? What were his hopes, dreams, and fears? She really doesn't know. [6]

Self-disclosure is a second approach to people-stressors, which usually can reduce tension and prevent stress build-up for everyone involved. As we shall see, however, self-disclosure is best used selectively. When used inappropriately it can increase, rather than reduce, stress.

What is self-disclosure? It is the process of revealing authentic, personal thoughts and feelings to others. Self-disclosure is allowing oneself to be seen, known, understood. Self-disclosure involves risk. Normally it is a risk worth taking. Discretion is needed, however, as suggested by Dorothy's experience above.

Self-disclosure occurs through the content of words (revealing or protective), the tone and quality of words spoken (harsh or warm), non-verbal behavior (eye contact, distance from listener, gestures, and facial expressions), and actions taken (reflecting deep love, vulnerability, or animosity, for example). Self-disclosure can take place in breadth (sharing a great deal of information about yourself, but nothing in much detail) or in depth (sharing intimate, deeply personal emotions).[7]

One book on self-disclosure refers to "The Lonely Society" to describe the fact that with urbanization, mobility, and the fast pace of life of most modern societies, self-disclosure becomes more difficult, indeed even risky.[8] Familiarity does not necessarily mean closeness. This is reflected in experiences with "familiar strangers," as described by the social psychologist, Stanley Milgram:

> For years, I have taken a commuter train to work. I noticed that there were people at my station whom I have seen for many years but never spoken to, people I came to think of as familiar strangers. I found a peculiar tension in this situation, when people treat each other as properties of the environment, rather than as individuals to deal with. It happens frequently. Yet there remains a poignancy and discomfort, particularly when there are only two of you at the station; you and someone you have seen daily but never met. A barrier has developed that is not readily broken.[9]

The "familiar stranger" phenomenon, indeed the absence of self-disclosure in general, is partly the result of a necessary decision to "screen out" most people we meet. We simply cannot give time and energy to be open in a personal way with the dozens or hundreds of people we meet each day. We would be overwhelmed.

Nor is full openness even in everyone's best interest all the time. "Plungers," who too quickly and too completely reveal themselves, often are scorned and avoided. So too are those who perpetually engage in "ego-speak" — the boosting of one's own ego by speaking only about what *we* want to talk about..."ego-speak," says one author is mental masturbation."[10]

Solitude can be golden at times. Insulating yourself from the opportunity to participate in self-disclosure sometimes is healthy and productive. According to Tillich, the theologian, solitude "is the experience of being alone, but not lonely." Henry David Thoreau once said, "I never found a companion that was so companionable as solitude."[11]

Full self-disclosure is inadvisable in certain circumstances:

— When you clearly would be rebuked or hurt.
— When revealing a thought, feeling, or intention would result in harmful reactions toward you.
— When the situation clearly calls for completion of a task rather than sharing of feelings.
— When the other person clearly is disinterested.
— When a feeling or thought is best reserved for intimate partners.

You probably can identify other situations in which concealment to some degree is appropriate.

On the other hand, a number of benefits often flow from self-disclosure.

— Expressing inner thoughts and feelings promotes self-awareness and self-understanding. By putting thoughts and feelings in words, they become clear to the sender.
— Communication becomes more complete. Intentions, background information, and associated emotions are better known.
— Emotional pressure is avoided or reduced, reducing chance of stress build-up.
— Expressing emotions promotes physical health. Unexpressed emotions block energy, get stuck in muscles and joints, help cause high blood pressure and other illnesses, perhaps even shorten the span of life.
— Expressing authentic feelings and thoughts puts the other person at ease, reducing his or her tension.
— The possibility of later depth, warmth, and honesty in a relationship increases.
— You open yourself to caring, verbal and action responses.
— You increase the chances of creative problem-solving, both by you and with others.
— You promote your own expansion of feelings, ideas, abilities.

317

In his lifelong study of self-actualizing persons, Abraham Maslow found that every individual he studied was fully open and disclosing to at least one or two other persons. Maslow concluded that the inability to be honest and revealing to at least a few others blocks growth and prevents fulfillment of potential. He recommends "when in doubt, be honest rather than not."[12]

A consistent research finding is that "self-disclosure begets self-disclosure."[13] Openness by A tends to elicit openness by B. On the other hand, a distant communication brings the same thing back. Thus, an important step to bring down unnecessary barriers both for you and for those you interact with is to be open whenever appropriate and possible. You thereby promote your own well-being and that of others around you — and you help build a social climate of support, forthrightness, mutual honesty and authenticity.

Exercise 11-7 — Monitoring Self-Disclosure

Which of the following statements best describes you?

_____ 1. I seldom share my true feelings with anyone.

_____ 2. Those with whom I work (or go to school) know little about what I'm thinking most of the time.

_____ 3. I usually feel better after expressing myself to someone I'm close to.

_____ 4. I wish I could get closer to others.

_____ 5. I wish I could open up more to others.

_____ 6. I would like to be more open to others and their feelings.

_____ 7. Being open with others usually ends up hurting me.

_____ 8. Others see me as quite honest and open.

_____ 9. My physical tension usually mounts when I hold in my feelings for very long.

_____10. My sleep is often disturbed by unexpressed bad feelings.

What can you learn from your answers?

Exercise 11-8 — Risking Self-Disclosure

During the next two days, take the following risks: express inner feelings to someone new and invite the same from someone new. What happened? What did you and the other person feel? What steps can you take to be more self-disclosing in the future? With whom? Through what specific actions of listening or talking?

Dealing With Anger

Anger is a familiar state that includes emotions, thoughts, physical arousal, and sometimes actions.[14] In Chapter 2, you read about "bound energy" resulting from arousal for physical action that remains unexpressed. Bound energy can evolve into tension, illness, emotional distress, and disorganized thinking.

Anger is a universal event, one of the most common distress feelings. How it is expressed can enormously affect whether stress is escalated or reduced.

A step toward understanding how to handle anger effectively is to recognize that it is often a secondary emotion, a cover-up for a prior, even stronger feeling that for one reason or another, we keep hidden. It can cover up each of the following, for example:

— Frustration
— Fear
— Self-doubt
— Feeling rejected and lonely
— Defensiveness
— Guilt
— Hurt

Anger usually arises in response to a perceived threat, frustration, or injustice. Perhaps the most difficult of all to allow into consciousness is anger from having been exposed, shown to be wrong, questioned, doubted. These are threats to personal worth. The greater the threat, the greater the potential anger. A key to dealing with anger as a cover-up emotion is to find out what the underlying emotion is, what is causing that feeling, and what can be done about it.

Anger commonly is aroused when we are in a zone of overload distress. It is then that we are especially short-tempered and irritable. Situations often trigger anger at these times when they would not during calmer times. When anger occurs, awareness of this fact may reduce its intensity.

Anger is best seen as a totally acceptable emotion. It is real, whether it is secondary or primary. It is primary when we are prepared to strike out because we feel we have been unjustly treated or when someone holds us back from something important. Such anger is real, but often is the result of displaced responsibility or blame. People who are prone to helplessness are angry more often than those who feel in control of their lives. Too often we have been told not to show anger under any circumstances — not even to permit it to exist in many cases. "Good girls don't get angry." "Christians should be free of anger." "It is not ladylike to get angry." The fact is everyone does get angry. "Anger energy is powerful and ignoring it will not make it go away. Often it will smolder until it bursts into flame, or dam up until it seeps out in ways that encourage illness."

As Rubin states in *The Angry Book,* many people have grown up in double-bind situations.

> *Don't hold it in — I can't stand you when you do — let it out! But when you let it out, I will hit you for being disrespectful. This damned if you do damned if you don't approach promotes severe conflict, much anxiety, great angry problems and emotional paralysis.* [15]

A number of constructive suggestions can be offered for dealing with anger in ways that minimize its unnecessary occurrence, acknowledge its existence, and allow for expression in harmless yet fruitful ways.

1. Occurrence of anger can be minimized when an attitude of patience, good humor, and tolerance is maintained. Anger is upset. Upset is natural from time to time. But is it worth being constantly or even frequently angry in the long run?

2. When anger is present, ask: What am I really feeling? Am I truly frustrated at being wronged, blocked, or misunderstood? Or is anger a cover-up for another feeling hidden beneath? If so, what is that other emotion, and how can I deal with it directly and constructively?

3. Waste no time in dealing with anger within the limits of what is appropriate. The longer it boils away, the greater the potential for physical harm and boil-over later on.

4. Ask: Is my anger partly the result of being overloaded? As pointed out earlier, anger often will partly or totally subside when this awareness is brought to the surface.

5. Get to the root of your anger. What can be changed in self, others, or the larger situation to reduce this anger and the chances that it will happen again?

6. When wanting to reduce anger, consider the following alternatives:
   — Talking it out without exploding to someone else.
   — Talking it out with whomever is the target.
   — Talking it out with myself through internal dialogue, rational or irrational.
   — Dissolving it through internal dialogue, with running, or with some other form of exercise.
   — Deny it exists and hope it will go away.
   — Dissolve it by waiting long enough.

Research at the University of Michigan suggests that blood pressure is highest among people who deny its existence or suppress it.[16] Second highest among those who explode with it, and lowest among those who talk it out with someone. I suggest a combination of exercise and talking it out probably is the healthiest of all.

7. In expressing anger to the target person use "I" rather than "you" openers.

   — "I am angry because dinner is late," rather than, "You are late again with dinner."
   — "I am upset at your failure to do your household chores this week," rather than "You failed again to fulfill your responsibilities."
   — "I feel really discouraged by your forgetting my birthday," rather than, "Well, you blew it again this year."

"You" messages set the stage for a defensive response from the listener. "I" messages lay the groundwork for understanding dialogue, and continuation of the conversation. This is a simple formula, but can work wonders for the person who is angered, as well as for the person who is the target of anger.

8. Avoid collecting anger credits for your "slush fund" of bad feelings, tense body tissue, and righteous indignation. Far better that you deal with them one at a time, piece-by-piece, immediately or soon after they arise. Otherwise, your bubble will explode or will eat away at your insides.

9. Express anger with forethought and good taste. Be rational about it. Does it really make good sense to explode at your 86-year-old father because of how he treated you when you were ten? Again, the key ethical questions are, what will the consequences be for others? And for myself? Is it moral to clear out my angry emotions in such a way that someone else clearly is hurt? Is there an alternative for reducing my anger while not inflicting harm on others? Obviously there is.

10. Avoid displaying anger at those closest to you who may be quite undeserving. A particularly common pattern is to transfer anger from job to family. Why? Greenberg suggests the following reasons:

    — They are available
    — They are safe to dump on (that is, relatively safe)
    — They won't hurt you (not in the way a boss or customer can)
    — Their personalities might be receptive to this
    — They will still love us
    — They won't reject us
    — They might understand us (if their emotional temperature is not too high)[17]

    Far better to handle work anger at its source — at work — or at least to talk it out at home and then leave it, rather than drip it out at home through poisonous darts or volcanic explosions.

11. Use techniques of giving negative feedback and assertiveness, both discussed later in this chapter, for expressing anger constructively, and for getting what you want, but not at someone else's expense.

12. Be available to your co-workers, spouse, children, and friends to talk out their anger, using techniques of active listening described earlier in this chapter. Help enlighten them about some of these principles for handling anger in the future.

13. Pick the appropriate time and place to express anger.

14. You need not feel guilty for feeling anger or for dealing straight on with it. It is a universal, completely acceptable emotion. Hurting others or unjustly blaming them for your problems, however, only adds unfairly to their distress.

Exercise 11-9 — Monitoring Your Anger

1. List several family situations in which you get angry.
   I get angry at home when:

2. List and discuss several work situations in which you get angry.
   I get angry at work when:

3. List several things about what you do or feel that makes you angry.
   I get angry at myself when:

4. List several other situations in which your anger is aroused.
   I get angry when:

Exercise 11-10 — Angry Answers

You are invited to answer the following questions from the *Wellness Workbook*. [18]

1. Messages I heard about expressing anger:

2. These things/events/people stimulate anger in me:

3. The last time I felt anger was:

4. Is it OK for me to feel angry?

5. Express it:

6. Unhealthy ways I express anger:

7. Healthy ways I express anger:

8. What I've learned about myself from these questions:

9. Share with a friend.

Exercise 11-11 — Monitoring Anger Sources and Reactions

For the next week or two, monitor situations in which your anger is aroused. Write them in your stress diary. Use the following questions as guides for your observation.

— Do any of them involve blaming others for your behavior or feelings?

— Might you have been less upset with greater patience, humor or tolerance?

— Was your baseline stress level too high to begin with?

— Exactly what did you feel emotionally and physically? At the moment? One hour later? And four hours later?

— How did you handle your anger?

— Was this a constructive or destructive response to your anger?

— Looking back, what might you have done differently in handling the anger?

Handling Negative Feedback

Among the most volatile interchanges between one person and another is giving and receiving negative feedback. If bungled, stress created by the original unhappiness is multiplied many times. Thus, an ensuing stress build-up mounts for both. The following format, can be applied at home, school, work, or in other settings.

> Assume you are under a time deadline at work. The deadline is tomorrow at noon, when you and your work team must turn in a report to management. Also assume that at 3:00 pm a member of the team has just produced a rather deficient segment which clearly needs more work and will require you as team leader staying up late tonight to revise it. You are quite angry and disappointed. This is not the first time he has come up short. Your patience is wearing thin. How can you best give negative feedback? You want to accomplish several things through this feedback: make known your own disappointment and frustration and let him know specifically what is deficient; let him know what the consequences may be for him, the team, and you; and indicate that in the future his performance must improve in specific ways.

Here is an approach developed by Steinmetz, both for you as boss in giving the negative feedback and for your subordinate in receiving it.[19]

1. Describe the situation and the deficiencies in specific and objective terms. Limit your remarks to the present, excluding, for now, the past. Give only what is directly useful and avoid overloading the recipient with unnecessary details or irrelevant points. Avoid sarcasm. Remain objective in order to minimize chances of defensiveness by the recipient. For example, "You had time available to work on this. We badly need it. It does not include these specific bits of information, which are vital to the overall report. Further, it is not written clearly."

2. Express your own feelings, using "I feel" messages. Share these feelings, rather than denying them. Avoid put-downs, attacks,

or accusations. For example, "I feel disappointed and frustrated."

3. Give the recipient a chance to respond here. If he or she agrees, you need not proceed further. An interchange with active listening both ways can be very productive.

4. Specify changes you want in specific terms. Be objective and firm. For example, "I will want such and such data by 6:00 this evening even though it may require staying overtime. Then I want to meet you at 8:00 am to go over what I have rewritten tonight."

5. Avoid being demanding, authoritarian, or patronizing. Simply be firm. "In the future, I would like you to ask if you are unclear about what is needed and to do a complete, thorough job."

6. Share your perception of the possible or likely outcome of the changes you request. Use positive terms, avoiding "you had better do it, or else" remarks. A threat of punishment muddies the waters. For example, "If you do, we all can be proud of our work, have better feelings as a team, and help out management."

A four-step format also applies in receiving negative feedback. Your goal is to focus objectively on the message being sent in order to remedy the situation through effective individual or joint problem-solving.

1. Describe the situation as you perceive it in objective and specific language.

2. Express your perception of the other person's feelings.

3. State in your own words the changes you think he or she wants.

4. State your perception of the likely consequences of the changes objectively, candidly, and specifically.

These formats must be adapted, of course, to specific people and situations. They can be effective for minimizing further negative feelings and for getting the job done well. The more these techniques are practiced and used, the easier and more natural they become.

Exercise 11-12 — Giving Negative Feedback

Think of a situation in which you gave (or wish you had given) negative feedback. Using the above format, write what you might have said below.

1.

2.

3.

4.

Exercise 11-13 — Receiving Negative Feedback

Now think of a situation in which you were given negative feedback. How might you have responded differently using this format? Write your answers.

1.

2.

3.

4.

Exercise 11-14 — Role-Playing Negative Feedback

With a cooperative partner, role-play the above steps, alternating between giving and receiving negative feedback.

Exercise 11-15 — Real Life Practice in Negative Feedback

Try the four steps described above for giving and receiving negative feedback in a real-life situation. Then answer the following.

1. Did the exchange accomplish what you had hoped?

2. What were the consequences for you? For your partner? For accomplishment of tasks? For others in the environment? Distinguish between immediate and longer-term effects.

3. What might you do or say differently next time?

4. What did you learn about yourself by using this format?

Assertiveness

Our framework of stress and stress management assumes that a stressor is perceived and appraised by the individual. Throughout this chapter, we have focused on constructive options for coping with people-stressors, active listening, appropriate self-disclosure, dealing with angry feelings, giving and receiving negative feedback. Another useful approach to coping effectively (that is, responding so you get what you want but not at others' expense) is assertiveness.

FIGURE 11-1
PASSIVE — ASSERTIVE — AGGRESSIVE TYPES[20]

Passive	Assertive	Aggressive
This person is:	This person is:	This person is:
Shy Withdrawing	Usually more extroverted	Somewhat hostile
Reluctant to assert rights and privileges	Aware of rights and privileges and uses them constructively	A vehement defender of own rights yet often violates or usurps the rights of others Unmindful of where own rights end and the violation of where other's begin
Socially inhibited	Socially productive	Socially destructive

328

Exercise 11-16 — Assertiveness Self-Assessment

Read the above chart carefully. Underline the items that describe you. Do you tend toward passivity, assertiveness, or aggressiveness? How does your behavior vary, if at all, at home, work, school, and social events?

Generally, assertiveness is desirable behavior for reducing tension in situations where there is potential build-up of resentment or anger, or when strength must be used to get what you want or to prevent someone else from imposing upon you unnecessarily. Yet we must retain choice and option. Aggressiveness is seldom called for, except perhaps in situations of physical attack or danger. Passive behavior sometimes is appropriate. Certainly, *temporary,* timely passivity represents simple good judgment in certain circumstances. Being quiet sometimes is best. Assertive behavior must be exercised with discretion and perceptiveness.

What are the specific characteristics of assertiveness? Steinmetz suggests the following:[21]

1. Eye contact: Steady, eye-to-eye contact while speaking. Not staring or glaring, but firm and unyielding.

2. Hand gestures: Use strong gestures to emphasize important points. Loses effectiveness if overdone.

3. Posture: Standing or sitting tall and straight, rather than slouching, slumping, or hiding.

4. Voice firmness: Maintaining a steady, firm volume, tone, and pace throughout, without imposing too much volume. Avoid yelling as well as weak trail-offs through drop of volume or "you-knows."

5. "I" statements: Just as with expressing disappointment, assertiveness calls for such openers as "I feel," "I want," "I need," I would appreciate." "I request." By contrast, the passive opener is "Don't you think that," while a common aggressive opener is "You should." "I" statements imply responsibility for what you are feeling and requesting.

6. Short sentences: These are clearly understood and imply firmness. Avoid long, rambling sentences that lose the listener and the potential impact of your message.

7. Pauses for feedback: Strategic breaks can both underscore what has just been said and provide an opportunity for clarifying a response.

Exercise 11-17 — Self-Monitoring Assertiveness During Next 24 Hours

Watch yourself for the next 24 hours. Enter in your stress diary what you observe about the fit between your overall pattern of behavior and the three described here. Also observe the degree to which you display each of the seven assertiveness behaviors just described.

Exercise 11-18 — Observing Others' Assertiveness

Repeat Exercise 11-17 with someone you know well. What do you see?

Exercise 11-19 — Recall Quiz

1. In your own words, what is assertiveness? Passivity? Aggressiveness?

2. What are the seven behaviors associated with assertiveness?

Exercise 11-20 — Role-Playing Assertiveness

Try role-playing more assertive behavior with a cooperative, safe partner. Create hypothetical, recalled, or anticipated situations. Reverse parts.

Exercise 11-21 — Assertiveness in Real Life

Now try to be more assertive in a real-life situation where it is timely and appropriate.

1. What did you feel?

2. How successful were you in doing what you wanted to do?

3. In getting what you wanted?

4. What were the consequences for self? Others?

5. What would you do differently next time a similar opportunity arises?

COMMUNICATION STYLE

In Chapter 1 we noted that many people are distress provokers, sometimes intentionally and with full awareness, other times quite unintentionally. In this chapter, we have reviewed a number of means whereby you can keep your own stress at a reasonable level without causing undue distress for others and while getting what you want.

Viewing your communication as a whole, do you give a preponderance of positive strokes (communication messages that add to others' self-worth or reduce tension) or negative strokes (acts that add to stress and lessen self-worth, comfort, and emotional well-being)? Of course, the communication process is never clearly one way or the other, but rather a mixture of the two. Most of us are somewhat in the middle. Yet the following principles generally are valid:

— Positive strokes prevent and reduce distress for others and, through a loop-back effect, for self.

— Negative strokes cause or add to distress for others, and, through the same loop-back effect, for self.

Karl Albrecht, in his excellent book, *Stress and the Manager,* has presented a list of positive behaviors.[22] We will re-label them "distress-provoking" and "stress-reducing."

Think of your own communication style as being either distress-provoking or stress-reducing (punishing or rewarding) for others. If those with whom you relate experience their exchanges with you as a positive, affirming to their own self-esteem, and productive for them personally, they usually will look forward to interacting with you. If they don't like the results, they will want to interact with you as little as possible. This principle provides a simple way to assess your communication skills and to identify the behaviors that cause or reduce stress for others.

Distress-Provoking (punishing) actions include:

— Monopolizing the conversation
— Interrupting
— Showing obvious disinterest
— Keeping a sour facial expression.
— Withholding customary social cues such as greetings, nods, "uh-huh," and the like.
— Throwing verbal barbs at others.
— Using nonverbal put-downs.
— Insulting or otherwise verbally abusing others.
— Speaking dogmatically; not respecting others' opinions.
— Complaining or whining excessively.
— Criticizing excessively; fault finding.
— Demanding one's own way; refusing to negotiate or compromise.

- Ridiculing others.
- Patronizing or talking down to others.
- Making others feel guilty.
- Soliciting approval from others excessively.
- Losing one's temper frequently or easily.
- Playing "games" with people; manipulating or competing in subtle ways.
- Throwing "gotcha's" at others; embarrassing or belittling others.
- Telling lies; evading honest questions; refusing to level with others.
- Overusing "should" language; pushing others with words.
- Displaying frustration frequently.
- Making aggressive demands of others.
- Diverting conversation capriciously; breaking others' train of thought.
- Disagreeing routinely.
- Restating others' ideas for them.
- Asking loaded or accusing questions.
- Overusing "why" questions.
- Breaking confidences; failing to keep important promises.
- Flattering others insincerely.
- Joking at inappropriate times.
- Bragging; showing off; talking only about self.

Stress-Reducing (rewarding) behavior includes:
- Giving others a chance to express views or share information.
- Listening attentively; hearing other person out.
- Sharing one's self with others; smiling; greeting others.
- Giving positive nonverbal messages of acceptance and respect for others.
- Praising and complimenting others sincerely.
- Expressing respect for values and opinions of others.
- Giving suggestions constructively.
- Compromising; negotiating; helping others succeed.
- Talking positively and constructively.

- Affirming feelings and needs of others.
- Treating others as equals whenever possible.
- Stating one's needs and desires honestly.
- Delaying automatic reactions; not flying off the handle easily.
- Leveling with others; sharing information and opinions openly and honestly.
- Confronting others constructively on difficult issues.
- Staying on the conversational topic until others have been heard.
- Stating agreement with others when possible.
- Questioning others openly and honestly; asking straightforward, non-loaded questions.
- Keeping the confidences of others.
- Giving one's word sparingly and keeping it.
- Joking constructively and in good humor.
- Expressing genuine interest in the other person.

Exercise 11-22 — Monitoring Your Communication Style

1. Check those items that apply to you most of the time.
2. Ask someone close to you to check which items apply to you most of the time.
3. Which communication actions would you like to decrease in the future? Increase?
4. Ask someone close to you which ones he or she would like you to increase or decrease.
5. If he or she is willing, tell that person what you would like him or her to increase or decrease for the sake of your own stress level.

OTHER CONSTRUCTIVE COPING BEHAVIOR

This chapter has focused on coping with people-stressors through effective communication. Sometimes stressors are not specific people or groups, as we saw in Chapter 4. They can be physical, a cluster of activities, an event, a personal illness or accident, and many more. Throughout the book a number of suggestions have been made which also are relevant here as we focus on your coping response toward specific stressors.

1. Which response is most appropriate to the situation and to your wants:
   — Changing the stressor?
   — Avoiding or withdrawing from the stressor?
   — Adapting to the stressor?

2. Remember to pace and space stressors whenever possible so you can stay within your zone of positive stress most of the time. The guidelines regarding Type A behavior (Chapter 7) apply here. Especially important is establishing priorities, written if necessary, among competing demands and opportunities.

3. Be aware of the need sometimes for collective group action to change or modify a stressor. Lobby groups, community special interest groups, unions, associations — all are in the business of doing just that. Join one, give it your energy, time, and money if it will help alter a stressor in your environment that can be dealt with only through collective action and that you strongly believe needs to be changed.

4. Withdrawal can be either constructive or destructive, as noted earlier in this chapter. Here are examples of withdrawal that may be constructive:
   — Leaving the scene for a while.
   — Taking a vacation, day off, or extended weekend.
   — Changing jobs, school, or classes.
   — Changing where you live.
   — Ending a romance, friendship, business relationship, marriage.

Withdrawing from the stressor may be a sound approach to coping with stress when other approaches have been tried, when the stressor cannot be changed, and when the remaining alternative is perpetual distress. But usually there are other coping responses through which you can reduce distress without leaving the stressful situation.

This chapter has included a number of practical guidelines and techniques for identifying and stopping destructive coping responses to stressors and for starting constructive coping responses. A key assumption underlying this chapter as well as others in Part II is that stressors do not cause distress. Rather, *we cause our own distress* by how we perceive, cope with, and react to those stressors. This chapter is intended to assist you in developing effective steps for coping with stressors.

Sometimes, however, distress does occur. How you handle that distress will determine whether you reduce or increase it and how long it will last. That is, your reactions to your own distress can be either adaptive (distress-reducing) or maladaptive (distress-increasing). Chapter 12 presents ideas and techniques for identifying and stopping maladaptive reactions to distress and for starting new, more constructive adaptive reactions.

REFERENCES

1. Regina S. Ryan and John W. Travis, *Wellness Workbook*. Berkeley, CA.,: Ten Speed Press, 1981, p. 181.

2. Jenny Steinmetz, *et al.*, *Managing Stress Before It Manages You.* Palo Alto, CA.: Bull Publishing Company, 1980, Chapter IV; Gerard Egan, *Interpersonal Living*. Monterey, CA.: Brooks/Cole Publishing Company, 1976, Chapter 6.

3. Modified from Steinmetz, *et al., Ibid.*

4. *Ibid.,* p. 64.

5. Ibid., p. 65.

6. V. J. Derlega and A.C. Chaikin, *Sharing Intimacy.* Englewood Cliffs, N.J.: Prentice-Hall, 1975, pp. 1-2.

7. *Ibid.,* p. 3.

8. *Ibid.,* p. 4.

9. C. Travis, "The Frozen World of the Familiar Stranger: A Conversation with Stanley Milgram," *Psychology Today,* 8, (1974), 70-80.

10. Derlega and Chaiken, *op cit.,* pp. 23-24.

11. H. D. Thoreau, *Walden.* New York: Random House, 1946.

12. Abraham Maslow, *The Farther Reaches of Human Nature.* New York: Viking, 1971, pp. 45-46.

13. Delega and Chaikin, *op cit.,* Chapter 3.

14. Theodore I. Rubin, *The Angry Book.* New York: Collier, 1969.

15. *Ibid,* p. 25.

16. *Executive Fitness Newsletter.* "How to Cut Down on Blowing Up." November 1, 1980.

17. Herbert M. Greenberg, *Coping With Job Stress.* Englewood Cliffs, N.J.: Prentice-Hall, 1980, Chapter 4.

18. Ryan and Travis, *op cit.,* p. 132.

19. Steinmetz *et al., op cit.,* Chapter VII.

20. Daniel Girdano and George Everly, *Controlling Stress and Tension.* Englewood Cliffs, N.J.: Prentice-Hall, Inc., 1979, p. 148.

21. Steinmetz, *et al.,* p. 81.

22. Karl Albrecht, *Stress and the Manager.* Englewood Cliffs, N.J.: Prentice-Hall, Inc., 1979, pp. 264-267.

CHAPTER 12

MONITORING AND MANAGING YOUR REACTIONS TO DISTRESS

The world in which we live is imperfect. We are imperfect creatures and forever shall be. The Garden of Eden went out some time back in Genesis. Hence, no one's life can ever be trouble-free. Distress is as sure to be part of human existence as eating, sleeping, paying taxes, and approaching death. Perhaps as some argue, distress will become an ever more central part of people's existence during the era of post-industrialism we are now entering.

There are, on the other hand, signs of optimism. Younger workers, for example, are less willing to suffer in mindless jobs. They expect more from work than did their fathers. Smoking is declining. The health promotion or wellness movement is rapidly gaining steam. The fitness boom is a good omen. Corporations support fitness programs for their employees. These are a few of many positive indications that, despite surrounding pressures, large numbers of people are taking care of themselves, building protection against unnecessary emotional and physical distress.

Still, the very fact of change — in the environment, in our own lives — inevitably will produce pressures under which many of us will begin to break at one time or another. In addition to all we have proposed thus far to manage stress wisely, one other key remains: to react to distress constructively so it will be reduced rather than destructively, which only worsens distress.

DELIBERATE AND SCRIPTED REACTIONS TO DISTRESS

Are your reactions to distress deliberate or scripted? If you react to distress with little awareness or deliberate choice, your response is likely to be scripted. Many children and young people use unconscious reactions to distress, copying what their parents do or did without realizing it. If you react in ways that *you* have chosen because they work and if you are aware of what you are doing, you are reacting intentionally and consciously. Unless you become aware of how you handle distress, you may be seriously limited by your lifescript — the blueprint for living discussed in Chapter 3. One way this can happen is by continually playing destructive "games" without knowing it.

Some years ago, Eric Berne wrote a book called *Games People Play,* in which he described ways in which people may keep themselves in a one-down, "not okay" position in life — an unpleasant, but familiar way of living out their lifescript.[1] Such games are ways of relating to others in which there are hidden, below-the-surface messages and "pay-offs," with one or the other person feeling bad as a result. Games played to keep yourself down include "kick me," "stupid," "ain't it awful," "yes, but," and "wooden leg." Games to keep other people down include: "Blemish," "corner," "bear trapper," and "rapo."

Games that keep oneself or others in a helpless, depressed, "crazy," or angry position represent destructive, unconscious reactions to prior distress that perpetuate banal or tragic lifescripts. Games are habit-forming, pushed on by the repetition compulsion. But they can be stopped through awareness, effort, and support from others. It is possible to gradually cease being a prisoner of script-supporting games and to move toward autonomy, authenticity, and constructive reactions to distress.

ADAPTIVE AND MALADAPTIVE REACTIONS TO DISTRESS

Very simply, adaptive reactions lessen distress for self, without adding to distress for others. Maladaptive responses to distress increase tension for self and/or others, in the long-run if not immediately. Examples of each are discussed throughout this chapter.

Targets of Reactions to Distress

In seeking to reduce distress, you can focus mainly on the source, that is, the stressors, or on your distress itself. One or the other may be the more adaptive or constructive, depending on the situation. At other times, both may be called for simultaneously. For example, to reduce work-related distress, you may need to try to improve the communication network at work, as well as to share your own frustrations with a close friend.

Combining the adaptive and maladaptive options with these two targets of reaction to distress, we have the four possibilities illustrated in Figure 12-1.

FIGURE 12-1
REACTIONS TO DISTRESS

		TARGET OF REACTION	
		Stressor	Own Distress
TYPE OF REACTION	Adaptive	Put communications problem on agenda for next meeting	Share frustrations with friend
	Maladaptive	Blow up at boss	Drink frustrations away

Extinguishing Maladaptive Reactions to Distress

Handling mental or physical distress maladaptively is to try to reduce it in ways that make it worse for self or others, in the long-run, if not the short-run. A great proportion of stress problems seen by physicians, psychologists, and stress consultants are not from reactions to original stressors, but the outcomes of escalation into something much worse through maladaptive responses to the original stress.

Just as one must identify and change destructive ways of coping with original stressors, so must we see and modify our maladaptive reactions to later distresses. Let us examine, then, some of these maladaptive reactions to distress, what effects they have, and how they can be reduced or extinguished. In each case, the key to stopping is substituting constructive alternatives — which usually are easier in any event.

Alcohol Abuse

One recent estimate places the cost of alcoholism to American society at about 15 billion dollars per year.[1] Ten billion dollars of that is for lost work time, two billion dollars for health and welfare costs, three billion dollars in property damage, medical expenses, workmen's compensation, and insurance. More males than females are alcoholics, although the gap is narrowing.

The incidence of teenage drinking is rising, and a progressive drop in age of first drink is appearing. Alcohol out-polls marijuana 79 to 38 percent in popularity in one recent survey.[2] While most youngsters drink "to relax" and "to feel better about themselves." estimates range from 1.3 to 3.3 million preteens and teenagers with drinking problems. As the ultimate destructive method of handling stress, alcohol-related traffic accidents kill nearly 8,000 adolescents and maim another 39,000 each year.[3]

Smoking

The bottom line is that smoking will increase chances of dying prematurely from heart attack, lung cancer, emphysema or bronchitis, pneumonia, or stroke. Roglieri estimates the increased odds of death from each of these causes increased as follows, compared with non-smokers.[5]

	1-1½ packs per day	2 packs or more per day
Heart Attack	80 percent	220 percent
Lung Cancer	480 percent	500 percent
Bronchitis/ Emphysema	70 percent	210 percent
Pneumonia	300 percent	300 percent
Stroke	50 percent	50 percent

But back to quality of life. That smoking reduces stress is a cruel illusion. Smoking decreases energy level for coping with daily hassles. By coating the lungs with tar and nicotine surrounding red cells with carbon monoxide, by making it more difficult for them to transport oxygen, and by accelerating heart rate, smoking means less ability to take in, circulate, and use oxygen — hence a greater struggle to do the same as a non-smoker can do more easily, other things equal.

Smokers may feel a lessening of tension from drawing that first smoke after a 20- or 40-minute break from smoking. But ironically, this is a slight reduction of tension caused by a mini-withdrawal crisis from going 20 to 40 minutes without a cigarette. The cigarette relieves tension caused by the very addiction to smoking. Smoking not only shortens life, decreases coping ability through less energy, and creates tension, it also decreases life chances and immediate discomfort for those who must inhale used smoke. It is expensive, and a poor example for children. Smoking is a maladaptive response to distress of the worst kind.

The American Cancer Society, The American Lung Association, The Seventh Day Adventist Church, and other groups now conduct very effective smoking cessation programs. Recent evidence suggests that stopping cold-turkey may be the most effective way. Social support from others helps make the struggle easier.

Drugs

Prescribed medications sometimes are temporarily useful and appropriate in reducing stress, as we will explain later in this chapter. Unfortunately, the "pill for every ill" approach is widely embedded in the popular mind and in medical practice.

Three groups of psycho-active substances are widely used to relieve tension.

— Depressants — tranquilizers, barbiturates, alcohol, etc.

— Stimulants — caffeine, amphetamines, etc.

— Distortants — LSD, mescaline, marijuana, etc.

In the short-run, all these may relieve distress by one means or another. However, in the long-run, they lose their effectiveness because of increased tolerance to the drug, because the stress triggers remain the same, because the person's ability to cope with the stressors remains undeveloped, or some combination of these reasons. The diminished capacity to cope through drug-induced numbness or psychological distortion may increase tension later. Psychological or physical dependency becomes worse and tension increases in the long-run. Yet illegal drug use continues to mount. And so does reliance by patients on prescribed stress-related medications. Valium alone is consumed to the tune of 3.2 billion pills per year in the U.S. — a 25 million dollar business in itself. Except for short-run, special situations, medications are a nonproductive, ineffective substitute for long-term relief of distress. Alternatives suggested in this book are far better.

Overeating

Curiously, calorie consumption per person in the U.S. has decreased since 1900, yet the percentage of the population at least 20 percent overweight has increased dramatically. This has been caused largely by decreasing physical activity throughout the population, as we have suburbanized, industrialized, mechanized, and "automobilized." An increased percentage of fat in our diets has contributed to a lesser extent. So too, no doubt, has been the tendency to eat in response to stress — especially when food is high in sugar or fat.

Eating to "relieve" tension often is learned in childhood. Mother feeds child at any sign of distress. As a consequence, the child may never learn to distinguish between hunger and emotions such as fear, anxiety,

343

and anger. Any state of arousal is experienced as hunger. In other cases, the child learns by parent example that a quick way to deal with tension is to stuff it, hide it, not let it out, by overeating.

I have found that about half of those I ask in workshops about appetite during stress report an increase, the other half a decrease. For many, it depends on the type of stress: overeating (often through hurried stuffing) during anger or irritation, but losing appetite during worry or apprehension, or vice versa.

Overeating is a maladaptive response to distress for several reasons:

— It often evokes guilt.
— It leaves the stress emotion not faced directly.
— It ignores the distress-producing situation.
— It adds weight. More weight means less energy. More weight often erodes self-liking.

Finding suitable substances for eating binges or chronic overeating in response to stress is vital. Regular aerobic exercise is perhaps the best alternative of all, because it will reduce inches and pounds at the same time that it helps relieve physical and emotional tension.

Escapism

Just as in coping with original stressors, escapism through T.V., flight, drugs, books, or fantasy, can be highly destructive. The stress response is likely to remain elevated, the distress emotion denied, the stress triggers unchanged. While temporary, intelligently used withdrawal may be constructive, escapism as a habit is potentially dangerous, both for self and others.

Spending Sprees

Often part of a manic-type response to tension, this can be devastating in its consequences. Like escapism, it is actually a form of evasion of true stress emotions and the original situation.

Physical and Verbal Abuse

Too often personal distress does not remain personal. Rather it is transferred to others in the form of physical and verbal abuse. Tragically, we seem to take out our frustrations on those closest to us — especially our spouses, lovers and children. Recent studies show a surprisingly high percentage of college students are involved in abusive love relationships. Most murders are inflicted on friends or family members. The incidence of wife beating and child abuse are among the most destructive of all reactions to our own distress.

Blaming Others

By blaming others, one can escape responsibility both for being distressed and for doing anything about it.

Overworking

Another form of deflection is overworking. Digging in harder sometimes is a way to reduce distress. Often, however, it is a temporary palliative, ultimately multiplying problems for health, frame of mind, and family.

Denial

The subculture of masculinity is especially prone to teach boys and men: "keep moving," "if you don't think about it, it will go away," "be tough," "boys don't cry," and above all "maintain an image of strength."[6] Temporary denial may be useful for seeing a difficult event or period through, but not when it is extended for very long. The result for both men and women who use this response to stress for extended periods is internal wear and tear until relationships and performances are seriously affected, emotional disturbances become extreme, or the body breaks.

Catastrophizing

In Chapter 9 we pointed out that mentally "making a mountain out of a molehill" can directly add to a stress build-up already started by other stressors. In essence, the stress response itself becomes a new stressor. This is a very common maladaptive reaction to stress which needs to be extinguished. One approach is to ask, what is the worst possible outcome of this situation? Usually, you will find you could live even with that outcome.

Martyrdom

Unfortunately, many people are habituated to distress — so addicted that they go out of their way to find it. This happens not out of deliberate choice, but because misery and pain are so familiar, the person seems to need his or her daily dose. The repetition compulsion overpowers the drive toward growth.

Self-created distress is perpetuated by rackets or games. Rackets are what people do inside their heads to keep themselves miserable — angry, anxious, or afraid. Games refer to interpersonal exchanges people use to make themselves or others feel bad. A "kick-me" game-player handles distress by encouraging others to make him feel useless or incompetent. A "stupid" player blunders again and again in order to be constantly reminded by others how inept or dependent he is.

Strange as it may seem, many people who have a history of distress go to great lengths to cope with their distress by creating more of it — thereby playing out their life script as a loser. This often is the tragic story of the alcoholic, the heroin addict, the habitual criminal, the psychotic. Changing this pattern requires enormous courage, awareness, and support. Most of all it requires overcoming the immense inertia of the repetition compulsion.

Except when very stressful circumstances cannot be changed or when temporary distress is self-chosen for a good reason (like preparing for a concert performance), the approach of simply living with distress is unacceptable to people who seek good health and self-development. There usually is a better way.

Lethal Effects of Maladaptive Responses to Distress

These, then, are illustrative of maladaptive responses to distress. Focusing on death, the ultimate distressful side-effect of maladaptive coping responses, Roglieri estimates that through the effects of overeating, depression (which he takes to be a type of coping rather than a distress symptom), smoking, heavy drinking, and high blood pressure, about five or six of every 1,000 white males aged 40-45 will die an early death directly as a result of "mismanagement of stress."[7] This does not include, of course, the contribution of the original stress itself to various causes of death, such as heart attacks or cancer. Roglieri argues that you are responding inappropriately to your distress if:

1. You light up a cigarette whenever challenged by a person, event, or situation.
2. You take a drink in response to, or in anticipation of, a stressful event.
3. You put your heart into your driving by speeding or driving aggressively.
4. You use food to calm yourself down.

5. You feel your heart beating rapidly, or your heart pounding when frustrated (indicating high blood pressure).

6. You use sleeping pills or tranquilizers frequently.

7. You become depressed (loss of appetite, loss of sleep, loss of libido).[8]

Roglieri concludes, "because prolonged dependence on these inappropriate mechanisms for dealing with stress leads to a lifestyle that increases your risk or premature death and disability, these habits have been referred to as 'slow motion suicide.' "[9] Short of that, these and other maladaptive responses to distress lessen the *quality* of life for others if not oneself.

Exercise 12-1 — Monitoring Your Reactions To Distress

During the past six months, how often have you used each of the following methods of trying to reduce your physical and emotional tension — Never, Rarely, Sometimes, or Often?

_____ 1. Drink alcoholic beverages

_____ 2. Smoke

_____ 3. Take a tranquilizer, sleeping pill, or other prescribed medication

_____ 4. Take aspirin

_____ 5. Take an over-the-counter relaxant

_____ 6. Drink coffee, cola, or tea

_____ 7. Eat

_____ 8. Yell, hurt, or otherwise take it out on someone else.

_____ 9. Forget about it and keep going

_____ 10. Use T.V., books, or something else to "escape" for awhile

_____ 11. Take a leisurely walk

_____ 12. Grin and bear it

_____ 13. Redefine the situation more positively in your mind

_____ 14. Change your approach to the person or stressor

_____ 15. Exercise

_____ 16. Do deep relaxation

_____ 17. Do a breathing or muscle relaxation technique

_____ 18. Talk it over with somebody

_____ 19. Pray

_____ 20. Use humor

_____ 21. Take a day off or a vacation

_____ 22. Other_____

_____ 23. Other_____

Exercise 12-2 — Reactions To Distress During Next Week

During the next week, watch yourself and others close to you.

1. Observe which of the above reactions to distress are used by you or others.

2. With what effects?

3. What constructive alternatives might have been used?

CONSTRUCTIVE RESPONSES TO DISTRESS

Assuming the individual is aware that something is wrong — mental or physical pain, discomfort or other signs of distress — what are his or her adaptive or constructive options? In suggesting constructive responses to stress, we draw together guidelines and methods already presented in previous chapters. Without being overly mechanical about it, consider the following possibilities.

First, be fully aware of stress signals, without fixation or hypochondriasis. What message do they tell me, if any, about disharmony in my life.

Second, what stress triggers have contributed to my distress? A single stressor? A cluster? Current or past? Internal or external?

Third, then consider the following options:

Changing stressor. Should I try to change the stressor? Can I do so through individual acts of my own? Through group or collective action? What are the gains and costs? What are likely outcomes and side-effects for me and others? My options include:

— pacing myself and my stressors better

— spacing my life changes better

— increasing my stress level if bored

— seeking to change a specific situation

— changing a physical stressor

— organizing time better

— tempering my own perfectionism or hurry sickness.

348

Adapting to stressor. Should I adapt to the stressor, but find new ways of lowering my distress? Some of these might be:

1. Change my perception of the stressor. For example:
   — alter irrational beliefs
   — take it less seriously
   — turn the "threat" into an opportunity
   — see this person or event as temporarily bearable
   — be okay no matter what.

2. Use new and better methods of controlling my emotional and physical response in this situation:
   — breathing methods
   — muscle relaxation methods
   — mental methods

3. Change how I act towards the stressor:
   — use active listening
   — be more assertive
   — be more self-disclosing
   — deal with my anger and resentment more effectively
   — give and receive negative feedback better
   — use a communication style that is less distressing for others
   — take more (or less) risks

4. Maintain a better lifestyle buffer to add to my ongoing protection:
   — exercise regularly
   — deep relaxation
   — eat well
   — use my social support network, especially those closest to me
   — strengthen my personal anchorages, especially my internal sense of meaning, value, and direction

5. Be careful to avoid destructive ways of handling my distress that simply make it worse:

   — alcohol or drug abuse

   — smoking

   — overeating

   — dumping on or abusing others

   — escapism

   — spending sprees

   — blaming others

Withdrawing from or avoiding the stressor. Should I withdraw from or avoid the stressor altogether? Can I? What are the gains and costs? Are all other options exhausted?

These then are a number of options. Through a patient process of rational appraisal and action, you will be able to increasingly break out of your "stuckness" and handle distress constructively. Distress inevitably will occur. If you can reduce or shorten it, rather than intensify or lengthen it, you will have taken important steps toward wellness productivity, and satisfaction for yourself and others as well.

ADDITIONAL COMMENTS

Below are several comments about specific methods and problems in constructive handling of distress.

Medications

Most stress experts believe medications are over-prescribed and over-used. Yet there are four conditions when they may be called for:

1. To reduce intense pain. Certainly medications are called for in cases of terminal cancer, post-surgery, or accident trauma, intense headaches, and other intensely painful stress-induced pain.

2. When a temporary crisis interferes with ability to carry on with daily life. A prescribed relaxant may help you to continue to function until the circumstances are resolved by lowering your anxiety level, raising your mood in times of depression, or helping you sleep.

3. Chronic long-term disturbances such as schizophrenia, hypertension, or manic depression may call for long-term maintenance on medication.

4. When life is threatened by elevated stress. For example, if a heart patient has anxiety-induced arrhythmias which could cause cardiac arrest, tranquilizers certainly may be called for.

After reviewing available literature on sleeping patterns, the National Academy of Medicine Institute of Sciences recently concluded that rarely, if ever, should sleeping pills be prescribed for longer than two to four weeks.[10] Similarly, other medications usually should be viewed as temporary treatment while attempts are made to find long-term coping and lifestyle buffer methods.

Solitude

When was the last time you were away by yourself, truly alone, for 24 hours? Forty-eight hours? A week? Ever? We are in almost constant contact with others — and need to be for emotional and practical reasons. Yet we also can benefit from being alone from time to time, perhaps routinely each year for a few days, perhaps occasionally to remove ourselves from stressful situations. As I write this, I am in a mountain cabin, truly alone and have been for many days. The experience is exhilarating — the opportunity to focus, rest, renew my spirit, appreciate the environment, experience simplicity. For more on solitude in modern life, read Anne Morrow Lindburgh's *Gifts From the Sea.*[11] This is a beautiful, inspiring personal statement about the beauty of solitude.

Music

Music can have a variety of effects: arousal, warmth, sexuality, playfulness. Music can create a sense of structure about you, it can rekindle nostalgia, it can create moods, and memories. It can stir you to action, add to your fear, make you angry or mournful, kindle religious sentiments, lower tensions, slow you down. Clearly, music can do many things, mentally and physically. People differ widely in musical tastes, and each person varies from time to time. Thoughtfully chosen music can indeed be restful, relaxing, renewing. Find which kind works for you for specific occasions. Try to disregard what your particular social group thinks you should like. Listen to your own body and spirit.

Play

George Sheehan, the runner-doctor-author, has stated that man is animal, child, scholar, and saint.[12] Perhaps it would be more accurate to say man is *potentially* all of these. For too often an imbalance is reached where man the animal and man the child are lost in the quest for money

351

and status. Play is part of a good balance. Whether through active games, dance, running, frisbee, cards, pranks, parties, or practical jokes, play can be enormously valuable in dealing with periods of distress — and in reducing chances of its occurrence in the first place.

Reflect on your answer to question 11 in the Quality of Life Index in Chapter 6. (How much fun and playfulness are you having?) How much time are you taking for your own playful self? What would you most like to do during the next two weeks that lift your morale and provide a fun diversion? If you have fallen prey to the trap of all work-no play, see what specific steps you can take to bring a better balance back into your life.

During periods of overload, trauma, or depression, play seems far away. Yet it can be created, rediscovered. One of the gifts children give to adults is to stimulate us to play every now and then. Try it.

Prayer

For centuries, prayer has been used to cope with tension. Prayer perhaps can be effective. Repetition of a verse as a focus of meditation can be relaxing. In fact, the relaxation response can be produced just as during secular methods of meditation. The time away to pray can lower activity level and anxiety. Prayer can increase hope and optimism. It can bring practical solutions. It can help tune in to one's "inner voice" which can be a source of enlightenment and direction. All these benefits can occur whatever one assumes about divine intervention — which may be the most important benefit of all.

Certainly, the belief in divine guidance and solace helps create a positive self-fulfilling prophecy. Unfortunately, the religious pathway sometimes leads to dependency and escape from personal responsibility for managing stress. Yet managing stress wisely through awareness of self-direction is entirely consistent with religious belief and practice. After all, God helps these who help themselves.

Intimacy

Unfortunately, marriage or courtship can be terribly destructive, adding to rather than lessening distress during difficult periods. Yet there is perhaps no more powerful antidote to weariness, tension, upset or depression than the authentic touching of two human spirits at the level of true intimacy. Something magical can happen which words fail to convey. Spirits rekindle, barriers come down, true emotion emerges from its submerged place, reassurance is given, distress lessens.

Massage

Massage can be beneficial in response to tension in a number of ways as Jane Madders explains:

> *Massage helps muscles relax. Physiological massage stimulates the flow of blood and improves the muscle tone. It assists in a clearing away of waste products, reduces muscle tension, and its assorted pain. It does far more than this, however. During massage, there is a subtle calming down of the whole body, a reduction of anxiety, a feeling of trust develops enabling the receiver to feel rather than to think. It offers recuperative rest from the turbulence of stress.* [13]

Learning to offer massage to one's partner is a true gift. Receiving massage is to receive a noble gift of love.

Massage for infants can promote bonding, as well as relieve tension in the child. My Center now conducts training programs for new parents in how to massage infants carefully and effectively. Vimala Schneider, author of *Infant Massage,* trained our instructor, Audrey Downes, in the same methods she is teaching other parents and instructors across the country. [14]

A number of different massage techniques for adults are available from professionals in most medium-sized and larger cities: chiropractic, accupressure, Rolfing, the Alexander technique, reflexology, Touch for Health, and more. Taking a class or receiving individual treatments can be most useful, both for immediate stress-reduction and to learn techniques for use at home.

Professional Assistance

This book is based on the principle of personal responsibility for one's health and stress control. In the past, far too much reliance has been placed on one or another professional: the doctor, the chiropractor, the minister, the psychologist, the marriage counselor, the social worker. The techniques presented throughout this book can be learned and used at home, using your own good judgement and willpower. Certain circumstances can be identified, however, when professional assistance definitely is called for, including, for example:

— To learn more about specific stress control methods such as aerobic exercise, meditation, massage, time management, and active listening.

— To express frustrations, worries, plans, and the like to an objective trained listener.
— To jointly problem-solve on a specific problem.
— To trace under careful guidance the present or past roots of a specific emotional or practical problem in order to leave or solve it.
— To receive a massage or other physical treatment.
— To receive inspiration to do something on your own.
— To receive group support for lifestyle change.

Hobbies

Favorite recreational activities such as gardening, woodworking, golf, backpacking, fishing, hunting, rock collecting, birdwatching, watching professional basketball on TV — all can help prevent or reduce distress in several ways:

— Diversion — getting away from the stressor
— Solitude
— Companionship
— Enhancement of self-worth
— Play
— Appreciation of the minor nature of your immediate problem within the larger picture

Handling Depression

As we saw in Chapter 3, depression is mental, physical, and behavioral. Recent studies indicate that physical exercise, especially running, is among the most effective antidotes to reducing and preventing depression.[15]

Exercise 12-3 — Reaction To Job-Related Distress

In his book, *The Stress Check,* Cooper identifies a number of maladaptive alternatives open to employees for dealing with stressors that produce unwanted distress.[16]

Stressor	Adaptive Response	Maladaptive Response
1. Overworked	1. Delegates work.	1. Accepts overload as unavoidable resulting in deterioration of performance.
2. Not aware of a company	2. Learns what policy is.	2. Guesses incorrectly and performs inappropriately.
3. Poor working relationship	3. Confronts issue and negotiates better relationship.	3. Attacks colleague indirectly through third person.
4. Under promotion	4. Leaves organization.	4. Loses confidence and becomes convinced of own inadequacy.
5. Company vs family	5. Takes a holiday.	5. Blames company for family problems.
6. Role ambiguity	6. Seeks clarification.	6. Withdraws from some aspect of work role.

The adaptive responses tackle the basic issue head on, thereby de-escalating stress. Unnecessary stress build-up is avoided. To check on your own stress responses:

1. Add other work-related stressors you have faced recently and list adaptive responses you have or might have used.
2. Have you observed yourself or others use one or more of the above maladaptive reactions? With what consequences for self and others? What constructive alternatives might you have used?
3. Develop a role-playing situation in which a stressful situation is created. Do the players adopt destructive or constructive alternatives?

Stress is an individual experience. Yet stress must be seen within the person's social and physical environment. In Chapter 13, therefore, we will focus on monitoring and managing the context of stress.

REFERENCES

1. Eric Berne, *Games People Play.* New York: Grove Press, 1964.

2. Karl Albrecht, *Stress and The Manager.* Englewood Cliffs, N.J.: Prentice-Hall Inc., 1979, p. 44.

3. John L Roglieri, *Odds on Your Life.* New York, Seaview Books, 1980, p. 94.

4. *Ibid.*

5. *Ibid,* p. 81.

6. Herb Goldberg, *The Hazards of Being Male.* New York: Signet, 1976.

7. Roglieri, *op cit.,* p. 197.

8. *Ibid,* p. 201.

9. *Ibid,* p. 202.

10. *Ibid,* p. 210.

11. Anne Morrow Lindbergh, *Gifts From The Sea.* Westminster, Maryland, Random, 1978.

12. George Sheehan, *Running and Being.* New York: Simon and Schuster, 1978.

13. Jane Madders, *Stress and Relaxation.* New York: Arco Publishing Company, 1979.

14. Vimala Schneider, *Infant Massage.* New York: Bantam Books, 1982. For further information about infant massage, including training programs for parents and instructors, write to: Audrey Downes, R.N., Infant Massage Programs, Stress and Health Center, Fifth Avenue and The Esplanade, N.T. Enloe Memorial Hospital, Chico, CA 95926.

15. T. Kostrubala, *The Joy of Running.* New York: J.B. Lippincott, Co., 1976; John H. Greist, *et al.,* "Running Through Your Mind," in Michael H. Sachs and Michael L. Sacks, editors, *Psychology of Running.* Champaign, Ill.: Human Kinetics Publishers, Inc., 1981, p. 5-31; John H. Greist, *et al.,* "Running As Treatment of Depression," *Comprehensive Psychiatry,* 1979, *20,* pp 41-54.

16. Cary L. Cooper, *The Stress Check.* Englewood Cliffs, N.J., Prentice-Hall, Inc., 1981, pp. 153-154.

CHAPTER 13

MONITORING AND MANAGING THE CONTEXT OF STRESS

Our primary focus until now has been on how you can better manage stress in your life. This single-person approach has been used on the assumption that, regardless of how you were raised or what happens around you, you usually can learn to keep stress from turning into distress and to react to distress, when it does occur, constructively. You, and everyone else, must manage stress wisely as individuals — no matter what others do, how badly you have been treated in the past, or how unfair the world around you seems.

Yet you do not experience stress and distress alone. You are vitally affected by the same social and historical forces that affect others in similar ways. Stress and distress are *patterned*. Many adults, for instance, experience heart attacks partly in response to the pressures of an accelerating, fast-paced society. Many youth become alienated and delinquent in part because of poor schools, limited job opportunities, and adult crime in their neighborhood.

If distress is to be minimized throughout American society, not only must individuals manage their own stress wisely, but social approaches to stress reduction must be followed.

SOCIAL APPROACHES TO STRESS MANAGEMENT: GROUP EFFORTS TO REDUCE SOCIAL FORCES WHICH CREATE STRESS AND DISTRESS, AND TO ASSIST PEOPLE IN DISTRESS

Social approaches can reduce harmful stress by:

Reducing contextual pressures which create distress (e.g., controlling neighborhood crime, improving schools, doing away with forced retirement, reducing chronic overload in the workplace, reducing child abuse).

Assisting individuals already in distress (e.g., through caring friendships, sensitive parenting, family counseling services, youth crisis centers, suicide prevention centers, emergency financial aid programs for senior citizens, halfway houses for people leaving mental hospitals).

MANAGING STRESS THROUGH THE FAMILY

The family can help children to learn about stress, to live so that stress plays a positive role in their lives, and to establish good stress-control habits for adulthood. If families can become more effective in teaching children to handle stress effectively, many instances of painful distress later in life may be avoided. Better stress management must begin in the early years of life — and the family is where the first, and sometimes the strongest, habits form.[1]

1. *Parents must understand stress and promote awareness of stress in their children.* Effective parenting depends on awareness of the nature, causes, and effects of stress and methods for its control — in parent and child. If children and young people learn more about stress, they also will be able to apply this understanding later as adults. Most people who are now parents need to learn more. Most of the ideas discussed in this book can be fully understood by 10 or 12 year olds if explained and applied in the normal course of family living.

2. *It is important for parents to provide unconditional love that in turn will contribute to positive self-esteem.* Many of the steps suggested in earlier chapters for managing stress wisely are based on self-control and conscious choice, which themselves depend on self-esteem. Self-esteem develops naturally when children are loved, not for what they do, but for who they are.

3. *Security and stability must be provided within the family.* No matter what else changes, no matter what the personal stresses, the child must sense that parents are there and that they care. Children also need a good deal of routine and predictability in their daily lives. Maintaining this climate is difficult enough in a rapidly-moving society in which family members often are involved in many activities outside the home. It becomes more difficult when families are troubled and go through divorce. The single parent often faces an even greater challenge.

4. *It is important to teach children to take responsibilities for their own actions.* In this way, they are more likely to grow into adulthood already able to choose wisely and used to taking control of events. They are less likely to grow up habitually helpless or overly dependent on others.

5. *Parents must promote early value clarification and choice — what is important, unimportant, desirable, and undesirable, valuable and not valuable.* Children and young people need to know what they believe

in — through their own thoughtful choices — as early as possible. This does not require a "hands-off" approach by parents. Controls and limits are important. But where the child's own welfare and the welfare of others are not at stake, promotion of the child's independent awareness and moral choice will help develop internal guidelines for action. In this way, the child will become self-directed and less like a paper boat on the stormy seas of change, option, an pressures.

6. *Parents should set an example by adopting a pace of life that is within their own comfort zone.* Children learn more from what they see than from what they hear. Parents who are perpetually either bored or overloaded are likely to raise children in the same mold.

7. *Parents should set examples of good health and fitness and constructive coping responses to distress.* The most important means by which parents can aid children in developing a good stress buffer and constructive coping responses is to practice sound habits themselves. It is vital for young people — before they marry and have children — to become aware of stress and to develop sound habits of stress management.

8. *To enhance family security, every family should be assured a guaranteed annual income — through paid work in private or public sectors or through family assistance grants; and discrimination in housing, education, and employment must be reduced.* Millions of children, youth, and parents encounter unnecessary distress because of poverty or discrimination and the family problems they cause. A nation genuinely committed to the "life, liberty and pursuit of happiness" among all its citizens must do everything it can, publicly and privately, to reduce discrimination and to promote economic security of families as a foundation for stress reduction.

MANAGING STRESS THROUGH THE SCHOOL

The school is the second major influence on children and youth. And the school, like the family, can minimize pressures toward distress and teach students how to deal with stress.

1. *Schools should provide more "affective" learning — that is, learning about emotions, relationships, and stress.* These topics in turn should be related to larger social influences. For example, students need to understand that many "mental health" problems are really stress-related and that they are caused partly by rapid social change. Affective

361

education can best be carried out through experiential learning. Students learn more easily if they can apply ideas to daily life or if actual life situations are simulated in the classroom through role-playing[2]. This type of learning should begin in the elementary years.

2. *The learning process must be designed to require high standards and offer enjoyment for more students.* Much of the distress experienced by young people is caused by oppressive, irrelevant, excessively standardized schooling. Research has shown that this is especially true for students who are not headed for college. Schools must recognize individual differences, provide for varied options along the way, be accompanied by reasonable rules and enforcement, offer many opportunities for involvement, — and be enjoyable[3]. Education must foster a positive sense of self-worth, as well as respect for others, among all who attend school. At the same time, schools should teach basic skills of thinking and communicating so that students will not experience unnecessary distress later in life because of poor preparation.

3. *Schools can reduce youthful distress by responding to deviant students in more positive ways.* Too often the feelings of anger, despair, and hopelessness among marginal and troublesome students are exaggerated by the way in which the school responds to deviants[4]. Too often the school emphasizes humiliation and exclusion rather than genuine concern and individualized handling of deviant cases. Often, substantial stress is created, setting in motion a vicious progression: rebellion, alienation, withdrawal, despair, dropping out, unemployment, and crime.

4. *Schools should enhance students' self-worth by offering varied opportunities for success.* Handling stress wisely, as we have seen, depends partly on a sense of control over events, which in turn is based upon self-confidence. Self-confidence can be fostered by providing every student with meaningful experiences he or she can master. Positive reinforcement from others builds self-esteem. This is one of the most important benefits of a wide-ranging extracurricular activity program, as well as community-related internships or field experiences[5].

5. *Learning should emphasize preparation for living in the world of today — and tomorrow.* Schools too often prepare youth for yesterday's world. And, as Toffler notes, "It is no longer sufficient for Johnny to understand the past. It is not even enough for him to understand the present, for the here-and-now environment will soon vanish." In his chapter, "Education in the Future Tense," Toffler provides many concrete examples of how schooling can be more future-oriented[6]. Included

are steps for emphasizing basic skills, for updating rapidly changing information, for relating to others in a fast-paced world, and for making wise decisions in a world filled with overchoice. Also needed are entirely new, creative alternative schools.

MANAGING STRESS IN THE WORKPLACE

Substantial distress often arises in the work setting — from oppressive supervision, higher worker turnover, meaningless routines, social isolation, and chronic overload.[7] A humane work setting should afford opportunities for creative expression and self-development and it should contribute to the physical and mental health of people who work there. A number of ways in which work organizations can minimize unnecessary distress and maximize self-development and good health can be listed:

1. The work organization should be attractive enough so that satisfaction is high and turnover low.

2. Role expectation in the work setting should be as clear and congruent as possible to minimize role conflict and role ambiguity.

3. Work should involve neither too much routine nor chronic overload.

4. A balance between continuity and change should be sought. While self-renewing change is needed in the workplace, such change must not occur at a pace so fast that it produces distress.

5. Supervisors and managers should provide continuing support and encouragement to their employees. Similarly, they should encourage the formation of cohesive, supportive work-groups among co-workers, or blue-collar workers such as carpenters, assembly-line workers, or auto repairmen.

6. To the degree possible, every person should be given maximum flexibility of work at the pace and manner that will contribute to good health, satisfaction, and self-expression.

7. Opportunities should exist for regular involvement of all employees in decisions affecting them in the workplace.

8. Responsible supervisors should be alert to work-related stress levels in the organization.

9. Guidance and supportive services should be provided to employees in distress.

10. Work organizations should provide opportunities to learn more about stress and distress, especially as these relate to work, and to par-

ticipate in physical fitness activities that contribute to health. Such opportunities can be provided within the workplace or in cooperation with outside community service agencies.

MANAGING STRESS IN THE COMMUNITY

Even the best family or school can do little to reduce stress if the youth who passes through them enters a community filled with strain, limited opportunity, and limited support for its residents. In a number of ways, the community can play a constructive part in minimizing stress, even in a fast-moving world.

1. *Communities must preserve the neighborhood, promote stability, and foster a sense of unity among residents.* Social anchorage is vital. So are mutual support and a lasting attachment to place and neighbors. These elements of good community life are constantly threatened by geographic mobility and perpetual change[8]. Programs and activities to support a genuine sense of community are most important.

2. *The community must provide programs for stress-ridden residents.* A good community is one that cares, and shows that it does, both by promoting person-to-person interactions and by meeting the special stress-related needs that cannot be met by individuals or their families. The latter includes, for example, family and individual counseling services, aid for senior citizens, youth crisis centers, child abuse programs, emergency housing services, and "re-integration aid" to those leaving mental hospitals and prisons.

3. *The community should provide varied opportunities for youth to become involved in constructive and meaningful roles.* For the past several decades, young people have spent most of their time in school. Relatively few part-time or summer job opportunities exist, and they are becoming fewer. Years ago, young people worked in the family fields, market, or shop. They had a sense of competency, belonging and usefulness. Now, most youth — especially those in the inner city — are uninvolved in meaningful activities and roles, because most of these have disappeared. Fortunately, many communities now are recognizing this need and are creating work — and school-related opportunities for young people, as well as opportunities for involvement in decision-making[9].

4. *Each community must carefully examine its rate of growth and, if it is too fast, slow it down.* Americans seem to be addicted to the idea that progress equals growth — growth in numbers of people, space, prof-

it, standard of living. There are two severe problems with this conception. We are rapidly running out of energy. And fast community growth inevitably means perpetual change. Rapid change means high stress for large numbers of people. Small alternative communities can play a useful role in illustrating stability, simplicity, neighborliness, and low energy use.

5. *Each community must find ways of integrating its senior citizens into the mainstream of productive, socially useful living.* American's way of handling the elderly is tragic: Out of sight, out of mind — but not really. The suffering of the elderly is great — in nursing homes, cheap hotels, isolated apartments, even next door. For many retirees, there is too little to do, too few who care, too little money, little reason to hope. The fundamental reason for this sad circumstance is that we isolate the elderly and exclude them from full participation. We must find ways of reducing their distress — by bringing them back into the workplace, strengthening their family ties, seeking them out in our neighborhoods, drawing upon their talents and wisdom in educating the young.

STRESS MANAGEMENT THROUGH LOCAL, STATE OR FEDERAL GOVERNMENT ACTION

Stress management must be the responsibility primarily of individuals, families, groups and the local community. It should be a local and private concern. But there are several important roles to be performed by government at federal, state and local levels:

1. Federal, state and local governments must provide some financial support for stress-prevention community services.

2. Federal, state and local governments should examine the stress-creating potentials of new policies and programs.

3. Federal and state governments should support research into the causes, consequences, and control of stress, as well as dissemination of knowledge gained by such research.

4. Federal and state governments should monitor stresses and distresses throughout the population through various "social indicators."

There are many social approaches to stress management. Only a few have been mentioned here. Social approaches must be aimed at reducing the structural social forces which produce distress. As the same time individuals must attempt to reduce their own personal stress levels. Attempts by government or social groups to reduce some of the causes of large-scale stress and distress should complement the individual approaches discussed in earlier chapters.

REFERENCES

1. For related views of child-rearing, see Claude Steiner, *Scripts People Live*. New York: Grove Press, 1974, Chapter 26; Dorothy E. Babcock and Terry D. Keepers, *Raising Kids OK*. New York: Avon, 1976: Thomas Gordon, *Parent Effectiveness Training*. New York : David McKay, 1970; David Elkind, *The Hurried Child: Growing Up Too Fast Too Soon*. Reading, Mass.: Addison-Wesley, 1981.

2. Charles E. Silberman, *Crisis in the Classroom*. New York: Vintage, 1970; Walter E. Schafer and Carol Olexa, *Tracking and Opportunity*, Scranton, Pa.: Chandler Publishing Co., 1971; George Leonard, *Education and Ecstasy*. New York: Dell Publishing Co., 1968.

3. Leonard, *Ibid.*

4. Kenneth Polk and Walter E. Schafer, *Schools and Delinquency*. Englewood Cliffs, N.J.: Prentice-Hall, Inc., 1972.

5. James S. Coleman, *et al., Youth: Transition to Adulthood*. Chicago: University of Chicago Press, 1973.

6. Alvin Toffler, *Future Shock*. New York: Bantam Books, 1971.

7. For selected readings on the nature of management of job stress, see, for example, Karl Albrecht, *Stress and The Manager*. Englewood Cliffs, N.J., Prentice-Hall, Inc., 1979; Arthur P. Brief, Randall C. Schuler and Mary Van Sell, *Managing Job Stress*. Boston: Little, Brown and Company, 1981; John M. Ivancevich, and Michael T. Matteson, *Stress and Work: A Managerial Perspective*. Glenview, Ill.: Scott, Foresman and Company, 1980. C.L. Cooper and R. Payne, editors, *Current Concerns in Occupational Stress*. New York: John Wiley and Sons, 1980.

8. Vance Packard, *A Nation of Strangers*. New York: Pocket Books, 1974, Chapter 19.

9. Coleman, *et al., op cit.,* Paris 3 and 4.

CHAPTER 14

STRESS AND COHERENCE LOOKING AHEAD

The most elementary acquaintance with history, with anthropology, and above all, with literature — be it the Bible, the Greeks, Shakespeare, Dante, or Dostoevsky — reveals the rarity of tranquility in human existence. [1]

- Aaron Antonovsky

This rather gloomy opinion on the possibility of human peace may or may not be valid, depending upon one's point of view and definition of tranquility. The history of the human species indeed is marked by considerable misery, illness, and struggle. In part, this results from humankind's continual need to adapt — to a changing physical environment, to ever-shifting technology, to neighboring tribes and nations, to the life cycle itself.

In short, stressors are ever-present. Adaptation is a never-ending process. Adjustment exacts a toll in wear and tear in mind, body and resistance to stress. Physical illness and emotional turmoil often result.

Yet there is reason for optimism, certainly at the personal level and perhaps collectively. For the medical and behavioral sciences have made great strides in providing guidelines on how we can face the inevitable, incessant stressors of living, yet survive — even thrive. This book has set forth a framework for understanding human stress and its effects, positive and harmful. Within this framework, we have examined a wide variety of specific techniques for monitoring and managing stress. These stress management methods fall under several headings:

- Monitoring early warning signs of distress
- Monitoring and managing stressors
- Monitoring and managing the lifestyle buffer
- Monitoring and managing perception of stressors
- Monitoring and managing the coping response
- Monitoring and managing reactions to distress
- Monitoring and managing the context of stress

By learning and using these techniques, you will progress toward the goals of stress management discussed in Chapters 1 and 5:

High level wellness for yourself
    Good Health
    Life satisfaction
    Productivity
    Self-development
Promotion of others high level wellness

Managing your own stress more effectively requires several qualities on your part:

    Effort, courage, will
    Patience
    Persistence
    Self-knowledge
    Action
    Garnering support from others

Assisting others close to you to manage better their stress will be enhanced by your own:

    Caring
    Patience
    Ability to listen
    Ability to explain clearly
    Timing of communication
    Persistance
    Respect for individual differences

Hopefully, insights and suggestions in this book will assist you both in your own quest for a high quality of life and promoting others' well-being.

COHERENCE, STRESS AND HEALTH

Antonovsky contends that effective stress management will produce an internal "sense of coherence" which in turn will promote wellness. In Antonovsky's words a sense of coherence is:

> ...*a pervasive, enduring though dynamic feeling of confidence that one's internal and external environments are predictable and that there is a high probability that things will work out as well as can reasonably be expected.*[2]

There are many routes to a sense of coherence. Having had parents who exemplified it helps. So do early successes in school and other arenas. Education itself, whether formal or informal, can yield the insights and sense of control over events that help with coherence. Being part of a social support network with unconditional caring, acceptance and love can breed confidence and predictability. Religious faith works for many people.

We live in a fast-changing, fast-moving world. By maintaining an effective lifestyle buffer, by thinking rationally and perceiving positively, by coping with situations and reacting to distress constructively, and by taking an active part in influencing our environments, we can deal with this fast-paced, potentially-distressing world armed with the kind of "resistance resources" Antonovsky contributes to a sense of coherence and a condition of well-being.[3]

Your own good health, of course, must not be achieved at the expense of others. Selfish pursuit of your own fullness as a person means nothing if others suffer. Self-realization assumes a progressive growth in your ability to foster the fullness of those around you. Hans Selye emphasizes what he calls "altruistic egotism" — earning others' love — as a guideline for achieving health and happiness and for making stress benefit both yourself and others.[4] Earning the love of others means doing things they will appreciate and for which they will extend their love. While it is vital to create conditions in which the health and growth of others thrive as well, this life-long goal can be attained only if you first take care of your own health and develop your own potentials.

George Sheehan, the physician who runs and writes, has stated that we live in a society where the body is a second-class citizen.[5] If you learn to manage stress well, your body can become and remain a first-class citizen — for the rest of your life. Your intellectual, emotional, and spiritual selves will flourish. And your actions will reflect the high regard in which you hold yourself.

If, at the same time, you direct your limited energies toward activities which are important and meaningful to you, then stress can be a positive force as you pursue self-development in your own unique way. For me, this means loving my family, running, teaching, speaking and writing. For you, it means whatever is special and meaningful; whatever expresses your inner drive for growth; whatever is your way to balance self-interest with caring for others; whatever is your path to wholeness.

371

Once you find this central, organizing focus — which can change several times throughout your life — managing stress wisely takes on special meaning. For then you can use stress constructively in reaching toward ever higher levels of growth.

REFERENCES

1. Aaron Antonovsky, *Health, Stress and Coping.* San Francisco, CA.: Jossey-Bass Publishers, 1980, p. 87.

2. For recent books on wellness, see Donald B. Ardell, *High Level Wellness.* New York, Bantam Books, 1977; Donald B. Ardell, *14 Days to a Wellness Lifestyle.* Mill Valley, CA.: Whatever Publishing, 1981; Donald B. Ardell and Mark Tager, *Planning for Wellness: A Guidebook.* Portland, Ore.: Wellness Media. 1981.

3. Antonovsky, *op cit.,* p. 123.

4. Hans Selye, *The Stress of Life,* Revised Edition. New York: McGraw-Hill Book Co., 1976, Chapter 20; Hans Selye, *Stress Without Distress.* Philadelphia: J.B. Lippincott, 1974.

5. George Sheehan, *Running and Being.* New York: Simon and Schuster, 1978.

SUBJECT INDEX

NAME INDEX

DIALOGUE BOOKS®

There are two other important DIALOGUE BOOKS by the same author, complementing WELLNESS THROUGH STRESS MANAGEMENT:

STRESS, DISTRESS AND GROWTH by Walt Schafer, Foreword by Hans Selye, M.D., ISBN 0-89881-040-X, 1978, $9.75.

This book by International Dialogue Press is intended to help people of all ages make stress work for them rather than against them. It discusses techniques for channeling stress toward useful goals.

CONTENTS

HANS SELYE, M.D., President of the International Institute of Stress, wrote the Foreword to STRESS DISTRESS, AND GROWTH. It is reprinted here in full:

FOREWORD

When I first started my research on stress over forty years ago, I did not fully realize its potential in terms of controllable human behavior. I had no idea that it would lead me and others to spend countless hours of work trying to dissect the complex and intricate mechanisms of stress.

I am pleased to see that the fruits of our manifold efforts are now being presented to the world through such books as *STRESS, DISTRESS AND GROWTH*. After all, the purpose of medicine and medical research is to heal and illuminate the path towards a healthy, more meaningful and rewarding existence.

Walt Schafer has shown a remarkable understanding of stress, as it has presented itself in all its manifestations to people like Ray Rosenman, Meyer Friedman, Thomas Holmes, Richard Rahe (and myself), to name a few. He has drawn from the extensive literature on the subject and has written a book that is easily understood even though it deals exclusively with this extremely complicated subject. I myself tried to do similar justice to all of stress research when I wrote *THE STRESS OF LIFE* and *STRESS WITHOUT DISTRESS* (two of my more popular books), but it appears that scientists rarely have the talent to clearly explain their work to the general public.

A mere glance at this book's Table of Contents will show that the author deals not only with the theory of stress and stress-induced diseases of adaptation but also with the stresses and strains of everyday life. Walt Schafer also discusses various techniques of managing stress and in doing so he has clarified a common misconception: that stress is always bad and should necessarily be avoided. He clearly explains that "stress is the nonspecific response of the body to any demand made upon it" and that we could not live without stress since we make continuous demands on our various organ systems - even when we sleep.

The fundamental principle is well brought out that it is not so much the nature of the problem we face that determine our reaction to stress but rather the various predisposing factors, particularly our personality type, that induce us to respond to a given type of challenge in a certain way.

The outcomes of stress largely depends on the way we perceive things. "It is not so much what happens to us but the way we take it." The more we accept the situation in a manner causing the maximum amount of pleasure, satisfaction and success (that is, good stress or eustress) and the more we avoid pain, sorrow and tension (that is, bad stress or distress), the more happy we are in handling the conditions that constantly face us all.

The author has learned so much about the scientific aspects of stress that, by combining this expertise with his extraordinary gift of presenting medical problems in a generally understandable and interesting manner, he has managed to write a book that promises to meet with much success by being very instructive and useful to many people. I believe it will be a best seller in every sense of the word.

I am also pleased to learn that *STRESS, DISTRESS AND GROWTH* will appear as a student manual. If we hope to make our society a healthy and happy one, we must reach out and show the way to our youth so that they can better harness stress to work for them. We must convince students, and even ourselves, that the inner resources are there. They only need to be discovered through awareness and by being in closer touch with our own selves.

Hans Selye, M.D.

STRESS, DISTRESS AND GROWTH features a separate Student Manual:

STRESS, DISTRESS AND GROWTH: A STUDENT MANUAL
by Keith Forman and Walt Schafer, ISBN 0-89881-013-2, 1978, $7.75.

This volume, available as a companion to the above text, presents verbal, written, and action exercises for both individual and group use.

"...adds a programmatic character to the suggestions made in the text."
—Contemporary Psychology

A third DIALOGUE BOOK is of great importance to personal wellness.

LOVE YOUR HEART by Leon Belshin, M.S. and Dean Mason, M.D., Foreword by William B. Kannel, M.D., ISBN 0-89881-011-6, 1982, $9.75

This book gives a vivid and clear message about proper methods for preventing heart attacks. The frequent use of highly interesting anecdotes makes the book read more like a story rather than a treatise on medical instructions.

CONTENTS
1. DON'T BE A CORONARY STATISTIC
2. EXERCISE: YOU SHOULD RUN FOR YOUR LIFE
3. PHYSICAL ACTIVITIES: USE YOUR HEART SO YOU
      WON'T LOSE IT
4. NUTRITION: DON'T EAT YOUR HEART OUT

ABOUT THE AUTHORS

LEON BELSHIN, M.S. served for several years as Public Health Educator for the Los Angeles County Health Department and taught Gerontology in the Los Angeles Adult Education Program. He is a Past-President of the Golden Empire (Sacramento) Northern California Chapter of the American Heart Association and a recipient of its Distinguished Service Award.

DEAN T. MASON, M.D. is Professor of Medicine, Professor of Physiology, and Chief of Cardiovascular Medicine at the University of California at Davis, School of Medicine and University Medical Center, Davis and Sacramento, California. Currently Editor-In-Chief of THE AMERICAN HEART JOURNAL, he has served on 20 Editorial Boards of leading Medical Journals. He has authored more than 1000 Original Articles for Professional Journals as well as 10 Textbooks on several aspects of cardiovascular science and clinical cardiology.

Dr. Mason is Past-President of the American College of Cardiology and a recipient of the Science Citation Index Award from the Institute for Scientific Information of *Current Contents* as one of the 300 leading scientists whose articles were most often cited in the world literature within the past 15 years.

WILLIAM B. KANNEL, M.D., Professor of Medicine and Medical Director, Heart Disease Epidemiology Study, National Heart, Lung and Blood Institute wrote the Foreword to this book.

FOREWORD

Epidemiologic studies over the past 3 decades have explored the way heart attacks evolve in the general population, suggesting in what ways those who ultimately develop coronary attacks differ from those who do not. From these investigations, a portrait of the prime candidate has emerged: a middle-aged male or elderly female, given to indulgence in too much of a too rich (fatty) diet, too little exercise, too many cigarettes, and unrestrained weight gain. Such a lifestyle often produces high blood pressure, high blood cholesterol, and elevated blood sugar. Yet the potential heart attack victim goes about with a sense of well-being, unaware of impending disaster, which usually strikes without warning.

Coronary attacks do not happen only to someone else. This disease and closely related strokes and heart failure are major health hazards, affecting one of every three Americans before the age of 60. It is not prudent to rely on modern medicine to save you once a heart attack occurs. Most occur without prior warning and can end fatally within a matter of minutes. Half of all heart attack deaths occur suddenly and unexpectedly. In one in five coronary attacks sudden death is the first, last, and only symptom.

Avoiding or correcting the predisposing "risk factor" is often difficult, since the coronary candidate is forced to swim upstream against a society that often promotes what they must avoid. However, the necessary changes in lifestyle are achievable without sacrifice of the good life.

This book which sets forth the hygienic advice needed to avoid a heart attack, is refreshingly free of incomprehensible medical jargon. The message is readily discerned, and the points are illustrated by interesting anecdotes. Co-authors Leon Belshin and Dr. Dean Mason, well-informed health educator and world-renowned cardiologist, make a good team and provide advice on how to protect yourself and your family from these leading causes of death.

William B. Kannel, M.D.

For more information on other DIALOGUE BOOKS, write or call International Dialogue Press, P.O. Box 1257, Davis, CA 95616. Tel. (916) 758-6500.